American Scene

a collection

by Dave Argabright

American Scene

a collection

© 2001 Dave Argabright
ISBN 1-891390-11-2

Published by:
Witness Productions
Box 34, Church Street
Marshall, Indiana 47859
765-597-2487

Cover photos courtesy of George Wilkins

Printed in the United States of America

*To my family, for
their love and devotion*

ACKNOWLEDGMENTS

There have been many, many people through the years who offered me help and assistance in some form, far too many to name individually here.

That said, I want to give credit to some key people. In 1982 Dick Berggren provided my first opportunity to write for a national audience in OPEN WHEEL MAGAZINE. In 1988 Jerry Gappens and Keith Waltz of NATIONAL SPEED SPORT NEWS talked me into doing a column there. Both publications have had a wonderful impact on my life.

Corinne Economaki has been a dear friend and supporter through thick and thin. Her steady, patient advice has guided me and inspired me. She agreed to edit this volume and I owe her many thanks for truly making my work better.

Bob Jenkins was kind enough to provide some supportive comments for this book, which I appreciate very deeply. George Wilkins went the extra mile to provide the cover photos for this project.

Ed and Susie Watson of Witness Productions provided much insight and guidance in the publishing process. To them I owe a mighty "thank you."

And finally, my family has been very patient as I selfishly pursued my craft over the past two decades. There were too many late nights when I forgot goodnight kisses and hugs because I was wrapped up in a story. I'm grateful that my wife Sherry has been incredibly patient, and my children have been understanding as well.

No man is an island; everyone needs good people around them for strength and inspiration. To all of you who have been there when I needed you most, one word: thanks.

Contents

FOREWORD

If Dave Argabright was a camera, he'd be a wide-angle model.

This observant Hoosier's view of auto racing extends a full 180 degrees.

Whereas most followers of motorsports are concerned to some degree with the hardware, the rolling stock, engines, chassis, etc., Argabright's focus is on its people.

All kinds of people. People in the cars, people who work on the cars, and people who watch the cars.

Argabright's uncanny feel for what it is that intrigues today's race fan is incredible. His sense of which nuance touches a nerve, catches an eye or fancy of this beholder or that beholder is what makes his writing so special, and him the most popular columnist in NATIONAL SPEED SPORT NEWS.

We're sure you will enjoy his columns in retrospect as much as we did, reading them for the first time they crossed our desk.

Chris Economaki
Editor
NATIONAL SPEED SPORT NEWS

INTRODUCTION

Some years ago as a rookie writer, I discovered something: every person has a story.

Through thick and thin, year in and year out, that discovery has served me well. For the past twenty years as a motorsports writer, I have met many interesting people, and I've always felt my job was to tell their story.

I never planned on writing this book. Along the way I wrote a bunch of short stories, and now they've wound up in a book. At the time they were written, I was so busy meeting deadlines I paid no thought to the idea of publishing them in collected form.

But one day not long ago I realized that I had put a lot of stories behind me. The years had swept past and my friends were getting gray hair and my kids were growing up and maybe it was time to go back and review some of the old stuff again.

Ultimately, I suppose I wanted to preserve my work. Every artist probably holds some deep-seated fear their work will be forgotten, and I'm no different. Few people keep old newspapers and magazines; a book is a more permanent.

As an avid reader, I delight in finding old titles from my favorite authors. Maybe a reader will find this book on the dusty shelf of a used book store twenty years from today and smile. That possibility is why I said yes to this book.

Writing can be wonderful and exciting and painful and lonely, sometimes even in the same story. Even in the same *paragraph*. But other than romance and friendship and fatherhood and a loyal old dog, I haven't found anything more emotionally rewarding.

Writing is a tremendous rush. I hope to do it for a long time, and I want very much to do it well. This volume is the best I could do.

So far.

Dave Argabright

Don't settle for writing it the way it's always been written; dare to write it differently, and maybe you'll write it better than it's been written before.

Russell Baker
The Good Times

In going where you have to go, and doing what you have to do, and seeing what you have to see, you dull and blunt the instrument you write with. But I would rather have it bent and dull and know I had to put it on the grindstone again and hammer it into shape and put a whetstone to it, and know that I had something to write about, than to have it bright and shining and nothing to say, or smooth and well-oiled in the closet, but unused.

Ernest Hemingway
The Short Stories

American Scene

a collection

by Dave Argabright

FAVORITES

FAVORITES

When I decided this book would become a reality, I began going through all my old stories, deciding which ones to include here.

Most of the time, I could recall the story just by reading the first paragraph. Others I didn't remember at all. And there were plenty of stories, especially those written in my earlier years, that caused me to wince and say to myself, "Man, that's terrible! Did I really write that?"

Others, though, brought a special feeling, kind of like looking at pictures of your children when they were very young. I have included some of those stories in this first chapter.

Some make me feel light and happy, while others make me feel very sad, and blue. But these are the stories I'm most proud of as a writer.

HOOKER'S KID

JULY 1989 - NATIONAL SPEED SPORT NEWS

Rick Hood needed no one to tell him he had just had a big night. As the heavy, moist late-night air enveloped the scene, he flitted among the many well-wishers who surrounded his black Gambler sprint car.

The crowd of people reached and touched him, shaking his hand, patting his back. "Nice ride, man," they said, one after another. His smile seemed to go on forever, and his staccato Memphis dialect was going at the speed of light. This was the spotlight; this was the big city. This was the Kings Royal at Eldora Speedway.

Fifty feet away Bobby Davis Jr. was wearing the winner's crown and picking up $50,000. Twenty feet away, Steve Kinser's machine sat in the runner-up spot. Two heavyweights, parked in a couple of their usual spots. Then there was Hood, who had sent virtually every one of the 14,000 witnesses home in an absolute fit. He had turned in an impressive—no, make that incredible—drive from deep in the pack to come oh-so-close to upsetting the very best at the very biggest.

To truly appreciate Hood's feat, one must first appreciate the Kings Royal. It has become the non-denominational All-Star game of sprint car racing. No sanctions, no politics. Just a few simple rules, and a lot of money. All the big boys, with their biggest, shiniest, most expensive toys.

And here was Hood, who has only been with the Danny Arthalony team seven weeks. Four weeks ago, chief mechanic Jerry Rone suffered a mild heart attack, and rejoined the team just days ago. Twenty-four hours before the Kings Royal, Hood's machine was severely crunched when a top wing failed and he crashed hard with Kenny Jacobs, whose Weikert machine went sailing over the turn-two wall in a crash that would have collected eight lives from any cat unlucky enough to be aboard. Both Hood and Jacobs walked away, and Hood's crew was forced to work through the night to repair the damage.

But, oh, was it worth it! When the hour came for Hood to shine, he stepped up and took his biggest swing. He started twelfth, and drove like a man possessed. By the midway point he was challenging Kinser for second, actually passing the Hoosier ace briefly before the King rocketed back by. But in dispensing with the lapped car of Chris Eash, Hood blistered a right rear, and was forced to settle for third.

It was the kind of ride which had stardom written all over it. The circumstances were all there, and it's likely to become a permanent part of the growing lore of the Kings Royal.

Hood has been winning here in the Midwest for several years, but has never quite achieved the kind of national success that makes a guy a household name like Doug, Sammy, or Steve (as in Wolfgang, Swindell, and Kinser). Hood enjoyed his greatest success from 1983 to 1985, when he drove Blackie Fortune's machines to two USAC sprint car titles and a Silver Crown title.

It's ironic that the titles were with the buttoned-down USAC, because Hood has nothing but renegade blood coursing through his veins. Perhaps it's a gift from his dad Hooker, who some say was the finest to ever strap in, and who was arguably one of the first to embrace the outlaw cause in the 1950s and 1960s.

Hood's "rebel" attitude was never more evident than in late 1984, when the USAC 4-Crown Nationals was rain-delayed a week or so. An outlaw event at Manzanita beckoned, and Fortune told Hood that if he ran there, he would lose his ride. Hood went anyway, and promptly got himself mowed down by an errant sprint car that shot through Manzy's infield. He had not only lost his ride, but was badly broken as well.

But the injuries healed, and so did his relationship with Fortune. They reconciled the following spring, and ultimately won both the USAC sprint car title and the Silver Crown title that season.

Since then, he has bounced around somewhat. With the Kings Royal, however, he has delivered himself back into the national spotlight. He and the Arthalony team face the remainder of the season with some momentum, and the conviction that on a given night, they can run with anybody.

Was there ever any doubt? Not in Hood's mind. After all, the trademarks Hooker always carried—pride, confidence, determination—all seem to be bulging from Rick's back pocket. "Hooker's kid" was a long time ago. Then again, maybe it was just last Saturday night.

CROCKY FACES THE WALL OF DEATH

JULY 1990 - NATIONAL SPEED SPORT NEWS

Roy Caruthers leaned toward the gasoline-soaked wood panel with his torch, the flame flicking in the gentle night breeze. In moments, the main straightaway surface at Lincoln Park Speedway would be illuminated by the inferno. Crocky Wright, who has seen seventy-one years, was ready to face the wall of death.

It's been a long time since Crocky tried the wall. Sure, he had the stunt mastered when he performed with Putt Mossman's International Daredevils way back in 1951. But considerable sand has passed through the hourglass since then, and his last attempt in 1981 was not completely successful.

But this time would be different, Crocky vowed. When intermission finally arrived at Lincoln Park on Saturday night, he was ready. He wore an ancient checkered helmet, a remnant from his days racing midgets, big cars, and bikes all those years ago. He paced nervously, directing the crew of helpers as they placed the wall on the track, pouring a white line from the center of the wall down the track toward turn four. When a man faces the wall, we can assume, he wants to see where he's going.

Finally, the old Honda was fired. In his jackboots and leather jacket, he looked like a cast member from an old Hollywood flick. He revved the engine and began a parade lap. The crowd stood and began to quiet. In the infield, racers and spectators stared and smiled.

As he twisted the throttle down the backstretch, maybe on this cool Indiana night it was like 1951 all over again. He was a young man, the wind in his face. He was the star. That's how it once was, so long ago. What man, who has stood and faced the cheers, does not want to hear them again, just one more time?

While his life hasn't gone exactly as planned, it isn't far off course. Long ago, he wanted to go to Indy. While he enjoyed moderate success on motorcycles, and loved racing midgets and big cars, he was never successful enough to find the Brickyard.

There were chances at marriage, but women just didn't understand why Crocky wouldn't give up some of his racing. The jobs came and went through the years, because employers didn't understand why Crocky needed so much time off. So the small kid born Ernie Schlausky seventy-one years ago has spent his entire life doing exactly whatever he wanted.

On this night, he wanted to beat the wall of death. As he brought the bike to a stop coming out of turn four, he looked toward the wooden structure in the middle of the track and thought of 1981 and the Indianapolis Speedrome. He tried the wall then, but things didn't go according to plan. He made it through the blazing structure, but wiped out and nearly broke his ankle. At seventy-one, he probably doesn't heal very quickly. He gunned the engine.

The signal was given to start the fire. An official poured gasoline on the structure, and stepped away. Caruthers, who came along as Crocky's assistant, fumbled with a lighter. His hands trembled as he tried nervously to light the torch that had been prepared. Finally, it caught, and he stepped toward the wall.

He reached out with the torch. Ambulance attendants looked on. When the small flame licked toward the gasoline-soaked wall, it ignited, and for a moment Caruthers himself stood too close to the blaze, his feet surrounded by flames. He dashed away, and people nearby stepped back and shielded their faces from the heat.

Crocky lowered his head. He snapped the Honda in gear, and gassed it. As he approached the wall, his tires ran along the white line that had been poured moments before. He lowered his head, and the Honda begged to be shifted to a higher gear. Every eye watched, every breath was held.

The front wheel hit the mark dead center. For a split second, Crocky and the bike were consumed in the hot, orange mass of fire. The wood shattered, with sparks flying, and in another moment it was over. There was Crocky, unscathed, racing toward turn one. The water truck rolled forward and crew members began spraying the flames, transforming what was the wall of death into a docile pile of smoldering wood.

Crocky made his way around the track and back to the main straightaway. The helmet came off, and friends and onlookers embraced the hero. The crowd cheered, and as the announcer struggled with a wireless microphone, Crocky was interviewed. He stepped through the gate at the flag stand, into a crowd of excited young children, all reaching to shake his hand, to touch the man of the hour. Crocky smiled and thanked them.

The track crew climbed into their equipment, to work the water that had doused the fire into the track. Racers and crews walked toward the pits, to ready their cars for the features soon to follow. After all, wall of death or not, it was Saturday night at Lincoln Park, and there were races to run.

Minutes later, when the leather jacket, boots, and ancient helmet were replaced with a light brown jacket bearing his name, Crocky again waded through the crowd of admirers near the concession stand.

"What a neat old guy!" exclaimed a kid of about ten years old to his buddy as he examined the autographed card Crocky had just given him. On the card were pictures of long ago, pictures of a young man aboard the racing machines he hoped would propel him to stardom. Tonight, it seems, they did just that.

Crocky Wright, star of stars. Yeah. What a neat old guy.

NIGHT OF DARKNESS

JULY 1990 - NATIONAL SPEED SPORT NEWS

The man struggled to catch his breath as he stood among a group of reporters in the Eldora Speedway press box. "Somebody just called," he began, his emotions capturing the attention of those around him, "said there was a bad one at Salem. Vogler...they think he might of, uh...uh..."

He couldn't finish, but everyone understood. As his words trailed off, fearful glances were exchanged. After an awkward moment a writer with the *Dayton Daily News* stood. "I'll call Salem," he said and headed for the door.

No one spoke for a moment. Surely this was a crank call, or some silly rumor that somehow sweeps through a race track crowd. After all, this just couldn't happen to someone as prominent as Rich Vogler. Could it?

Attention returned to matters at hand. They were ready to push off the Kings Royal. Some of the best on dirt ready to put it all up for fifty grand. The stars were there, the crowd was there, and we were ready. But the lights just didn't seem as bright as they had just moments before.

With the sounds of sprint cars firing and pulling away from push trucks echoing in my ears, I thought of Vogler. I remembered a phone call four years ago when I asked to interview him for an ANDERSON HERALD feature. He agreed to meet me after work at a restaurant on Indy's northwest side.

When I walked in that night, there he was. USAC champ, midget master, Indy 500 veteran. Willing to spend a January evening with a guy itching for a story. There was his wife Emily, smiling and tending to the young child in the high chair. Rich faced me across the table, with his hands folded neatly in front of him, and answered every question. When there was nothing left to ask, he thanked me for my interest in writing about him.

My mind drifted back to reality, as the field for the Kings Royal roared to life. It was shaping up to be a Steve Kinser/Doug Wolfgang showdown. When I looked upon the sweeping Eldora surface, I didn't see the same twenty-four sprint cars I had been watching all night.

Instead, I saw machines that are too light and too powerful and too fast and ready to devour people. I saw mortal, vulnerable human beings ricocheting around a small dirt surface at nearly 150 miles per hour. They were husbands, fathers, brothers, sons, and friends.

We've been gently lulled into forgetting that race cars, especially sprint cars, can be unforgiving beasts with a mean appetite. We've come to view wicked-looking shunts as footage for the highlight films, not a grisly scene with profound and grievous results. If the tragedy does occur, we think to ourselves, it will involve an unknown guy and not one of our household-name heroes.

Today we believe in helmets that absorb and protect, gloves and firesuits that repel heat and flames, and straps and buckles that hold. If any of the above fails, we've learned to rely on brilliant surgeons with sophisticated technologies to make everything all right. But they can't make the reality of racing fatalities go away.

The crowd cheered as Kinser gained slightly on Wolfgang. I thought of the Salem spectators, who must have been in a state of absolute shock at that very same moment. Maybe it was a crank call, I thought. Just maybe.

Lap twenty-two came and Jack Hewitt took a soft rollover in turn two. During the stop, I went downstairs for an update. The guy from the Dayton paper said he couldn't get anyone at Salem, but called a friend who was watching the Salem race on ESPN. "It doesn't look good," he said.

The Kings Royal restarted and moved to its closing stages. Wolfgang had 'em covered, with Kinser not far behind. When Kinser's last-lap contact with the turn-two cement vaporized his hopes for a $15,000 second prize, the group of writers stood and headed for the start/finish line, to greet the victorious Wolfgang.

The Williams team was elated in victory lane. Wolfie, always a class act and tonight a deserving champion, smiled. $50,000 is a lot to smile about. As he struggled to remove his arm restraints, he leaned over to kiss a family member.

I thought of Emily Vogler. I wondered if, at that very moment, there was a scene of anguish and grief in the chilly confines of a lonely hospital emergency room. The fun was over at Eldora. It was time to go home.

The pressing crowd made the walk up the track longer than usual. Already, whispers could be overheard. "You hear about Vogler? Is it true...?"

The grandstands were virtually empty. Rounding the corner and heading for the exit, I saw the Dayton writer coming out of the press room. I asked if he had heard anything official.

"Oh, it came over the wire," he said quietly. "He's dead."

I had had about an hour to prepare for his statement, but it still took the air from my lungs. I thanked him numbly and walked outside. The bright lights of the t-shirt trailers lit the way, and I turned into the darkness that enveloped the parking lot. It began to rain. It was to be a long ride home.

WARSAW FINALE

AUGUST 1990 - NATIONAL SPEED SPORT NEWS

There is no line at the pit shack at Warsaw Speedway, as the crowd has already arrived for the track's final night of competition after forty-two years in business. A small sign reading "Thanks for the memories" is taped up for all to see.

Behind the backstretch wall, down the dirt path to the pits, people are sitting on cars, in lawn chairs, in trucks, watching hot laps. Thirty yards behind them, lapping gently against the Indiana clay, lies beautiful Winona Lake, ringed by estate-like homes.

Nine people living in those homes successfully sued the Warsaw fair board to permanently close the facility, citing dust and noise problems. A negotiated settlement called for tonight to be the final show for 1990 and forever. Sadness hung in the air.

"It's like a death, really," said Becky Sechrist, who has worked here as a gate attendant for two years. "People who have come here for years are walking in tonight with very sad faces. Some have said they feel like they're going to a funeral."

The finale has certainly brought the people out, as a packed grandstand awaits the first heat. Tonight also marks the final night of the Kosciusko County 4-H Fair, which hosts its annual one-week run each August. Down the midway, brightly painted booths offer Ice Slushies, Elephant Ears, sweet corn, melons, and Jumbo Sliced Onion Rings.

Around five o'clock or so, folks began their trek through the walkways that snake through the fair, past the Hy-5 Ferris Wheel, the Paratrooper, the Kamikaze, the Rock-O-Plane, and the Thunder Bolt. They made their way toward the grandstand facing the quarter-mile clay oval. They were ready for "the races," some making their annual visit. Some have made this night a family tradition for more than forty years. This will be the last chapter.

Kim Baney, who has worked PR for the track for several years, fights to control her emotions. "This is going to be a tough night," she says, with a nervous smile. "When you know something you love so much is going to end, it's hard to face it. This track has been a part of my life since I was six months old. It's never going to be the same."

On the track, the sprint dash lines up as dusk approaches. A boat lazily powers out from the near shoreline toward the center of Winona Lake, its white marker light fading as it moves away. Two kids in a pedal boat twenty feet from shore stand in their craft, craning their necks for a glimpse of race cars. You wonder if they'll ever get a chance at a closer look.

Announcer Jeff Abbott calls the action from the officials' stand, naming drivers and their sponsors with rhythmic verse, honed from weeks of watching the action. Nearby, a cassette deck records his comments. Since his Saturday nights are going to be free from now on, he's cutting a "demo tape" to see if he can land a job at another track.

Bimbo Atkins, the local hot shoe, wins the dash, but not before Randy Woodling gets upside down on the last lap. Bimbo, track champ here in 1989 and points leader this year, is a Warsaw kid who began his racing career here twelve years ago. There will be no more easy tows on Saturday night.

"We have to go three hours in any direction," he says, gesturing about. "It really makes me sad, and I guess it takes money out of my pocket. It's going to be an emotional night, you can feel it. It's like a graveyard down here."

Across the way, driver Van Gurley also feels the emotion.

"I've been coming down here for ten or twelve years, and the people here are nice, they treat you well, and you get out of here at a decent hour," he says. "I didn't really think about tonight very much till I signed in, and I saw that sign that said 'Thanks for the memories.' I realized I'd probably never see some of these people again. That's really sad."

The grandstand buzzes with talk of Shady Hill Raceway, about an hour away. The rumor is that Shady Hill, long a Saturday night stock car track, will begin featuring non-winged sprint cars. Folks here are looking for an alternative.

The sprint car feature is lined up on the main straightaway, and for the final time the drivers are introduced. They solemnly belt in, and eighteen fire-breathing cars are soon circling the oval for a parade lap. Abbott implores the fans to get on their feet for a final sendoff, but everyone is already standing, waving as the winged sprinters idle past, with gloved hands waving a return salute. A few cigarette lighters are lit: tiny flames dancing in the moist night air. Maybe it's the methanol, but you see folks dabbing their eyes with tissues.

Atkins brings them off turn four, and quickly takes charge. Kenny Haynes, who is always full of excitement, pressures. On a restart from a minor yellow flag, he pokes his nose under Atkins and gives him a try. But Atkins—known locally as "B.A."—has 'em covered, and is soon back out front.

The crowd notices Jeff Walker, on the move from deep in the pack. He gets around Haynes, then presses Atkins. On lap nineteen he pulls alongside coming off turn four, and the crowd roars as he passes Atkins and backs it into turn one, already starting to pull away. Haynes hangs in to pass Atkins for second on the final lap, and the three pull to a stop on the main straightaway for their trophies.

Some of the crowd leaves, many turning for one last glimpse of the track. Ron McKenzie will take the Hobby Stock feature, Harvey Hayes the street stock main, and finally, Jim Hughes wins the mini sprint feature. It's over, but many still hang around.

In the pits, Atkins serves as an unofficial party host. His trailer is open, and racers and fans enjoy refreshment from a chilled keg sitting nearby. Memories are shared, stories are exaggerated, and laughter is all about. The pit lights are left on to accommodate the gathering, and soon the season point money is paid, bringing to a close all official business. Across the way, Walker is a happy winner, and some people remember that it was here at Warsaw that he captured his first career victory several years ago.

"My dad (Don Walker) raced here for years, and once won eighteen straight races at Warsaw," he says, loading the trailer for the two-hour tow home to Arcadia. "I wanted to win this last one, mostly because he had been so successful here. He always kids me that he won more races here than I have, but now I can say I won the last one."

It's after two a.m., and the lights are all gone now. There's nothing but the quiet chirping of crickets, and the gentle lapping of Winona Lake. The moist, cool air comes in off the lake, giving the night air a chill. Several yards away, the Warsaw Speedway surface is silent and dark. Forever.

Thanks for the memories.

BUTCH

MARCH 1992 - NATIONAL SPEED SPORT NEWS

He sits high upon the auctioneer's stand facing nearly a hundred people, his eyes searching through the crowd for a bidder. His staccato voice goes like a machine gun, rifting syllables into the microphone. Every few seconds he opens his mouth wide and draws a quick breath of air, then continues with another gust so quickly you don't even notice the pause. This is life today for Butch Wilkerson.

Twenty years ago, he was one of the hottest guys going in outlaw sprint car racing. He was brash, cocky, arrogant, young, and healthy. And he was sensational in a sprint car.

Life takes some funny turns, doesn't it? He was a young lion, headed for stardom, and instead winds up operating an auction house in tiny Scipio, a wide spot on Indiana Highway 7 between Columbus and North Vernon.

When he was at his peak in the 1970s, he was one of the few guys who could consistently hold his own against the emerging powerhouse team of Karl Kinser and Dick Gaines, one of the best-ever combinations which was also at its prime during the same period. Wilkerson was full of fire and excitement, and seemed to go through life with a chip on his shoulder and his chin jutted out, just waiting for somebody to try to stop him.

Now, his ambition is simple. He wants his auction barn to be the best in southern Indiana. He works hard, and takes a lot of personal pride in what he has accomplished.

"I work about a hundred hours a week getting this stuff in here for Friday night," he says, gesturing about at the stacks of widely varied merchandise. "I'm serious about this place. I want it to be the very best in the state."

That same intensity and drive led Wilkerson to the end of his career. Unlike many of his contemporaries, his was not a quiet retirement. He had a dream of racing at Indy, and knew he had to get involved with USAC to make that happen. He was racing Sherman Armstrong's sprinter at Winchester in 1979

33

when he slammed into the turn-four wall with such force that it probably should have killed him, given the violence of the crash.

But the world wasn't finished with Butch Wilkerson. Instead of pulling the sheet over his head, doctors watched him hang on. He suffered dreadful head injuries, and his recovery stretched from months to years. His personal life was in shambles, he was broke, his ability to race was gone, and he still had some butterflies. He was only thirty-four years old, and his life wasn't a pretty picture.

"My life for eight years after the crash was junk," he admits. "If I had a few coins in my pocket, and could chase a good time, that was all I cared about. I had no drive, no ambition, and had no direction in my life."

He decided to get his auctioneer's license, then in 1989 had the opportunity to lease the auction house here in Scipio. He has worked hard to build a successful business, and to guide his life back to respectability.

He deals in lots of different products, and his customers are mostly local folks looking for a Friday-night bargain. They shuffle in wearing work clothes, and their boots are worn. They look at the merchandise moving through the sale process at a fast pace, and listen to the man with the beard and glasses, a cowboy hat perched on the back of his head.

A lady bids successfully for a box of merchandise, and the real fun is looking through the box to see what she's bought. She finds a chess board that has a power cord, and she looks at it closely to figure out what the power cord is for.

"Maybe you push a button and the pieces move ther'-selves," says her husband, winking at an older man sitting alongside. A woman nearby stares intently at the game and says, "Really?"

The woman turns the game in her hands, examining it, and says, "I guess," and the men laugh out loud. This isn't about buying something; it's about having fun.

Wilkerson knows his customers, and knows the name of the game is entertainment. That's nothing new, because he was certainly fun to watch in a sprint car. No matter where he started, or finished, you knew you would see him racing hard. If there were a hairline opening, or any chance at all of making an opening, he would put 'er in there. Sometimes it worked, sometimes it didn't.

During one stretch many years ago, the legendary car owner Dizz Wilson actually had both Wilkerson and Gaines in his two cars as a team, as did Karl Kinser at a later period. The story at the time had Dizz helping both get strapped in for the feature, then walking over to his truck to take a tranquilizer.

Wilkerson had dodged a few bullets before his fateful day at Winchester. He was hired to drive Cecil Beavers' aging machine in 1976, and they were doing well. He landed a full-time job in September driving a truck for the winter, and had to make a decision: race the next Friday night or take a load of cattle to Peoria, Illinois and earn $190. If he won everything that Friday night at Bloomington, he made $140. He climbed into the truck and headed for Peoria.

Beavers put popular Calvin Gilstrap in the car, even though the veteran driver had been semi-retired for months. Gilstrap cut an excellent lap on his first circuit, good for second-quick time. Using his left hand to crank more outside weight in the car, he caught a small rut in turn three on his second lap, and crashed mightily. He died two days later.

Wilkerson was undeterred, like most racers. He continued racing just as hard as ever. His duel with Bob Seelman in the 1979 Little 500 is one of the most memorable performances of all time. For nearly 150 laps he and Seelman went through traffic like scared pups, both putting banzai moves on each other, moves usually saved for the last lap. Both drivers were simply too stubborn and aggressive to save their race for the end; Wilkerson later broke a torsion bar, and Seelman took second in a very controversial finish.

And then it was over. Like a wisp of smoke that disappears over the hillside, Wilkerson's talents were never to be seen again. But today, in this quiet little town, he has no regrets, and the same cocky smile and bravado are still present.

He was lucky enough to find Mary, a strong woman who has helped him get his life in order. They are talking about getting married, and the forty-seven year old Wilkerson says this gal will take good care of him. The parties and fast life, that was a long time ago. He went to only three races last season. This is the life he wants today.

Those who saw him race at Lawrenceburg remember the magic. It's sad it will never return, but there is happiness in his life, happiness he has found something that satisfies him nearly as much as driving a sprint car.

He holds the gavel tightly as he talks into the microphone. The audience leans forward to study the item up for sale, and he grins as he begins the bidding.

It's not Lawrenceburg; but for him, it's close. This is his world today. The excitement is not over for Butch Wilkerson.

ROGER'S COURAGE

NOVEMBER 1992 - NATIONAL SPEED SPORT NEWS

He sits quietly in the brightly lighted office, smoking a cigarette as he looks at the papers scattered across his desk. It's a gray Monday in Indianapolis, and another day of courage for Roger McCluskey.

Gone is the familiar mane of black hair, leaving a shiny, bald pate in its place. He is a bit weak as he goes about the business of his official duties as USAC director of competition. Very settled, unemotional, down-to-earth. Ready to face whatever challenges are thrown at him.

The past couple of years, those challenges have been significant.

Three years ago, he got sick. He was on a business trip out West, and a severe pain in his back led to an early return to Indianapolis. He went to a doctor; the news not good.

He had cancer, the doctors gently told him. He could fight, and might win. But it would not be pretty.

He's still fighting. And regardless of the outcome, he has risen to display the courage and determination that reveal the stuff of which he is made. The valor of his every day is beyond what most of us display in a lifetime.

36

He doesn't talk much about his illness. No need, really, since he isn't looking for sympathy or pity. His is a private war, the kind we all fear and pray we will never face. It has been a roller coaster of hope and disappointment, as he wins a couple of battles, then loses a couple.

"This last round was pretty tough," he says of his most recent bout of treatments. "But that's life in the big city."

These are the glory days for Roger McCluskey. It's like years ago, when his successes were much more public as he fashioned a brilliant driving career with USAC. Two sprint car titles, eighteen Indy starts, 1973 National Champion, five championship car victories, two stock car titles, 230 championship starts.

McCluskey was known as an intense, never-give-up racer who would fight you bitterly for a single inch on the track.

That kind of determination has returned to serve him well.

He thrived in a dangerous era that saw many of his friends die young. His closest friend, Don Branson, perished in the 1966 season closer at Ascot, California as McCluskey clinched the USAC sprint car title. Even in happy times, there was tragedy.

But he fought through it, and eventually concluded his driving career with a triumph at the 1979 Milwaukee 200. He was ready to step up to a new and different challenge as a USAC official.

He is a powerful man today, with a great responsibility. He is optimistic about the future of USAC, and although the challenges are great, he firmly believes he has the team in place needed to address those challenges.

But nothing brings out the gleam in his eye like sprint cars. He still remembers his era, when cars had names instead of part numbers, when words like "Konstant Hot Special" and "Fike Plumbing Company" and "The Miracle Power Special" could make a grown man's hair stand on end.

What is striking is the quiet manner in which he fights on, sitting up straight in the wheelchair that aids his mobility. Nobody knows about his war because he says so very little. Does he feel he is an inspiration to people?

"A few people have told me that," he admits. "But on the other hand, I'm selfish. I like livin' here."

And there it is, that wide grin. The smile that pierces any depression or doubt. The smile that says he believes.

"You got what you've got, nothing's perfect," he explains. "Whether your problem is physical, or mental, or emotional, whatever, you've got to stand up and battle it the best way you can, and find the right people who know how to help you. I've had lots of really great help. I'm still hanging with it."

So he goes back to work. Outside, the cars roll past on 16th Street and the afternoon turns into evening and another day closes.

Tomorrow will be more of the same. He will get up, and while most of us hop out of bed and head for work, he must struggle through mind-numbing pain for the chance. Never giving up, always pressing, refusing with all his will to yield one single day.

Somewhere, there are a couple of guys sipping a cold one and remembering trips to Reading, or New Bremen, or Winchester, or Eldora. Their hair has a touch of silver now, and they smile as they recall the names that roll easily from their memory. Foyt, Larson, Sachs, Rutherford, Marshman, Andretti, Branson, Hurtubise, Jones.

"How about McCluskey?" one will inevitably add. "Remember him? Man, he was always one tough dude."

He still is, friend. Fighting, fighting, fighting. For every single inch.

THEY CAME TO SAY GOODBYE

SEPTEMBER 1993 - NATIONAL SPEED SPORT NEWS

The crowd filed quietly into the building, escaping the heat and humidity of the Hoosier summer day. They spoke softly, straightening neckties and nodding greetings to one another. They were here to mark the ending of the story. They were here to say goodbye to Roger McCluskey.

The aisles of the large auditorium known as Clowes Hall on the campus of Butler University in Indianapolis sloped gently toward the stage, where a large curtain loomed floor to ceiling. Everyone sat in dim surroundings without speaking, alone with their thoughts and searching for a key to the sadness of the moment.

Bob Jenkins, Henry Ryder, and Hunter Floyd took turns at the podium, each offering splendid memories of the man. The audience laughed and cried, remembering McCluskey for what he was, an invincible and powerful giant of a man who never gave up the laughter.

On stage stood the memories. Several large framed photographs, each telling a story, draped in cloth and flanked by beautiful floral displays. There was McCluskey the racer of sprint cars, stock cars, dirt cars, and Indy Cars. McCluskey in victory lane, McCluskey the official, and in the very center of the group, McCluskey pictured with a racing hat and his impish, broad smile, the happy man whose spirit and character touched nearly everyone he met.

The speakers were eloquent as they stood in the spotlight, yet it would be difficult for anyone's mere words to describe McCluskey as well as that one photograph. Strong and dynamic, expressive and happy, his image seemed to leap from the stage into the hearts of those who had gathered to remember him.

He had great success as a race driver, yet that just didn't seem important at this moment. Instead, it was clear McCluskey had many, many friends who loved him, something far more important than mere victories and losses.

They spoke of his courage. For four years, McCluskey fought the cancer that ravaged and eventually claimed his body. But not cancer, nor anything else, could take his spirit. That, to the very end, belonged to Roger McCluskey.

He survived the harrowing days of the 1960s, when death and destruction were frequent visitors to the race track. It forged his character, teaching him to live every day to the limit, never forgetting it might be his last.

He came out of it alive, never losing the smile, never forgetting the little guy. As an official at USAC, his was an open door. He was the calm, cool character who was the anchor the organization needed at just the right time.

Seated in the front of the audience sat Jean, his wife of twenty years, who, when Roger became ill in 1989, seemed to rise to the occasion. She never hesitated, never faltered, standing by his side through thick and thin. An example of why the phrase "in sickness and in health" means so much to those who are really in love.

Each speaker eased the pain with their words, guiding us through our grief to the happy memories Roger left behind. Beautiful music played during several interludes, leaving each person to think longingly of the days when the man with the broad smile was a voice on the telephone, or a hand to shake, and not just a memory, not just a photograph.

Jenkins finished his remarks by reminding us Roger lived life just the way he wanted, then slowly walked to his nearby chair and sat down. As everyone sat in silence, the music of Frank Sinatra began, telling us about living life "My Way."

The curtains closed nearly all the way, leaving only the center picture visible. Through the emotion and the sadness was the broad smile of Roger McCluskey, lifting the hearts and souls of everyone in attendance. Soon, the music ended, and the crowd slowly stood and filed in silence from the service.

Outside, they walked to their cars, looking over their shoulders at the gathering clouds of a thunderstorm. Life, in its infinite greatness, was going about the business of going on. In a few moments their headlights searched through the rain as they remembered the man who was everyone's friend.

The memories are all they have now. Those memories are much like the spirit of Roger McCluskey. May they live forever.

IRONHEAD

DECEMBER 1993 - NATIONAL SPEED SPORT NEWS

It was a cool, autumn Saturday night at the race track, and in the middle of the infield a man sat alone in a lawn chair, drinking beer and catching a now-and-then glimpse of race cars. It was the cheap seats, but he seemed as happy as he could be.

I thought of Ironhead.

Terry was his real name, but to the rest of us it was just Ironhead, another face in the crowd. His was a life full of stress and strife, marked by unhappiness. "Goin' to the races" always seemed to cheer him up, as he never turned down a chance to pay his way in.

I sometimes wondered if hanging around the race track was therapy for his troubled soul. He was a working stiff who held back a few bucks to pay his way in the front gate, often stretching a weekly paycheck enough to catch only a couple of shows a month.

The noise, the people, the night air, that was his kind of deal.

He worked at the glass factory, fitting swing shift hours around a lifestyle we are now taught to avoid. Booze, women, smoking his mind on rock and roll, he fit them all in. But when all was said and done I saw him happy in only one environment.

Sitting in the bleachers, watching race cars.

Our worlds connected when I was much younger, the wild-and-woolly days before there was a mortgage or a light bill. We shared a shift at the glass plant, him a "lifer" and me a kid just wandering from job to job and nailing down the first planks of a life. He was older by about ten years, and I saw him as a worldly guy who had been around the block. He had a zest for laughter that seemed to cover a dark, sad inside.

He was always good for a hell of a time.

There are great stories I recall, like the night he sat perched on a barstool in the small-town tavern near the plant. He was ready for another round, one more longneck now sitting empty before him. Nobody knows how these things

41

get started, but he and the bartender began to discuss how fast one could empty a tall cold one.

Ironhead killed one in ten seconds. I wonder, said the bartender, could you drink six in a minute?

Five minutes later, a crowd had gathered to watch the experiment. Someone went across the street to the other bar in town and brought that audience over as well. The bartender lined up six on the bar, telling Ironhead if he drank them in a minute or less they were on the house.

As the sixth empty hit the bar, a glaze settled over Ironhead's eyes. The corners of his mouth curled up slightly, and the crowd of about thirty people cheered. He made a couple of steps toward the bathroom, and then he, well, erupted. When the bartender said the beer was on the house, he couldn't have been more prophetic.

For a couple of years he and I made a few races together, local shows where we would sit in the stands and dream there might be a place for us in the racing game.

They seemed like good days, days of laughter and a simple good time. I finally quit the glass plant and moved on to something else, but we tried to stay in touch. When we would run into each other in town he always began the conversation the same way.

"I been to a some real good races here lately," he would say, eyes wide with genuine excitement. He asked when we could get together, maybe take in a local show and catch up on things. We'll do that, I said. We'll sure get around to it.

Just as easily as our paths had crossed, our lives drifted apart. Partying and running the bars faded, and we didn't seem to hook up at the race track any longer.

I heard through the grapevine that Ironhead was doing well. He had met a good woman and settled down. I wondered if she was a race fan, and I wondered if the happiness Ironhead had missed for so many years had finally caught up with him.

A few years later I was at Anderson Speedway, watching the stock cars on a warm Saturday night. A drunk was staggering down the aisle in front of the main grandstand, his pants barely hanging on his hips as he tried to tuck his shirt in with hands that wouldn't seem to work properly. The crowd began to laugh at the man, who was oblivious, as he shuffled along. My gaze fell on his face as he turned to look over his shoulder, and my heart sank.

It was Ironhead.

I didn't know quite what to do. So I did nothing but watch him shuffle off into the night.

A couple of years ago, I was away on business when I made my nightly call home to check in. The usual stuff. Then my wife remembered that a buddy had called.

"He said somebody you knew died," she began. "Somebody named Iron Kid or something like that. Had a heart attack."

I think of him sometimes when the night air is just right, when you can sit under the stars and watch race cars and dream. Young will always turn to old, but dreams never really die.

They say racing has become a complex business. Somewhere in that complexity are everyday people, to whom the simple pleasure of watching a couple of race cars means a hell of a lot. The little guys who count their nickels and dimes and sit in the rain for a chance to make all the struggles in life go away, even if it's just for a little while. Nobody loves it more than they do.

Ironhead taught me that.

GOODBYE, ROBBIE

MAY 1994 - NATIONAL SPEED SPORT NEWS

Author's note: This column was written three days after Robbie Stanley was killed in a racing accident at Winchester, Indiana.

I'm going to miss you, Robbie.

It's been a pretty tough couple of days since you last climbed into a race car, days filled with doubt and grief and sadness, mixed with the busy excitement of another conclusion to another month of May.

I had become complacent, because I had forgotten that getting killed is a very real part of racing, a part everyone hates. I had laughed and joked with you so casually, forgetting that in one fleeting instant, the laughter could be silenced forever.

To put it simply, you're the first racing buddy I've ever lost. And I guess I'm having a real hard time dealing with it.

Some of the guys who have been around a while tell me it's part of the game; you have to accept it and go on. "Reality," they call it. They say it will always be there, the issue of danger in this sport. But maybe I don't want to face that because I'm not sure how to laugh and smile and joke with someone who might not be here when the night is over.

I suppose you would tell all your friends to keep going, that you don't want them moping around thinking about what happened to you. I suppose you would want us to keep our chin up and go on with whatever it is that we do.

That's what we tell ourselves, anyway, probably to help us through the hard times. We tell ourselves you died doing something you loved, and all that, and nod our heads at each other and somehow put one day together, then two, then three, until we've accepted what happened and fallen back into our routine.

That's what I'll do, I guess, fall back into the good old routine. Work at the office, drive home, kiss my wife, play catch with the kids, pay the bills, go to the races and have a good time. It will all keep going, just like before. But now there's going to be some emptiness at the races. And I can't do a damned thing about it.

You were a neat guy to work with, Robbie, I can tell you that. When you won, you had plenty of time for my dumb questions, when I tried to find an interesting angle to your winning yet another feature.

And I also saw you lose some tough ones. Just a few weeks ago at Terre Haute, you had one in your pocket when Cary Faas got under you with just a lap or two left to steal your thunder. I came walking up to your trailer about fifteen minutes later, and you looked at me and smiled.

"I've lost 'em before," you said, speaking quietly, "but these kind are hard to take."

But you didn't gripe. You didn't blame the car, or the track, or the flagman, or anybody else. You hated it, but you simply admitted that you got beat. That night just reaffirmed what I had figured out a couple of years ago, that you were truly a class act.

Coming back from Winchester on Thursday night was a long ride, I've got to tell you. I thought about a lot of things, little things, and I really couldn't believe it was over. I remembered you storming these hills when you decided to go pavement racing in 1991, and you had hardly seen the place before. You made our eyes bug out, and scared us, but you were fast.

That's all you ever really wanted, you told me, to go fast and make it as a race driver. Some people called you fearless, but of course that was never true. You just had what it takes to be a winner. Nobody can ever deny you that, because you won in them all: pavement, dirt, with wings and without.

You had some really neat people to help you get there, that was obvious. Your family helped you through the lean times, and you always made sure they got the credit for that. I think about how little "quality" time most parents get to spend with their kids, and I realize now that you and your folks could measure yours in years and years and years.

I remember hopping in the car with you and Michele last spring and riding to Winchester. It was a great time, you won the feature that day, and we talked a lot of good racing on both ends of the trip. But I remember one thing that really stands out in my mind.

That day was your first ride at Winchester in the Hoffman car, a car Steve Butler had vacated during the winter. Now, at the opener, you won the feature event in his old ride. We weren't a mile from the track when you told me you felt bad for Steve, because you knew what it felt like to get beaten by your old ride the next time out.

I was kind of amazed, to tell the truth. There you were, the day's big winner, and you were worrying about somebody else. But that was right in character.

I had the habit of making sure to look you up every time we were at the same race track. Not that either one of us had anything really important to say, but you always put me in a good mood. We would joke and laugh, and you always found something to smile about.

Right now, it's hard to smile.

A long time ago I read a quote from some philosopher that went something like this: "I've studied life in great detail, and I can sum it up in three words: it goes on."

Yes it will, it will go on. With one less smiling face, one less classy guy, one less racer. Maybe we'll hook up again later, somewhere where there isn't any unhappiness, where racing buddies never go away. I'll keep that hope in my back pocket.

For now, I've got to go find something to keep me busy, to keep my mind occupied on some busy work. Because this "reality" stuff hurts my gut. And it's going to be a while before it quits.

MARVEL SEEKS THE TITLE

SEPTEMBER 1994 - NATIONAL SPEED SPORT NEWS

It looked like just another season finale at any one of a hundred Saturday night race tracks in America. A new champion was being honored, having raced season-long for the honor of adding his name to the long list of track champs.

But perhaps we don't understand.

It wasn't just anywhere else, and it wasn't just anyone else. It was Brad Marvel, winning the season championship at Lincoln Park Speedway.

For other men, it might have been viewed as a ho-hum award, to be stashed in the trophy room to gather dust and be forgotten. But success is always a matter of perspective.

It is difficult, if not impossible, for us to realize how meaningful this single accomplishment is to one man and his family. For Brad Marvel, who stood with tears brimming in his eyes, wiping sweat from his face as others fought to control their emotions, it was sweet, sweet, sweet.

Less than one year ago, Marvel looked back at his lifetime of racing, and prepared to say goodbye. From quarter midgets to sprint cars, he raced and had fun, living and breathing the intoxicating vapors of this sport and experiencing its stranglehold on the human imagination.

He didn't want it to end, but he had no choice. Since he was eight years old, diabetes has stalked and ravaged his body, a constant foe that takes, takes, takes, never giving any ground back to its victim. The blood vessels in his eyes were the latest concession, and he readied himself for several surgical procedures that doctors insisted would end any hope of driving a race car.

At night he could visualize the cockpit of a sprint car, running lap after lap in his mind, and wondered what it would be like to never see the sight again. Soon, as he was consumed by anesthetic, he bid goodbye to his love, his passion, his racing.

But, ahhh, not so fast. As his vision began to return following the surgeries, Marvel made a startling and exhilarating discovery: he could see far better than even the most optimistic medical prognosis.

He had driven sparingly in the past few years for Dr. Tom Black, a Terre Haute cardiologist who has the relatively odd hobby of driving and campaigning a team of sprint cars. One of Black's cars had carried Kevin Thomas to the Lincoln Park title in 1993, and he looked to Marvel as a contender for the same honor this season.

It began as a difficult season, with the loss of Robbie Stanley in May. Stanley and his family had enjoyed a very close relationship with Marvel since the beginning of their sprint car exploits, and it was a moment of profound grief for Marvel.

Grief was nothing new. In 1983, when Brad was running Stanley's sprint car, his brother Billy died in a sprint car crash at Lincoln Park. It was a major upheaval for Brad, as he wanted to simply crawl into a hole and pull the world in behind him.

He eventually emerged from his cloak of sadness, and in time would come to embrace the same Christian beliefs and lifestyle that Billy had so joyfully espoused. Brad's attitude softened and changed, and as he approached his mid-thirties, he became perhaps the friendliest guy at the track.

His smile was contagious, beaming through every pore in his body, nearly every moment. When life is hard he smiles, and steps it up another notch. When sadness is here he smiles, quietly providing the light that helps guide others through the darkness.

The potential loss of his vision provided an extra incentive, he admits, because it reminded him that this season, this race, this life, you get one chance and one chance only, and then it's over. So he stood on the gas and raced with a new-found aggression and hunger, with a renewed desire to win a title.

Perhaps some of his desire was because Lincoln Park is where Doc Black likes to race. Perhaps some of it stems from Lincoln Park being one of the toughest, most stern tests of a team in the country, with a level of competition that regularly sees some of the big dogs on the trailer when the feature is pushed off.

48

And perhaps he wanted to do it for Billy.

He raced hard all season, and it looked to be all gone after a devastating and violent crash in mid-August, when his car flipped high into the air. The resulting impact broke his shoulder, virtually locking him out of the title chase with several races left.

But the next event was rained out, and the following week a special winged program was scheduled, with no points awarded. By week three, Marvel had a gut check and crawled back into his car, ready to fight on.

Now, as a massive crowd gathered at Lincoln Park for the season closer, the Non Wing Nationals, there was another hurdle when Marvel's car broke the driveline early in hot laps. Out on the track was Brian Hayden, in a position to lock up the title if Marvel did not make the main event.

Led by Marvel's crew chief, "Cuz," a group of men thrashed and worked, sweating as the daylight faded into night. Marvel worked among them, wallowing in grease and dirt. Soon, it was buttoned up, and he climbed aboard and tightened the restraints. As the push truck chugged behind him, his heart sank.

The engine was locked up.

Now, it was another crossroads. He raced down pit road to the team car of Robbie Rice, parked with engine problems. Despite low oil pressure, he made a late qualifying effort. Afterward, he and his crew again went to work, figuring out the problem and correcting it.

He transferred through his heat to the feature, while Hayden was forced to come through the B main. Marvel lined up twelfth in the feature, right behind Hayden. Hayden needed to beat him by at least eight positions, and went to work early. As Marvel raced conservatively, Hayden roared into the fray, fighting and working the cushion and passing cars on the outside.

But ten laps into the event, Hayden's luck soured when he spun and brought out the yellow, moving to the tail for the restart. Now, if Marvel simply finished in the top ten, the title was his.

As the checkered flag waved, Marvel came home seventh, three spots ahead of Hayden.

The race, the night, the season, it was over. There were no bright lights, no mob scenes, just a loyal group of friends and followers who embraced and enjoyed their achievement.

Marvel stood among them, exhausted and overwhelmed, a forty-one year old first time champion, thankful to everyone for their help. Soon, he was headed down the road, the noise and the lights fading behind him.

He would think about his championship, and Billy. He would remember Robbie Stanley, and those many years of struggling and working to keep himself going in this crazy business. He would pray words of thanks for one more chance, the one he would give everything of himself to make the best of.

Just another track championship? I don't think so. It was an eloquent example of a man who rose above all the obstacles to prevail. That, it seems, is something one seldom sees on just another night.

THE HERO RETURNS

OCTOBER 1994 - NATIONAL SPEED SPORT NEWS

The big man stared straight ahead, fidgeting with his gloves. He tugged at his shoulder straps and scooted his body farther into the seat of Dick Briscoe's sprint car, as a push truck gingerly rolled toward his rear bumper ready to send him away. Just as it did, bright sunshine broke through the cloudy skies and washed over the grounds of Bloomington Speedway.

Then again, maybe it just felt like sunshine.

Here he was, the real-life Dick Gaines, having blown out the candles on sixty-one birthday cakes. Here he was, back in a sprint car for the first time in twelve years. Here he was, giving people a chance to see him in uniform, perhaps just one more time.

To some, he might have been a joke. Whatever possessed him, they asked, to do such a dumb thing? Why was he trying to do something that couldn't possibly be done? What was he trying to prove?

He seemed hardly interested in proving anything to anyone. He was investing this Sunday afternoon on himself, fulfilling desires that have brooded in him the past few years, stalking him on race weekends as he quietly lived his life miles from the lights and the noise that made him a star. He was, you see, a real star.

For more than thirty years he raced among these hills, eventually becoming a national champion and earning a spot in the National Sprint Car Hall of Fame, enjoying the enduring and widespread recognition it brings. Yet, to many on this day, he was a curiosity, and some of the younger people stared at him with a look of puzzlement as they whispered, "Who's Dick Gaines?"

The rest of us didn't have to ask. In a younger time, Gaines was one of the giants, one of the reasons for wringing a few hard-earned coins out of our pocket to watch him and his rivals thrill us and scare us and excite us and give us an addiction to racing that will hopefully never be cured.

He was a big man in size and stature, and some continue to say he has never been fully recognized for his awesome talent. He was, and is, a curious sort, somewhat the loner, but friendly. He speaks "hillbilly," that wonderful dialect that peppers words and phrases about with machine-gun speed, exaggerating one moment then masterfully understating the next.

He has never tried to be anything he isn't. In his day, he was an enormous talent, but he was not the kind of guy today's sponsors would likely want to back. He was just too straightforward and matter-of-fact to spend time talking up somebody's product, or talking about himself.

His life revolved around sprint cars, and little else. He climbed aboard Dizz Wilson's car back in the early 1960s and proved the two were far more than a couple of local racers, winning so many events that nobody really knows the official count. And, while Karl Kinser was destined for greatness, it was his pairing with Dick Gaines that helped him take some major steps outside of southern Indiana.

Lord, there are great stories of those halcyon days, when Gaines was one of the major players within an impressive pool of sprint car talent here in the Midwest.

"When I was racing," said Butch Wilkerson, himself full of horsepower before he was felled with a severe injury in 1979, "that was the guy I always considered myself number two to."

Indeed, among his rivals, few mention Gaines with anything but respect and reverence. They laugh as they tell yesterday's stories, but there wasn't much funny back then, when he drove to victory after victory and left many biting their lips in frustration.

After blowing an engine at Paragon, he once pleaded with Keith Ford to let him drive Ford's big-block sprint car in the feature. The car, purchased earlier from Karl Kinser, was appropriately called "Big Bertha."

Despite the fact that Ford had timed third quick, and would be starting up front, Gaines eventually talked him into giving up his seat to allow Gaines to start on the tail. Gaines insisted to Ford that, "I won't lift 'er."

Ford told Gaines he didn't have the male organs to do that with a big-block car. Gaines stared at him and said, "You and I both know better than that."

"He passed eleven cars on the outside on the first three-quarters of a lap," remembered Ford, his gaze far, far away as he told the story. Then he crashed, crashed, crashed. When Ford arrived breathlessly on the scene, Gaines had a complete and thorough explanation.

"I forgot to lift," he said.

His years with Wilson were productive and at times barely tolerable, as the cantankerous, tempestuous car owner was delightful one day and miserable the next. However, in his defense, having on-the-gas men like Gaines in your car probably doesn't allow a man to relax.

But those days are gone. It is not 1967; it is 1994. A look through the pits reveals that only one of his great rivals is still racing, the fellow legend and powerhouse Bob Kinser. Kinser and Gaines were never friends, and to this day it would be awkward to get them together socially. That's hardly remarkable, considering that they were two strong-willed, high-talent fish swimming in the same pond. What is remarkable is that two men, born in the same generation within fifty miles of one another, would *both* rise to such greatness.

Now, on this autumn afternoon in the autumn of Dick Gaines' life, he wanted to put the throttle down just once more. He says the lure of $7,500 first-place money at the "D.O. and the King Race Fest" brought him off the couch, but money had little to do with it.

While Dick Gaines stopped driving race cars twelve years ago, he never really quit being a racer. His body could still perform, but the keen eyesight was nearly gone, leaving him following a violent, tumbling crash at Champaign, Illinois in 1977. He still talks reverently of the car Karl Kinser had put under him that season, although he nearly rode it to his doom.

"You could get 'er sideways, and just step on the gas, and—whooomm—that 'ol thing would straighten right up," he said, his face animated as his hands contributed to his story. "Ain't never been a car like that, I tell you. Ain't never been."

He managed five more years of driving following the Champaign crash, but his vision after dark was simply too poor to continue. So he "retired" to relative obscurity in nearby Mitchell, selling a few cars and mobile homes and carving out a living among these hard, tough hills.

He stayed almost completely away from the race track. He may never admit this, but it would be impossible for him not to miss the glory, the competition, and the friendship.

"Dick's pride," said Wilkerson, "just wouldn't let him come to the races. He didn't want to look like an old guy from the past."

But he wasn't just standing around watching today. His vision wouldn't be a factor, with the race held under the afternoon skies. An expected sixty-plus cars, plus three other divisions, would likely turn the track dry-slick, so why not get out here with the kids and have some fun?

He hot lapped, ran his heat, missed the show, and his day was over. Nothing spectacular, just a few more laps for a guy who has earned the respect and admiration of virtually everyone who knew him.

He didn't pass anyone, he didn't set any records, and he didn't show a hint of his former greatness. But for many of us, it was Mickey Mantle up to bat one more time. He didn't have to be sharp to be magic. Just him being here, in the midst of dust and noise and people, was enough.

When it was over, he disappeared over the hillside, perhaps to return to his contemporary world far removed from the methanol and the clay. The cool autumn night soon nipped at one's nose as the parking lot began to empty, and there was nothing but inky blackness of the sky as the day was long gone.

But it still felt like sunshine.

GREAT DAY FOR THE RACER

DECEMBER 1994 - NATIONAL SPEED SPORT NEWS

He awoke with a start, morning sunlight peeking through the bedroom blinds. He reached for the alarm and rolled out, and when his feet hit the floor felt the soreness come over his body.

It had been a late night in the shop, arriving home past midnight, another too-short night in the middle of a too-short week. He dressed and headed downstairs, his work uniform stiff and clean upon his back.

It was too early for the rest of the family, and he ate a quiet breakfast alone. Last one to bed, first one awake, as usual. He thought about the race car, and the same overwhelming feelings swept over him: it needs to be ready by Friday, and it's still got a long way to go.

He climbed into his pickup truck, backing out the driveway and heading up his quiet suburban street. He braked to a stop at the end of the block; it was time for a decision. To the right was his job, where he was expected; to the left was the shop, where an incomplete race car waited.

His mind was jumbled as he debated. He knew his boss wouldn't mind, but knew his family needed the money. Yet, how could he get the car done in just a couple of evenings? He cursed softly and pulled the turn signal lever down.

He arrived at the shop, unlocking the door and fixing a fresh pot of coffee. He called the plant, telling them he needed to work on the race car. His boss understood, and said there was no problem. He hung up, knowing that not everyone has this much freedom. He also thought of the money that would be missing from his next paycheck.

It was one of those days when he felt like he was in a vise. He was a family man, a working man, and a racer. Yet, no matter how much he tried, the priorities were often completely reversed. He loved his wife, loved his kids, enjoyed his job, but this damned racing thing. How could it have gotten such a hold on him?

He liked to think he did it for the fun, but laughed at the thought. Yeah, some fun. Work like a dog on this stupid old car, spend every dime you've got, and for what? Just so you can get a rush of excitement and accomplishment when you pass somebody on the race track?

He had been through this thought process before, over and over and over. He could not justify the amount of effort he put into racing; but no matter how logically he approached the issue, it never made any difference. He would always be back here, with the wrench in his hand, working as hard as ever.

The coffee was hot, and the cup warmed his hand as he sat on the workbench. He looked around at the worn walls of the building. It served as race headquarters, but it was really nothing more than an old alley garage, with two bays covered by sagging doors. He thought about the big operations the high-dollar guys have, and chuckled.

There had been chances, years ago, to get in those cars, but he was too stubborn. He liked doing it his way, and besides, he reasoned, when you own the race car you get to keep all your winnings. Plus, he just loved to get his hands dirty.

But today, the tools didn't look so appealing. He was tired, and another soul-searching crossroads had arrived. There had been no major crisis, no watershed event that had driven him back to analyzing his situation. Rather, it was many things: time, and money, and family, and energy, and success.

Yes, there *had* been some success. He always brought far less equipment to the race track than anyone else, but he was always competitive. He won a couple of features every season, local shows far from the limelight but enough to give him a tremendous emotional boost.

He finished his coffee and went to work. With the radio music in the background, he slid his toolbox open, grabbing the pieces he needed. Within minutes he was lost in his own world, working silently and quickly, knowing exactly what goes where and why.

At midmorning, he made a parts run. First he stopped at the bank, where he ran across a high school buddy, and it shocked them both to realize it had been twenty years.

"You're doing some racing now, is that right?" asked his friend. He nodded, and they talked about the local short track and Saturday nights.

"I bought a shoe store out at the mall a couple of years ago," his friend explained. "I don't have any money, but it might be fun to get my name on your race car. I can't do much, no more than, say, $750 for the year. But if you're interested, call me this winter and we'll talk about next year. Maybe I can buy you a couple of new tires."

Deep inside he cringed at how cheap he had become, but it was little deals like these that kept him going. It wasn't much, but that $750 could go toward something new. He took the guy's card, and they shook hands.

He spent the afternoon crawling around on the floor, making some progress on the car. This was not a good day for thinking, because he couldn't keep the depression from his mind. From the far recesses, the voice was nagging him, growing in urgency and volume: Why the hell are you bothering with all this? Why don't you quit this stuff and get a real life?

The doors were open now, allowing bright afternoon sun to pour inside. He discovered a couple of additional parts he would need, and wasn't sure how he was going to pay for them. He picked up the phone, and soon heard his wife's soft voice.

"Hi!" she exclaimed, surprised with his call. Within an instant, though, she knew. "You're not at work, are you?"

No, honey, I'm not. I just had to get the car together, that's all. There was no other way. But the boss wasn't mad, so that wasn't a problem.

"Gee, that's at least ten days this summer you've missed, but I guess that's okay," she said, her voice trailing off.

Honey, I need to pick up a couple of things, I think it'll be about $150. Can we cover that? Is that going to put us in a bind?

"No, we can get it covered," she answered. They talked a moment, then hung up. She sighed as her hand rested on the telephone. She knew they needed another day's pay in the budget, but there was no point in reminding him of that. He knew.

Fifteen years, and it only gotten worse. She loved racing in the beginning, and still enjoyed going and being involved. But it just didn't seem like much fun anymore, and she laughed as she thought of all the money they had spent over the years. But even though she would be elated if he were to become nothing more than a spectator, she never forced the issue, because she was scared.

Scared by the fact that if she backed him into a corner and said, "Racing or me," she honestly didn't know what his decision would be. They loved each other, but he loved that damned racing, maybe even more.

Late in the day, his buddy arrived at the garage. He was the kind of friend one should treasure, because he gave much more than he ever received. Every week, sometimes every day, he came and helped. He always came along to the races, and wouldn't even let anyone pay his way in. He just loved to be involved, and it gave him some satisfaction to help make a car go faster.

As his friend worked, the racer headed home for dinner. His family was talkative at the table, and it was a nice, happy scene. He and his wife had three beautiful children, good kids who worshipped their dad.

"Dad, do you think we could go for a bike ride tonight?" asked his oldest boy.

Not tonight, son, I've got to get back down to the shop. We've almost got the car ready, and only one more night to work on it. I can't take the chance. We'll do it another night, I promise.

His funk deepened as he headed back to the shop. The bugs swirled around the light bulbs, and soon he was alone again, his buddy heading home around eight. He spent the next three hours making a needed part, a part the big guys would have bought.

It sobered him, as he considered: my time is almost worthless, because I don't have the money to make it valuable. He finished the part, and decided he'd had it for the night.

He closed the garage doors, and paused to look over the scene. He stared at the old car, showing her age but sitting proudly. He could always get the most from the least, and he was damned proud of that. But tonight, he didn't feel proud about much of anything.

He drove home, and the house was dark. Only the front porch light glowed, his wife knowing he would be along sooner or later. He parked the truck and made his way up the sidewalk.

The grass needed cutting, and his mower wasn't working right. The garage door had been broken for three months, but he hadn't found the time to fix it, so they simply parked outside.

His wife's car needed tuning, but there hadn't been a wrench on it. He began to feel overwhelmed with the futility of his situation.

Once inside, he showered and washed away the sweat and dirt of a full day. But his blues remained, and he headed downstairs, not ready for sleep. He opened a beer and sat, a lone figure under the kitchen light.

He thought about everything he didn't have: money, prestige, freedom. He would never have been rich, but if he had taken every dollar he'd spent on racing for the past twenty years, and put it in the bank instead...

He hadn't been to a movie in five years. He had never been to a concert. He missed many of his kids' school functions, because he was busy racing. He had never been to a high school reunion. Mother's Day, Father's Day, Memorial Day, July fourth, Labor Day, he had raced through, and past, all of them.

And what did he have to show for it? A house that was falling down, a worn out race car, a few lousy trophies, and a tiny bank account. He finished his beer, walking up the darkened staircase as the downstairs clock sounded a single chime.

He could hear his wife's soft breathing as she slept soundly, and he quietly slipped into bed. As he lay on his back, his eyes grew accustomed to the darkness and he stared at the ceiling. It was a deep, depressing moment, as he was slipping toward the moment he had always feared, when he would seriously consider quitting racing.

Then, suddenly, the voice came back to him. The scene in the bank, and the words: "Maybe I can buy you a couple of new tires."

He smiled broadly, rolling over and pulling the blanket up around his chin. No problem sleeping tonight, he thought. It had been a great day...

THE GOOD MAN

FEBRUARY 1996 - NATIONAL SPEED SPORT NEWS

Getting there, someone once said, is half the fun. From Kokomo to Lincoln Park, Tri State to Avilla, Anderson to Terre Haute, making the trip to Hoosier speedways can be an adventure. Scenic from the vast flatlands of the north to the rolling hills of southern Indiana, nothing is more pleasant than an afternoon trip followed by a good night of racing.

In fact, when I think of the great times from the past twenty-plus years of racing, some of the more memorable events took place far from the race track.

There was the ride to Eldora on a freezing day in the back of Steve Remington's pickup truck; a hundred-mph run from a Kokomo traffic cop with an unnamed racer at the wheel; a blown right-rear tire on an old Corvette that gave me a hairy ride through the weeds; on and on.

But perhaps the greatest memory comes from twenty years ago; when late on a summer night I learned that Indiana people really are the finest in the world.

I headed for Lawrenceburg Speedway on a Saturday afternoon, to hook up with a brother-in-law for sprint car racing at the fabled 'Burg. Riding my new motorcycle, I was just out of my teens, still young and wild, with a few bucks in my pocket and living every inch of life.

It was a beautiful, sleepy Indiana day; the kind of summer afternoon that seems locked in place, to be repeated until the end of time. The locusts screeched as I rolled through the Hoosier countryside, warm air washing over me as I drew nearer to speedway, where legends waited. A few miles outside Lawrenceburg the bike faltered, and I switched to the reserve fuel tank without losing a moment.

I had come to see the stars: Dick Gaines, Butch Wilkerson, Bobby Black, Calvin Gilstrap, Bob Kinser; every one of them larger than life. In the county-fair atmosphere of Lawrenceburg, it was another night of mud-throwing, sideways sprint cars riding hard into the cushion and bicycling, before brave men gassed them in the other direction.

When the racing was over, I climbed on the bike and headed toward North Vernon, where I would sleep for the night. I remembered the fuel situation, and like an idiot rolled past open gas stations in Lawrenceburg and Aurora. I'll just stop in Versailles, I figured.

It was just before midnight when I cruised into Versailles, a quiet little place that apparently likes to go to bed early. There wasn't a gallon of gas to be had, as every business had closed hours earlier when they rolled up the sidewalks and locked them away. I began to sweat.

Several miles out of town the bike sputtered, coughed, and went silent. I coasted to a stop off the highway, dropped the kickstand and climbed off. Pulling my helmet off, I looked up the road.

There was not a light in sight. Behind me, I could see faint lights at a small farmhouse about a half-mile back. There was nothing but the sound of crickets as I turned the bike in the road and began pushing.

As I drew near the house, I could see the front door was open. Inside the front room was a family watching television, oblivious to this silent stranger in the night. The gravel in the drive rustled slightly as I pushed the bike off the highway, finally parking it before walking toward the house.

It was after midnight, and my throat was dry as I walked toward the door. I was scared and vulnerable, cursing myself for my stupidity and putting myself in this situation. I stepped onto the porch and into the light, where moths and June bugs battered quietly against the screen. The people in the room before me were still mesmerized by the flickering box, and my hand silently reached upward, rapping gently on the wooden door.

They were startled, and in a millisecond every eye in the room was on me. An adult rose from his chair, as several children jumped up from the floor to investigate this surprise.

"Howdy," he said with a smile, walking toward the unlocked door. "Can we help ya?"

I explained my problem and that I needed some gasoline to be on my way. I apologized for the interruption, feeling very foolish.

"Hey, now, that's jest no problem a-tall," the man said. He turned to one of his children and said, "Now, you go get me the lantern, and fetch me my keys."

He stepped outside, followed by at least six children. "Ain't it a beautiful night?" he asked, reaching down to tousle the hair of a small child at his side. "Why, we was a-watchin' the late show, just fixin' to go to bed. Lucky you come along when you did, cause once I gets to sleepin' I wouldn't get back up fer God hisself if he ran out of gas!"

We laughed that kind of warm, heartfelt laugh of innocence. I was amazed at this man, and his wonderful demeanor. Someone had come along with an uninvited intrusion, and this man was happy, kind, and friendly. He owed me nothing, but was willing to step up because I needed help.

In a moment, a little one delivered to him a flashlight and a small key chain. We walked across the yard toward an old white shed, all the children surrounding us as we walked, their bare feet making tiny prints in the grass dampened with summer dew. As we drew near the shed, he handed me the light as he fumbled for his keys.

"Here, shine me the light," he said, squinting at his keys until his fingers had found the right one. He lifted the tiny padlock, turning to grin widely at me.

"These knotheads 'round here will steal ya blind if ya ain't careful," he said, and in a moment the door was open. He found a small can of gas, and in a moment we had poured its payload into my bright orange tank. What would have cut his grass was now going to take me home.

"Well, I sure thank you," I said, my hands drawing some money from my pocket.

61

"You put that money away," he said. "Gallon of gas ain't never hurt nobody. I ain't no businessman. You get on up the road."

I argued, but of course he wouldn't hear of it.

"I'll tell you what," he said finally. "Next time some `ol boy runs out of gas by your house, you help him out. That'll make us even-up."

The kids waved and shouted as I fired up the bike, my headlight cutting through damp night air. I gave one final thank you, and in moments was in fifth gear, rolling away from a scene that would be etched in my memory forever.

Over the years, I have traveled many times down U.S. 50 along that stretch, looking at each house and wondering if it was the one. The exact location may have faded over time, but certainly not my memories of a good man who was willing to help a dumb kid get out of a jam.

Those folks, and the idea of helping a total stranger late at night, were wonderfully innocent; an innocence that is probably gone forever from our society.

Later that summer, the radio brought shocking news that Calvin Gilstrap was dead, killed in a Bloomington sprint car flip. I was stunned beyond words that these wonderful, exciting, beloved sprint cars could kill. An innocence of another kind died that summer, I think.

Now, twenty years later, I look at calendars with surprise, amazed so many pages have turned. It is still a great ride to Indiana races. Just remember to gas it up before you go.

HERBIE

APRIL 1996 - NATIONAL SPEED SPORT NEWS

It was the type of night that tests the mettle of any race fan, from the passive now-and-then spectator to the most hardened race junkie. It was about forty degrees, with a stiff twenty-mph wind out of the north.

But they came to Anderson Speedway this Saturday night for the season opener, ready to see another year of stock cars on this historic quarter-mile bullring. Winter has been grudgingly, gradually releasing its grip on the Midwest, and people seemed anxious to forget the cold and get the season underway.

A big man stands near his race car, watching the wrenches work. He is ready to tee it up one more season, knowing it is possible that this is the last one. This is the thirty-sixth season opener for Herb Rose, all here at Anderson Speedway.

It's hard to grasp how much this scene has changed from that first one in 1960. He was a tall, lanky kid who liked cars, just spreading his wings and becoming a young man. Track owner Joe Helpling had introduced the "Fabulous Figure 8s off the High Banks" at what was Sun Valley Speedway, and like a small child chasing a firefly, Rose was drawn to this race track with its bright lights and roaring engines.

Now, in 1996, he isn't a kid anymore. His face shows the years that have passed; each line like a chapter in a long and drawn-out book. He became a journeyman race driver, able to handle anything, anytime. He kept his nose clean, took care of his car, and didn't get himself hurt.

Yet, he never really left Anderson Speedway. Oh, sure, in the mid-1960s he did some ARCA racing, and had some great runs, but he just didn't have the backing that many of the factory teams had at that time. When that era was over he eventually found his way back to Anderson Speedway.

Rose became part of a group of incredibly talented and colorful race drivers who had a specialty: the Figure 8. Yeah, most of them were also very good oval racers, but there was something about "the 8" that made them special.

Among them were Gene Huston, the intensely aggressive daredevil who may well have been the greatest Figure 8 driver of all time; Darwin "Hook" Blankenship, the free spirit; Bob Fields, who won so many races here nobody can count them all; Dick Hinshaw, the quiet tradesman; and Gene "Cookie" Cook, who at his peak could dominate. All were here every Saturday night for more than twenty-five years, come hell or high water. There were others, too: Johnny Keller, Junior Shirley, Mike Williams, Bill Keep, Bill Lemon; it was a heck of a crew. And right in the middle was Rose, the tough racer who only needed an inch to beat you, any night, any spot.

Of course, like all race drivers, age has eventually taken most of them out of the game. Only Rose, Blankenship, and Huston still choose to battle with the kids every Saturday night, winging their way through the crossover with the precision needed to stay alive.

You look at Herbie, and you wonder why he races. He has spent far more money at this game than he's ever going to take out. He's been banged up, punched, taken out, set down, and broke. I guess the flip side, winning races, and championships, has been enough to sustain him.

You shake your head, thinking here is a guy who has raced his guts out for thirty-six years, and has never received the kind of recognition that goes with being a champion. Sure, he's got a little bit of local notoriety, but outside of this small circle...well, you just don't see a guy like this in the spotlight.

Probably like a hundred other guys, or maybe a thousand, at tracks like Anderson, or Thompson, or Hialeah, or Devil's Bowl, or Skagit, or Berlin. Great racers, great heroes, great guys, but only if you're lucky enough to catch their act at a local level.

It's funny. When you've had an opportunity to see some great racers around the country, you finally realize that some of the very best were right there in your hometown. That's where guys like Herb fit, for me, right up there at the top where the big names park.

There is an episode I remember, from about ten years ago. At the big Labor Day stock car show at Winchester, Rose was set to drive Kenny Jones' car, a good car in good hands that was a favorite to win that day. It was hot and muggy, and Rose came home second. Moments after the race, someone told me Herbie had keeled over when he climbed from the car.

I ran the length of the pits, my mind working overtime. His heart, maybe? I got to the pit and Herb was seated in a lawn chair, his big hands holding his side. His face was white and he was having trouble breathing.

Our eyes met, and I quietly asked him what was wrong. Nearby, someone yelled that an ambulance was on its way. Herb, between gasps, explained he had hit a bump very hard down in three, and it jarred him so hard against his seat that he had busted his ribs.

"What lap, Herb, when did it happen?" I asked. "I think the first or second..." his voice trailed off. Soon, the medics arrived, ready to take him away to fix his ribs.

To this day, I'm amazed when I try to grasp what the man did. With several broken ribs, he fought Winchester's treacherous banks for nearly fifty laps, holding off several challengers and bringing the car home in second place.

This year, he says he'd like to win a few more races and have some fun. He'll run his own low-budget late model, and he's got a great, great ride in Tony Bargo's Figure 8 car. He knows, deep down, that a lot of people expect him to win the Figure 8 championship. He never says it, but you can see the desire in his eyes, just like it was 1960 all over again.

Parked next to his car is another No. 99, with another guy named Rose lettered over the door. Herb's kid, Ronnie, began racing two years ago at age seventeen, and you can sum the kid up by saying he's his father's son. He's steady, smooth, consistent, and takes care of his race car. Give him an inch, and suddenly he's alongside you. I wonder where he gets that stuff?

Herbie laughs when he thinks of his kid racing, and his future. To really blow your mind, consider the length of Herbie's career in this perspective: If his kid races as long as Herb has, he'll still be cinching up the belts in the year 2030.

Soon the races are over, and midnight is not far away. Cold weather has cleared the place out quickly, and shortly after the Figure 8 feature you see Herbie all alone in his pickup truck, with the race car on an open trailer behind. His headlights pierce the darkness as he heads home, another among hundreds of racing nights before.

There are no groupies hanging on him, no PR men getting quotes, no television lights in his eyes. I smile when I think the fans here probably don't understand what a great career this guy has posted.

I head for the car, through a now-deserted parking lot, and look around and know this isn't Daytona. But that's the beauty of this gig: It doesn't have to be.

JUST THE BEGINNING

MAY 1996 - NATIONAL SPEED SPORT NEWS

The bright colors of the Menard car were vivid under gray skies, and Tony Stewart sat patiently waiting for a green flag. It is his day of days, when the kid who is in high gear hopes to make his mark on the biggest venue in all of racing, the Indianapolis Motor Speedway.

A track record? The pole position? Both are expected of him, and he doesn't want to disappoint. The light blinks green, and a crew member stabs the electric starter into his machine and engages the trigger.

"Whhhhirrrrrrrrr....boom, bubba boom, vroom, vroom..." The gearbox complains with a grind as he searches for first gear, and the Menard engine moans as he labors out of his pit and down pit road. It is a raw, cold Saturday morning, but the chill is thawed by the enthusiasm and intensity of his crew and dozens of onlookers in the pit.

In nearby grandstands, thousands of people huddle under blankets and sheets of plastic, cheering lustily as cars take to the track for another practice session before qualifying begins. Stewart quickly tops the charts with a 235.7 mph lap, and it looks like he is ready. He is called back in, and comes down pit road and inadvertently stops several lengths short at another Menard pit. Nervous, perhaps?

"Go get him!" shouts Team Manager Larry Curry, sending crewmen scurrying down pit road to push their boy home. When he is pushed into place they engage the air jack and change his tires, as he sits perfectly still in the car with the visor up on his brightly painted helmet.

Finally, he pops his belts and wiggles from the car. Pulling off his helmet, his hands tremble slightly as he peels the tape that holds his radio earpieces in place. Immediately people in the grandstands begin shouting, "Tony...Tony...over here, Tony...go get 'em, Tony..."

He smiles nervously and waves, and begins walking back to the garage area with Curry and team owner John Menard. He enjoys a few minutes of quiet and some lunch: the calm before the storm. Away from shouting crowds, roaring engines, and the pressurized confines of a race car, he perhaps thinks for a moment about the position he is in.

A year ago, the only job he could find here was as a pit-crew stooge. Now, he is ready to gun for the pole in one of the fastest race cars this place has ever seen. Don't look for such a fast-forward button on your machine, because that kind of warp speed advancement is unlikely for most of us.

Soon it's time to face the challenge. Stewart walks from the garage, and sits next to Curry on a golf cart. Neither speaks. You get the impression Curry wants to make sure he keeps Stewart close, not letting anything or anybody play any games with the kid's head. After all, a rookie mind can be fertile ground for the wrong kind of thinking.

Stewart's car is placed in the qualifying line, and he prepares to reenter the cockpit. He fiddles with his visor a bit, and a nearby friend from his short-track days softly calls out to him.

"Relax, Tony," he says. "Just think of it as a really big Silver Crown race."

Stewart's face breaks out in a broad grin, and he raises his head, turning to look at the man. He shakes his head, and then mouths the words, "Nice try."

The car moves up one more spot, and there is a reunion. Nelson Stewart, Tony's father, is working for Pennzoil this month here at the Speedway. Tony sits on the pit wall, taping his earplugs in, and Nelson moves up behind him and pats him on the back.

Nelson's shirt is Pennzoil yellow, while a couple of feet away Tony's car is painted Quaker State green. But it is blood, not oil, that binds these men.

No words are spoken as Tony works with his helmet and Nelson's hand rests on his son's shoulder. All those lonely hours in the pickup truck hauling the go kart, a million memories and a million miles. It all ends here, it seems...or does it just begin?

Nelson blinks at tears in his eyes, his hand clutching his boy's shoulder. Finally the car is pushed forward, and it is time to move down the line. Tony turns to his father, and their eyes meet. They shake hands, holding the grip several moments as they stare at one another. Then, the younger man stands, turns, and walks forward with a look of intensity.

The crowd moves with Tony, and as photographers jostle around him, Nelson is left standing alone. His glasses are off, and a handkerchief dabs away the tears.

Tony pulls on his helmet and is strapped in. Davy Jones sets a track record and Stewart sits unflinching in his car, with no movement but the slight heaving of his chest as he breathes. He is now within a couple of cars from the front of the line, face to face with thus far the single greatest moment of his career.

Johnny Rutherford walks around the car and leans down, putting his face directly in front of Stewart's visor. He says a few words, and Stewart nods. Rutherford stands and walks away. What could one possibly say to a driver in this situation?

"I told him just do four smooth laps, just like he's done all week," says the four-time winner. "That's what I always told myself when I was getting ready to qualify."

Did his advice ever work?

"Well, I got the pole here twice," he says, a smile crawling across his face until it was an unabashed grin. "I guess it did."

In a moment, Chief Steward Keith Ward reaches into the cockpit to shake Stewart's hand, as do Menard and finally Curry, who gives some last-minute soothing to his hired gun. Again, the message is clear: just be smooth, just like practice.

The engine is fired, and it is Stewart's turn to qualify. He engages the clutch and the car is away. The crowd, sensing that the boy is going to deliver, rises as he heads toward the most exciting two-and-a-half miles of asphalt on earth.

Menard and Curry aren't cheering. They aren't smiling, either. This is crunch time, baby, and they have their game faces bolted on tight. They head to the pits to wait.

Stewart blazes around the course at more than 233 mph, turning in four smooth, consistent laps that for most of the day earn him the pole. Tom Carnagie's booming voice reverberates around the grounds, informing us that it's a one- and four-lap record.

In a moment, as the next gladiator takes to the track, Stewart's No. 20 comes growling down pit road, the crowd cheering lustily as he brings the beast to a stop. There is jubilation and emotion, and you know this is a moment he will never forget, nor will those around him.

There is a mob of media, crew members, and fans to greet him, and he seems swallowed up by it all. At every turn he is patted on the back, his hands shaken, microphones thrust into his face.

Behind the crowd is Menard, saying nothing but allowing his smile to speak volumes. Is he disappointed with the 233, given that Stewart had practiced several miles an hour faster?

"You always want to go faster," says Menard softly, nodding his head, his smile intact. "But maybe that's all there is today."

He would wind up second-quick, but it's hard for anyone to be disappointed. Up above, gray clouds fill the skies, but it is far from gloomy for Tony Stewart as he lives his day of days. From stooge to star, in a blur. And it is just the beginning...

DUSTY OLD PHOTOGRAPHS

MARCH 1997 - NATIONAL SPEED SPORT NEWS

They were just old photographs, discovered in the bottom of a box.

The colors were vivid, the bright blue race car, the yellow and white letters that had been quickly applied, the beautiful green grass from the sunny afternoon, and the black-and-white cloth patches from the checkered flag the driver held proudly outside the car's window.

It had been more than twenty years since those pictures were taken; long ago pushed back into some obscure corner of memory. Only now did the recollections rush out of hiding, prompted by the images.

His name was Mike Riddle, and we had worked together at the factory. He was a buddy, a certifiable wild man. We were both just kids, but since he had married very young and already had a wife and a couple of babies, he seemed like the old man between the two of us.

Anderson Speedway had introduced a new class of race cars that summer, something called street stocks. Cars poured from every corner of the region, and it seemed like every man within five counties who had access to a welder had built one of these cars.

Just a couple of weeks after they announced the new cars, I went to Anderson one Saturday night and was shocked to see that Riddle had built a race car, an old Buick Special with a small V8. I was shocked because, to the best of my knowledge, the guy had never even been to a race track before.

He had been on vacation the week before, when somebody mentioned they were thinking about building a car. That was all there was to it; in just a few days, he was a race driver.

Because I was already a track rat, I naturally pitched in, since he was the first guy I was ever close to who actually raced. After the Buick was history, we decided to build a bigger car during the winter.

He found a 1966 Chevy somewhere; we also found a 348-inch Chevy, an antique even in those days; a big hunk of iron with weird-looking valve covers. We rolled the junk to his garage, and he let me come over and help.

Pity the man who puts a wrench in my hands; anybody who does so is going to get exactly the quality of work he deserves. But this deal was different, because the first thing we had to do to the old car was strip it out. Ripping seats from their moorings; gouging the dash from its natural home; cutting out fender wells; suddenly I found work I was qualified for. Just don't ask how to put any of it back together.

Soon, we had a rolling race car. The old engine had a ton of torque, but you couldn't keep it cool on the North Pole. We had raced many times at Anderson, but it was soon time for a road trip. We made the Saturday-night show at Anderson, then dragged the remains of the car home for quick repairs before a Sunday-afternoon show elsewhere.

I remember it was light outside, probably around 5:30 a.m., when Mike had to weld something on the car. He fired the car up, surely shaking the windows in his neighbors' homes, and drove right up to his back porch. He rolled his welder up on the porch, and I asked him what was he doing.

"I need juice," he said simply. "Here, help me move this dryer."

We dragged his wife's dryer away from the wall, and Mike quickly "redefined" the usage of the 220-volt outlet, busily welding away in his back yard while his wife and kids and a few of the neighbors still slept.

As we wrestled the dryer back into place, I remember thinking that Darrell Waltrip probably didn't have to mess with stuff like this.

We were so proud, heading up through town, with an honest-to-God race car on the trailer behind. Kids yelled and pointed, other motorists looked us over as they passed, and we might as well have been heading to Daytona, with the smile on our faces.

We went to a little track about an hour away, a place called Mt. Lawn Speedway. It remains today a beautiful old track, originally built where a baseball diamond once stood.

Flat and egg-shaped, it was a challenge for the best of 'em. And when it came to minor details like chassis setup, we didn't have a clue. One of the other racers must have felt sorry for us, because he came over and offered some basic advice on springs and shocks; and while Mike may have been listening, the guy may as well have been speaking in Russian, because the conversation went sailing right over my head.

But Mike did quite well in qualifying, and sure enough started up front in the feature. He took the lead and hung on, driving with a clenched jaw, the 348 crackling and popping as he lifted for the corners. Just don't get hot, I remember thinking; just don't get hot.

We were all acting like fools, jumping and yelling and screaming as the laps wound down. He had never before won a race of any kind, and if you've never been there it's not really possible to describe what that feels like.

Soon, he took the checkered, and in the euphoria I grabbed my camera and headed down from the stands. I dashed to the pits and across the track, trying to focus and get ready for the victory picture. Not only had he never won before; I had never before taken a picture in focus.

It is a warm feeling, thinking about that moment. He had taken the checkered flag from the starter, and was taking his victory lap. As he slowed for the first corner, I ran close to the track, and we looked at each other and just laughed, a joyful, deep laughter that comes clear from the toes. I raised the camera and clicked off memories, recording the moment—and the feeling—forever.

It wasn't the last race he won; he eventually moved up a division and raced for about ten years, the wild man becoming a pretty fair race driver.

The pictures don't show it, but some bad memories were part of the package, too. There was the night he took a massive hit in the driver door, the kind of shot everyone immediately knows is bad. It is a sobering, somber feeling, standing there helplessly while your friend begs to die as they are trying to cut him from a shattered, broken race car.

I remember the sound of the ambulance door slamming shut, none of us knowing if he would make it as they hauled him away. Nobody ever knew it, but I went to my car and I cried.

He made it, and raced again. Eventually, he hung it up and gave up race cars, while I gave up the cameras and somewhere along the line picked up a note pad. I've never regretted that move; at least you don't have to focus a word processor.

The sins of the father really are visited on the son. Last summer I made a trip to Anderson, and guess whose kid is driving a race car? Another young Riddle, this one named Doug, was rookie of the year in his division this past season. Ah, the circle of life remains unbroken.

I wonder if the kid has any friends who have a camera? I hope so, because everyone needs to record those moments, so that they too can find memories at the bottom of a box. Just a bunch of old, dusty photographs.

THE PROMOTER'S GHOST

APRIL 1997 - NATIONAL SPEED SPORT NEWS

His ghost is here, you know.

It is a cool evening in central Indiana, with mothers and fathers and children zipping jackets and pulling on coats as they make their way into Anderson Speedway.

For forty-nine years this old place has welcomed them, sitting in silence throughout the week and coming to life on Saturday night, the most sacred few hours in traditional short-track racing.

People line up at ticket booths, trading a few dollars for a tiny ticket to paradise. It's funny, watching the transactions take place; everybody seems to give up their money with a smile.

Their walk quickens as they pass through the entry gate, as if something deep inside is urging them on, anticipating fun and excitement. There is something inside all of us that seeks the excitement, as we walk with the body of a man and the spirit of a child.

The parking lot is filling fast, and drivers are concluding their meeting in the pits, just a few minutes before race time. The crowd sounds are all around, as the announcer's smooth voice recites news and information about tonight's event.

Children squeal and giggle as they hold tightly to their parents' hands, their eyes widening as they pass by the concession stand. Perhaps they dream of treats to be bargained for later, ranging from sweet, sticky cotton candy to the salty, familiar popcorn.

You stand and look at all this, and you begin to understand that this is what old Joe had in mind.

He was an odd fellow, make no mistake about that. Joe Helpling was a square peg in a world filled with round holes. He was quirky and eccentric, and some of his thinking was downright bizarre.

But he gave us Anderson Speedway, fifty years ago.

He's gone now, leaving the earthly world some twenty years ago. But on this night, for the first time in years, I look around this comfortable old race track and realize that Joe Helpling lives on, perhaps forever.

He liked to dream, and when he bought a parcel of ground from the City of Anderson in 1946 he envisioned a bowling alley here at 25th Street and Pendleton Avenue. But something along the way changed his mind; although he had never before seen an auto race, he decided this site would be just dandy for a race track.

He was right about that.

He sketched a high-banked quarter mile on a single sheet of paper, and hired a crew of men at $1 an hour. By early 1948, he was ready to race, and he called the place Sun Valley Speedway.

He was, I must admit, ahead of my time. When I was a young boy, discovering this place, he was a hollow, aging shell of his former self. But I grew up listening to the stories of his promotional genius, and today understand that he was a gifted man whose talents will probably never be fully appreciated.

He liked to try different things; some were hailed as bold and innovative and others as downright daffy. He once held an event that saw a field of cars go five laps counterclockwise, and as the leader crossed the finish line on the fifth lap, he reversed direction and ran clockwise the remaining five laps, meeting his followers head-on until the frantic field could reverse themselves.

Many of his ideas had historic implications, such as the Little 500 sprint car race. He was called a lunatic at the time, when he proposed thirty-three roadsters going 500 laps. Call it visionary or hard-headed; but Joe believed the idea would work. And it did. While the roadsters are long gone, since 1949 the Little 500 has become a cornerstone in the identity of this town.

I walk to the main grandstand, and look at the people sitting there, chatting happily between events. It isn't hard to remember my early years when I would beg and plead with my dad to take me to the races. He did, along with a brother-in-law who allowed a car-crazy twelve-year-old boy to witness the scene of methanol-breathing sprint cars here on Wednesday nights.

It was a religious experience.

When I was old enough to drive, I came over here every time the gates opened, sometimes dropping my last dollar at the ticket window. I had many friends, but none felt the spirit quite as powerfully as I did, so I sat alone in the grandstands, taking it all in.

Despite all those hours in science class, I still believed the earth's rotation centered around Sun Valley Speedway.

On this chilly spring night, everything seems so modern, so fresh and clean and up-to-date. I look behind the grandstands, and I can imagine Joe, walking right over there, with the shuffle of a very old man whose time had come and gone.

He wore clean white coveralls, with red lettering on the back that boldly proclaimed, "FABULOUS FIGURE 8'S OFF THE HIGH BANKS." Kids made fun of the old guy as they raced past, while adults looked and rolled their eyes, probably considering the strange old man to be much like the town jester.

He was a shadow, a man who was truly misunderstood. He slowly, steadily lost the handle on this place, and by 1975 was in serious financial trouble. Old Joe, it was alleged, didn't pay his taxes.

By early 1976 an auction was scheduled, and six local men came together to buy the track. Joe quietly faded from sight and a year later died.

The six were good caretakers of the place; through a series of buyouts their team was eventually reduced to two, John Hellis and Rex Robbins. Earlier this year, they decided their run had finished here, and they sold the track to some newcomers.

Hellis and Robbins, along with their former partners, left this place in far better shape than when they got it, and anyone who loves racing here owes them a bit of thanks.

The new guys are interesting. Rick Dawson is a quiet accountant with a strong business sense; Skip Waymire is a well-known local man with years of work in local politics; R.J. Scott is the fired-up promoter whose ideas just never stop coming.

Together, they have visions for Anderson Speedway; their faith and optimism is evident in every conversation. I can't help but wonder if old Joe isn't here somewhere, whispering in their ear when they think up an idea that might seem a bit too bold, a bit too risky.

He had it right: Give people a good show for a fair price, and they'll be back. Keep them excited. Don't be afraid to try new things. Listen to your customers.

I wonder about the people throughout Joe's life who ridiculed him and thought him wacky. I wonder if they ever had ideas and dreams, and if they ever tried to turn them into reality. I wonder if their life's work outlived them.

Joe's did.

"JESUS, COME AND GET ME..."

SEPTEMBER 1997 - NATIONAL SPEED SPORT NEWS

It was a quiet ending to a very large life.

Sometime in the early morning hours of September 4, life ebbed from the body of Jan Opperman, freeing his troubled soul from sixteen years of imprisonment. It was a passing that was as blessed as it was sad, because it just isn't fair to ask a person to suffer forever. All the same, there is no joy in saying goodbye to a man who was a friend to everyone, whether they had met him or not.

Jan Opperman had a profound influence on modern sprint car racing, more than he could have ever imagined. Out of the West nearly thirty years ago came this beaming, longhaired man who smoked pot and talked about Jesus. At a time when American society was being wrenched by a tumultuous cultural upheaval, Opperman arrived to transform sprint car racing as well.

Because of his controversial persona, his acceptance in the sport did not come quickly. But his awesome driving ability would eventually open the doors, as people from every corner acknowledged that this man represented a rare, special talent.

He captivated all of sprint car racing, literally from coast to coast. Perhaps it was his hippie lifestyle that made him such a compelling story; or maybe it was his breathtaking skill and bravery behind the wheel. But open-wheel fans who saw this warrior were transfixed, mesmerized by his very name.

Those who didn't know him personally would look at his hippie lifestyle, his frayed jeans, his floppy hat, his outspoken love of Jesus. He made them squirm, because he was different than anyone they had ever seen before.

But he proved time and time again that he was truly great in the seat of a race car, and he eventually forced people to look past the long hair and the lifestyle. Whether he wanted to be or not, Opperman was an agent of great change in sprint car racing.

Before Jan Opperman, conventional wisdom said that an outlaw racer was a notch below USAC and other leading organizations. Nobody had ever really challenged that thinking. Until Opperman. It is true other racers made a dent— Kenny Weld, Bubby Jones, Rick Ferkel, to name a few—but it was Opperman who truly broke through, capturing the public's imagination on several occasions as he won against USAC's best.

It was suddenly okay to have long hair, to be anti-establishment, to walk your own path exclusive of others. A clear trend can be traced to Opperman's arrival in the sport, as being an "outlaw" soon became as acceptable as running USAC.

This, to those who did not experience it, was a truly profound shift in attitudes.

Alas, no man is forever, no matter how great. Opperman won races from sea to shining sea and is accepted today as one of the greatest by any standard, but he was not bullet-proof.

His devastating crash in the 1976 Hoosier Hundred ended it all, for all practical purposes. He was struck in the head by another car's bumper after getting upside down at the Indiana State Fairgrounds, and it was actually something of a miracle he survived.

Like the great lion he was, Opperman refused to give up. Slowly, steadily, he worked through rehabilitation for many months following the accident, until he climbed back into a race car less than a year later.

For the next five years he searched desperately for the magic that had left him, driving anything, anywhere, as if looking for something he would never again find.

He sought to turn the story of his life into one of hope and recovery, but instead found it destined to be filled with tragedy. His second major head injury came at Jennerstown, Pennsylvania in 1981, taking the driving skills and the ability to function as a normal human being.

After his crash, Jan Opperman was once again something of a symbol, but it was not as a vibrant, brave, dashing race car driver. Rather, he became the tortured image of what you and I fear most: incapacitated, incoherent, and dependent on others for even the most basic human needs.

Of course such tragedy is usually followed by love, and Jan Opperman's story was no different. His mother and father, refusing to send him to an institution, devoted their lives to caring for him, spending sixteen steadfast and loving years by his side and making his life as good as it could possibly be. Great parents are a much finer gift than material wealth; in that regard, Opperman was blessed beyond description.

During the years that followed, several people helped Opperman in a variety of ways and should be commended, because they truly improved his living conditions and his life. Dick Berggren of OPEN WHEEL MAGAZINE was the first, as his haunting and brilliant story in May 1986 reached the hearts of race fans throughout the country. Robin Miller of THE INDIANAPOLIS STAR made Opperman the beneficiary of several fundraisers at Indianapolis, while WFBQ (Indianapolis) radio's Bob Kevoian and Tom Griswold raised more than $100,000 to help support Opperman and his family.

Harvey Shapiro and Ed Watson produced a book about Opperman's life and donated the proceeds to Jan and his family; so did Joe Scalzo and Carl Hungness. Noted attorney Cary Agajanian donated countless hours administering a trust fund through which money steadily helped the family.

Race fans never stopped sending money to help Jan Opperman. Sometimes it was a check for a hundred bucks; or it might be an index card with $.85 in coins taped to the back with the words "Merry Christmas, Jan" scrawled on the front.

That should be the measure of the man, more than the hippie lifestyle, more than the brilliant driving ability. Here was a person who touched thousands of people, touched them in a way in which they were never really the same after the experience. That is a level of love many aspire to, but few achieve.

His heartbreaking injury made communicating difficult, and Opperman experienced great peaks of emotion as he tried to talk to those around him. Inexplicably, during the week prior to his death he became more lucid, at times speaking in entire sentences.

"Jesus, come and get me...after while would be all right, but now would be better," he pleaded.

The heartbreak of Jan Opperman is over. The lion is free at last, free to roam once again and find beauty and joy and happiness in a place he always believed awaited him.

His floppy hat, his bright eyes, his hair blowing in the evening breeze, that is what we remember of Jan Opperman. The powerful slides into the corner, blinking through the blood in his visor and staying with the fight. The loud, deep laughter that came from deep within. The long nights in his old station wagon, driving hours and hours to another race track. All were the essence of Jan Opperman.

Let us know that his was a life that will never be duplicated.

He once belonged to all of us; now he belongs to God. May we remember him forever.

COLUMNS

COLUMNS

Ed Hamilton was easy, and that's what started it all.

It was 1983, and I had been writing for THE ANDERSON (Indiana) HERALD for three years as a "stringer." A stringer was a part-timer who covered local sports on the weekends, primarily high school sports.

I loved covering basketball and football, but I was a race fan at heart. In 1983, Ed Hamilton came to THE HERALD as our new sports editor.

Since my arrival in 1980 I had lobbied for more racing coverage, to no avail. So when Ed came to town, I immediately explained that the paper needed to expand their auto racing coverage, figuring this would allow me to attend more area races.

"Great idea," he said. "You're our writer. I want you to write a weekly column. We'll pay you the regular stringer rate."

Never mind that the "regular stringer rate" didn't even buy a tank of gas; I was absolutely overwhelmed and intimidated at the thought of writing a column. News writing is simple; you gather the facts and report. But writing a column isn't so narrowly defined, and you're expected to express—gasp—an opinion.

But once I got started, I loved it. I had found my niche. I could express myself and have fun, completely uninhibited by the boundaries that normally come with news writing. The column, called "Track Talk," ran from 1983 to 1987 in THE HERALD. I stopped writing the column when I moved from Anderson to Fishers, Indiana, because I believed (and still do) that local writing should feature someone very close to the local scene.

Sometime in the mid-1980's, Jerry Gappens and Keith Waltz began asking me to write an Indiana-based column in NATIONAL SPEED SPORT NEWS, which is considered the most important trade publication in all of motorsports. Jerry was the publisher at that time, and Keith was the editor.

Talk about intimidated. *Wow. I simply couldn't imagine myself writing for a national audience. So I resisted for a couple of years, and Jerry and Keith would bring it up just about every time we talked.*

Finally, in early 1988 I agreed to give it a try, with one condition: if any of us received feedback that the column wasn't very good, I would stop. Jerry and Keith agreed, along with the great Chris Economaki, and "Indiana Scene" was born. Later, we renamed the column to "American Scene."

That column was one of the most important things that has ever happened to me. It expanded my horizons more than I could have ever imagined, and opened a whole new world.

It's been thirteen years now since it began; I hope it continues for a hundred more.

The SPEED SPORT columns are what this collection is all about. I have included some feature stories (in another chapter), but it's the columns that I have especially enjoyed writing.

I'm grateful the people at SPEED SPORT gave me the opportunity to do the column, and I'm especially thankful that you, the reader, have come along for the ride.

EIGHT YEARS IN THE MAKING

FEBRUARY 1988 - NATIONAL SPEED SPORT NEWS

Big victories often hasten a young driver's rise to the top. With that in mind, Roy Caruthers has his fingers crossed.

Caruthers' victory in the recent Hoosier Dome Invitational in Indianapolis is the greatest on-track accomplishment, to date, in the twenty-six year old Indy native's career. It came in front of nearly 15,000 people, and his share of the $25,500 purse was around $4,000. It's not Belleville, but it beats sitting at home watching reruns on a January Saturday night.

Caruthers used a brilliant late-race pass to take the lead from Johnny Parsons, Jr. in traffic. He downplayed his role as driver ("The car was perfect," he would later claim) to praise the work of his crew and the people who helped him get there.

"Getting there" has not been easy for Caruthers. He is the adopted son of the late Doug Caruthers, a well-known car owner. His stepfather is veteran Indy Car crew chief Johnny Capels. Roy Caruthers began driving while in high school, but his career has maintained a modest growth.

Gene Crucean, the fun-loving, talented photographer who teamed with John Mahoney to produce the unforgettable *Sprint Car Pictorial* from 1968 to the early 1980s, was convinced by Caruthers to buy a midget and go racing in 1980. While Caruthers has occasionally driven for others, he and Crucean have been together since.

The pair campaigned in CORA, WWAR, USAC, and lately the AAMS series throughout the years. While Caruthers earned the 1987 CORA points title, big victories have eluded him.

Until the Dome. Actually, his 1987 showing was also impressive, when he dogged Rich Vogler for much of the hundred lap grind, giving onlookers a glimpse of talent that perhaps hadn't yet been discovered. But a broken rocker arm ended his ride, and it was the same old story. Close, but no trophy.

This year he was ready. The team, which is not a big-buck operation, decided to skip the other indoor midget events throughout the Midwest during the weeks preceding the Indy show. They wanted to conserve their limited capital and tire budget for one show, rather than come to the Dome with used rubber and no money. It worked.

"The car has always worked well in the Dome and at the Speedrome," Caruthers admits. "But with those new tires, it hooked up perfectly."

The first-place showing prompted a riotous celebration, aided by the fact that Caruthers had prevailed in front of the home crowd. Well-wishers and backers from the past eight years crowded around the team as they exulted, eyes glistening in the haze that hung in the Dome air.

Caruthers took it all in stride. Within a couple of hours of the victory, he was home in bed. Crucean, however, couldn't suppress his happiness, and he and followers left the Hoosier Dome and headed for a downtown Indy club called The Slippery Noodle Inn.

There, to the music of Harvey and the Blue Tones, they savored the team's accomplishment, eight years in the making.

Author's note: The above story was my first column in NATIONAL SPEED SPORT NEWS.

GUT-CHECK TIME

FEBRUARY 1989 - NATIONAL SPEED SPORT NEWS

For the umpteenth time in his long career, it's gut-check time for Chuck Amati.

Amati has won a lot of races in his twenty-five-plus years in sprint car racing. He's traveled all over the country, and his charm and character have built him a loyal following. He has overcome virtually every obstacle placed in his path.

However, sprint cars have displayed a voracious appetite for Chuck Amati's body and soul. He has been broken, burned, bruised, and beaten. He invested his last dime into his own team a few years ago, only to be left with a twisted, worthless pile of junk following a massive Eldora crash.

But he always came back. In 1964, he crashed through an antique wooden fence in Milan, Tennessee. A flying timber tried to rip his right arm from his body. It nearly succeeded. The damage was so severe that he couldn't lift his arm for months. He fashioned a leather harness to hold his limp arm at his side, and raced. And won. They called him the One-Armed Bandit. He was young, cocky, and aggressive.

Twenty-five years later, Amati now faces perhaps the greatest challenge of his life.

He and car owner Darryl Tate had won fifteen features and two Indiana track championships (Paragon and Tri-State) in 1988, and they decided to try to make the season-closing event at the Talladega short track in Alabama. Amati had not seriously crashed all year long. At Talladega his luck ran out. His machine got caught in traffic and flipped ten times, end over end. The car was destroyed, and so was his right shoulder socket. Crumbled. Finished.

Now, Amati must once again decide how much he wants to drive a race car.

"I'm doing better every day," he insists. "The doctor has designed a leather harness that will brace my arm to keep it in its socket when I race. He says that a big jolt, like hitting the cushion hard, will let it pop out of socket again."

To really appreciate what Amati is facing, one must examine his lengthy career. He was the journeyman outlaw, racing and winning all over the country. The injuries suffered back then were to a young man, and were dealt with quickly. As he grew older, however, mending took longer. And it became increasingly difficult to find quality rides.

Following the big-league crash in 1984, Amati found himself physically hurting and financially broke. It seemed as though he had nothing left. For three long years, he languished around his Illinois home. In 1987, he finally got a one-race ride at Lawrenceburg. Despite the long layoff, he amazed everyone but himself by winning the feature. He was still without a ride.

The dream didn't die. Tate, who had wrenched Amati's Jerry Shields ride in the early 1980's, had built his own chassis and the pair lined up limited sponsorship money. They decided to race the tough southern Indiana circuit.

Amati's comeback was nothing short of brilliant, leaving absolutely no doubt he could still drive a sprint car.

But now what? While he doesn't divulge his age, Amati is not a young man. His shoulder injury is serious. But he says he isn't a quitter; still wants to win.

"I'm very confident about this season," he says with his trademark smile. "I know what it's like to drive hurt, and I can do it. A man has just got to deal with the fear that builds up inside, deal with it in your own way. The only way I can overcome that fear is to get back in the car and get the job done.

"When I came back last year, after being off three years, I was so, so scared. Not scared of getting hurt, but scared I would fail. The fear almost overwhelmed me for a good six weeks. The only way I could make it go away was to let my desire and ambition challenge that fear. All year long, my race was with myself. I just wanted to beat that fear that had been with me every day for three long years."

Amati admits his Cinderella comeback with a low-buck team was "the most glorious event of my life," especially because so many people had written him off. The success was even sweeter because of the strong emotional ties that have bonded he and the workaholic Tate, along with the rest of the team, through some lean weeks in 1988.

Not everyone believed in Chuck Amati a year ago. But those who did were people like Jim and James Hall, of Hall's Racing Engines. Like Charlie and Scott May, whose Carterville, Illinois excavating and construction company helped bankroll the team because Amati had been Scott's childhood idol. Companies like Brodix, Marsh, McCreary, Schoenfield, Afco Fabricating. It was as much for those people, as for himself, that Amati wanted so much to succeed.

Despite all the physical evidence that might make one think otherwise, the key ingredient that will bring Amati back in 1989 is desire. It will be with him every moment, and his goal is to win a feature and the track championship at Bloomington Speedway, a track he insists is "the toughest weekly show in the country."

His injured arm is never mentioned. The shattered bones could just as well be invisible, nothing more than a minor irritation, just as the leather harness will be. But through his pain and suffering, in front of all those people who said it couldn't be done, Amati will be there.

You can bet the farm on it.

ORDINARY GUYS

MARCH 1989 - NATIONAL SPEED SPORT NEWS

A couple of ordinary guys got together on a recent Sunday afternoon, and it was their first reunion in a while. They did the same things most old friends do, chatted and remembered days and nights gone by.

For the most part, Larry Dickson and Gary Bettenhausen are ordinary guys. But they did some extraordinary things during "The Larry and Gary Show" twenty-or-so years ago, and theirs is perhaps the greatest chapter ever in USAC sprint car history.

That was the reason Dan Wonn of the Hoosier Auto Racing Fans put together their reunion before a packed house at a UAW Hall on Indy's southwest side. Between reels of classic Dick Wallen sprint car action, the two men who made history allowed emcee Larry Nuber of ESPN to talk with them about the way it was.

Bettenhausen took his first sprint car ride at Ascot, California in November 1967. He liked it. In 1968, he drove A.J. Watson's four-cam Ford at Reading, Pennsylvania to open the USAC season, where he finished second to Dickson. It could be interpreted as a harbinger of things to come.

Dickson was already tough in a sprint car. He came from the tough outlaw supermodified circuit, earning his stripes along with the bruises and bloody noses which were part of the territory. When he saw his first USAC sprint car race at Reading in 1965, he watched what he thought were "out of control" racers doing things with sprint cars that sent chills up his spine.

The two began an intense war that would last for four years in reality and forever in memory. Dickson claimed the USAC championship in 1968, with Bettenhausen second. Their roles were reversed in 1969, and in 1970 Dickson won again, with Bettenhausen runner-up. Finally, in what would be the last year of "The Larry and Gary Show" in 1971, Bettenhausen earned the title with Dickson right behind.

USAC was the pinnacle of sprint car racing during that era, and it is often overlooked that while Dickson and Bettenhausen monopolized the series, open wheel legends such as Rollie Beale and Sammy Sessions were relegated to third place or worse. Larry and Gary raced against the very best of the very best, and left everybody in the weeds.

On this day, as Nuber prodded with questions both seemed to enjoy answering, it was apparent just how much the former rivals had mellowed. The laughter was easy now, giving no hint of the intensity and emotion that had once motivated Bettenhausen to tape a photograph of Dickson on the dashboard of his Willie Davis sprinter.

Their rivalry was the final element that pushed them out and ahead of everyone else. The media always asked one about the other. "What about that guy...do you like him? Did you hear what he said?" They weren't just racing against the field, but especially "you know who," wherever he was. It's a good bet each knew exactly where the other had finished when they were putting it on the trailer for the ride home.

Dickson is the quiet man. He says Bettenhausen is "the most determined man I've ever met," but Dickson isn't exactly a pushover himself. During their many confrontations there were inevitably some harsh thoughts, but very few harsh words.

Like many other things, "The Larry and Gary Show" was never officially over, it just went away. They had left their mark on a sprint car world that was changing all around them, from roll bars to cages, from bandanas to full-face helmets. Their lives and careers were changing as well.

Dickson "retired" from racing in 1972, and when everybody had completely written him off, made an incredible comeback by subbing for an injured Bob Frey in Ernie Ensign's machine at the Little 500 in 1974. Dickson easily won the grueling event, convincing himself and the rest of the world that he still had what it took. He capped his comeback by winning the 1975 USAC title, and continued racing up until recently, when one could quietly note that his name was found less and less frequently in USAC Silver Crown results.

Bettenhausen found himself in Roger Penske's Indy Car in 1972, and he continued to enter a limited number of sprint car events despite Penske's concern of a serious injury. An incredibly violent crash on a fateful July 4 afternoon at Syracuse, New York in 1974 nearly paralyzed his left arm, and only after a gutsy comeback did he once again enjoy success. He continues to race Indy Cars and USAC Silver Crown machines today.

Their Sunday afternoon conversation no regrets. Dickson pointed out he was simply happy the two men had lived to tell their story. When one considers their wars were waged on the hills of Salem, Dayton, and Winchester without a roll cage, perhaps that is the brightest and most significant factor of all.

It has been a number of years since either has won a sprint car race. But as an appreciative reunion audience showed them, memories of their success remain bright and vivid. Larry and Gary are, well, two of a kind. Extraordinary talent. Extraordinary courage. Extraordinary personality.

Pretty big stuff from a couple of ordinary guys, sharing their lives on a Sunday afternoon.

"YOU'LL GET ALONG JUST FINE WITHOUT ME, KID."

NOVEMBER 1989 - NATIONAL SPEED SPORT NEWS

When the November winds drive autumn from the Indiana skies, I think of Bob Byrne. That's when he went away.

He was one of the most knowledgeable men ever involved in Indiana racing. He was the chief scorer at Anderson Speedway since its 1948 completion, and until his death in 1983 he was involved in every single event ever held there.

Bob's command of racing facts, dating from the very beginning of the sport, was simply incredible. He knew virtually every story, from every little bullring in Indiana, from Jungle Park to the Speedway. He was a well-known writer, and a frequent contributor to NATIONAL SPEED SPORT NEWS.

He knew everybody, it seemed, in the Anderson area. He worked many years at General Motors, and was one of the most staunch of the rabid Anderson

Indians basketball fans. He could recite every starting lineup that "his" Indians put on the floor since 1920.

He knew a lot about things like that. He also knew how to help people.

For a number of years, Bob authored a racing column in the ANDERSON BULLETIN. I remember, as a kid, running to the mailbox every Wednesday evening, ripping through the paper until my eyes found the familiar words "Let's Go Racing," next to the picture of a smiling man wearing a worn USAC cap.

What he did was important to a lot of people. Along with that came some heat. A story was told, back in the 1960s, of the Little 500 driver who was upset because he felt Bob scored him incorrectly. Late that night, after the race, he jumped Bob and gave him a violent beating. Bob was unruffled, and it never seemed to dissuade him from making the tough call when it was needed.

The Little 500 was his baby. He was present on the afternoon the late Joe Helpling announced the pioneering event, and Bob never missed one until the 1984 race, six months after he died. He knew every driver, and every car, and every story through the years, just as a father can recall specific events in his son's life. He was nothing less than a fixture, and many well-known people walked away from Anderson with great respect and admiration for the guy in the little town who knew so much.

Behind the scenes, however, Bob had more than his share of heartache. His two broken marriages left their mark. He struggled to raise his children alone. He was never afraid to speak his mind, and made some enemies. He carried some grudges to the grave.

Memories are kinder to Bob today, and those things don't seem as important as they once were. It's much easier to remember Bob for the good things he tried to do.

The BULLETIN had a rival in town, the ANDERSON HERALD, which offered very little coverage of racing. I had covered plenty of football and basketball for the paper, and the HERALD sports editor gave me a shot at my own racing column. I was somewhat overwhelmed. I knew I would be competing with Bob, and in terms of racing knowledge knew I wasn't in his league. I didn't know him personally, and didn't know what was in store for me.

It would have been easy for Bob to try to run me out of town. He didn't. He went out of his way to help. He gave me scrapbooks and reference materials. He answered my late-night inquiries as deadlines loomed. He introduced me to people who would be good contacts. Most of all, he offered moral support.

Then the heart trouble came.

There had been too many late nights, too many cigarettes, too much heartache for it to be any different. His health slipped away, and he could only struggle on in frustration. He kept writing, and he kept his job as the PR man at Anderson Speedway, despite his hospital stays.

Late in the 1983 season, we planned to share a ride to the All-American 400 in Nashville, but at the last minute the doctor ordered Bob to stay home. You'll have to go along without me, he said. I remember his very last words to me: "You'll get along just fine without me, kid." His words still have a haunting sound when I think of them some years later; a couple of days after Thanksgiving, he died in his Chesterfield home.

There have been many changes since that night five years ago. For me personally, it's a different life in many respects. But one thing hasn't changed; I still hold great memories of Bob. He taught me that it's better to give to those who need a break. In that respect, I hope time will stand still, never robbing me of my memories of a fine man indeed.

A WORLD FILLED WITH HOPE

AUGUST 1989 - NATIONAL SPEED SPORT NEWS

Just a few days ago, her world was normal. Her life was filled with family and racing, as she traveled the Midwest watching her husband become a talented driver on various midget circuits.

Today, instead of sitting among cheering crowds and the long trips towing the race car with Eddie by her side, Joan Horne's days are filled with doctors, medication, emotional peaks and valleys, and a husband who is badly hurt.

Her world is filled with hope. Hope Eddie will get better. Hope they will be home soon. Hope they will overcome the inevitable financial burdens to come. Hope she and her husband can explain the situation to their two year old son.

When she watched Eddie touch wheels with Bob Cicconi late in the thirty-lap feature a few days ago at Indianapolis Raceway Park, she held her breath. Eddie doesn't crash much, you see. Joan saw the car glance off the wall and slide to a stop in the middle of turn three, one of the fastest points of the five-eighths-mile oval. She saw Mel Kenyon's car slam violently into Eddie, and was frightened.

The first night was like a hazy, faraway dream. The first few minutes blurry as they carefully removed Eddie from his devastated racer. The helicopter ride took Eddie to Methodist Hospital in Indianapolis, just minutes away. Not knowing if her husband would live or die, not knowing what her world would be like when the sun came up tomorrow.

They carefully explained Eddie's injuries to her. Basal skull fracture. Broken hip. Badly bruised arm, probably broken. They told her what they knew, and what they didn't know. She didn't know what to expect. She prayed.

When they took Eddie to Intensive Care, she couldn't see him much. That was tough, she says. She wanted to be close by his side, even though there really wasn't much she could do, especially since Eddie wasn't really in any condition to talk. Just the same, she wanted to be there, every minute.

About that time, she began to realize there were people there to support her. The doctors and staff at Methodist were supportive and kind. Her family was right behind her. Other racers offered what they could. Mel Kenyon, whose lacerated leg required thirteen stitches, called. She knew she wasn't alone.

She didn't have to wait long before her hopes began to come true. Eddie regained consciousness, and began to speak to her. X-rays revealed that his arm was not broken. Doctors were encouraged.

They moved Eddie to a private room, where she could sleep on a cot. She had been staying in the hotel across the street, the one reserved for patients' families. Now, she could spend every minute with Eddie, helping and being there for him. They were both happy with that.

There are two major concerns with any patient. Their physical well being which includes broken bones and other such ailments in which doctors and nurses are expert in dealing. Then there is their emotional well being, the mental condition that often determines not just *if* a patient will recover, but how long it will take. She will let doctors and nurses take care of the first part, and is determined to help with the second.

Like anybody in his predicament, she says Eddie's spirits have been up and down. He's happy that lots of his friends have called and sent cards, because it reminds him that people care very much about him. But the pain is tough, and the medication he's given to deal with it very powerful. She knows how important her positive influence is right now, so she tries to talk and think positive all the time.

No matter how much she ever thought about Eddie having a big crash, she says she didn't expect it to be like this. It was always the other guy, you know? But this time, she is married to the other guy. This time it's close to home.

She wonders if they will ever race again. When Eddie first began talking after the accident, he said no. But when you are in intensive care, she wisely points out, who wouldn't say that? She thinks about the car, back in their shop, all bent and broken. She knows eventually Eddie will have to make the decision: race again or quit.

Right now, she is more concerned about Eddie's stomach. With the drastic change in his body, he's having difficulty keeping anything down, and feels nauseated a lot. Doctors say this is normal. "It will pass," they say. It makes Eddie feel pretty rotten, but he says it won't stand in the way of his recovery.

The next bright spot will be leaving Indianapolis, returning home to Defiance, Ohio. When Eddie can keep solid food down, he can be transferred. She is excited. She knows it will happen, because she has hope.

She misses their son, Chad, who is staying in Ohio with Grandma and Grandpa. He doesn't understand what happened to Daddy. This weekend is worth waiting for, she says, because Chad will come visit. That will brighten their spirits.

When she reflects on the past few days, she is thankful. It could have been lots worse, she says. When she thinks about that helicopter, she knows just how much worse it could have been.

There were several thousand people at IRP the night of Eddie's crash and probably a million more watching on television. After it happened, they all worried about Eddie, and then went back to their own busy world, probably wondering once in a while how he was doing. In just a few days, they will actually forget it even happened. That's not cruel, that's just the painful facts of life.

The cheering crowds are gone now, but Eddie is not alone. He has Joan by his side; ready to face challenges most of us cannot comprehend. Together, they can recover. Together, their lives are filled with hope.

ORNERY

OCTOBER 1989 - NATIONAL SPEED SPORT NEWS

His black shoes pound the firm infield soil of Winchester Speedway as he walks among Goodyear tires, carrying an air gauge. Onlookers seem oblivious to his presence, instead focusing on the bright green No. 88 with Buick sheetmetal nearby. He is wearing a black jacket over a plaid, untucked shirt, and a very large frown.

Mike Eddy is having a great time.

The scene was just prior to the start of the twentieth-annual ASA Racing Series Winchester 400. The two-time "400" champ would soon slip on a familiar driver's uniform and proceed to put the wraps on an unprecedented fifth ASA Racing Series championship.

It was fifteen years ago that a pudgy, determined kid with long blonde hair took his first ASA title in 1974. The years that have passed have produced a leaner, cleaner, and yes, meaner Mike Eddy. His intimidating stare and terse replies to questions have earned him a dubious reputation with the media, as he has sent more than a few interviewers retreating to the sidelines waving the white flag of surrender.

Now, two-and-a-half hours later, he is ready to talk, but only a little. He finished fourteenth after breaking a Heim joint early in the race and losing twenty-five laps, but needed only to finish sixteenth or better to clinch the title. ASA PR Director Al Stilley delivered Eddy to a pack of writers and broadcast reporters who have already interviewed the top three finishers: Butch Miller, Ted Musgrave, and Tony. Eddy slips almost unnoticed into a chair in the corner of the brand new Winchester press room.

"I find that if everybody thinks I'm ornery, they leave me alone at the race track," he says quietly, allowing a smile. "When I'm runnin' around there, sizing tires, getting the car ready, I'm in my own world, and I love it. I'd like people to leave me alone. I guess I am a pretty hard guy to get along with, but I have less trouble with people that way."

Eddy is the working man's racer. During the week, he does all of the maintenance and repair on the car at his shop. On weekends, he drives the tow rig to the scheduled ASA show, and at the track doesn't let up, with help coming from a crew of volunteers. Eddy is not just the driver; he is virtually the entire organization. Why does he handle what must be an enormous workload?

"I don't have any money to hire mechanics," he says matter-of-factly. "All of my sponsor deals are for equipment, not money. So I've gotta make it go all by myself. I've been with teams that all I had to do was show up at the track with my helmet, but when things go wrong, you can't correct it yourself. Now, if the race car breaks, I got nobody but myself to blame."

He hasn't had much to blame himself for this season. Of 4,050 possible ASA laps in 1989, he completed an impressive 4,001. Earlier in the day, when the Heim joint failed, the car had scarcely stopped in front of his pit before Eddy was squeezing through the side window, goggles still in place, headed for the tool box.

Now, with his fifth ASA title in place, it's on to bigger and better things. Or is it? Many of Eddy's former playmates have left the ASA town and headed for the bright lights of Winston Cup. Mark Martin, Rusty Wallace, Dick Trickle,

Jim Sauter, and Alan Kulwicki all traded paint with Eddy on a weekly basis, but now they are gone.

"I'm very happy right where I am, with ASA. If I were to run NASCAR, that would take up two hundred percent of my time, and I'm just not willing to give up my family life and my home life for that."

He also knows self-promotion is a necessary part of being a successful career driver in today's world. But that's not part of his deal, blowing his own horn.

"As far as I'm concerned, that's the most distasteful part of this business. I love the driving, workin' on the car, the travel, all that. But I hate facing the press, the interviews, talking about all of this. I know it's bad to feel that way, but hey, that's me. Working with the media is the least-liked part of my job."

Now, Stilley calls Eddy's name out to the writers in the room, introducing him as the 1989 ASA Champion. A smattering of applause echoes as Eddy takes his seat in front of the room. Miller playfully asks Eddy if he jumped out of the car when it broke and fixed it himself, and he doesn't seem surprised when Eddy says yes. Some of the reporters are amazed when they learn Eddy actually works on the car himself, even during the race.

They shouldn't be surprised. Everything Eddy has accomplished in his career has been the result of determined, gritty, sweaty, hard work. He's been on top of the mountain, fallen painfully, and climbed back up. As he sits on the pinnacle today, he recalls just three years ago when he began his new team with some equipment and $5,000 from Howe Enterprises.

"They told me to race until it was gone," he says, allowing the soft smile to play upon his face once again. "I'm still goin'."

That $5,000 check was one of the best investments Howe Enterprises ever made. If anybody ever gives Eddy a check with more than one comma, he might go on forever.

Frowning all the way.

THE FIRST SIXTEEN

JANUARY 1990 - NATIONAL SPEED SPORT NEWS

Sometimes at night you can almost hear their names in the wind. Their images still plays in our fading memory, when we think of what used to be. Their names bring a smile to the face of an old-timer, and sometimes a look of puzzlement to a kid. They are the legends, the heroes, the unforgettable souls who made their mark on sprint car racing.

Some are still around, with a few wrinkles, gray hairs, and joints that hurt when the weather changes. Some didn't get out alive.

They now have a chance at immortality. In April, sixteen individuals will be named on the first induction ballot for the National Sprint Car Hall of Fame in Knoxville, Iowa. There will be sixteen added each year, but getting in on the first ballot will perhaps be the ultimate measure of greatness.

Eight will be former drivers; four will be former owners, mechanics, builders, or sponsors; and four will be former promoters, officials, media members, or event sponsors. All will be unforgettable.

These are the guys who brought us to where we are now. If it hadn't been for their showmanship, courage, desire, and ability, sprint car racing would have died long ago. Instead, they electrified us with their brilliance, filling our hearts and minds with dreams that we too someday might be great. They made us forget our own limitations, and they made us want to come back, forever. Even though the sport changed and they all would eventually go away, the seed was planted, and for most of us, it refuses to die.

It began with the drivers, who made us squint through the dust and cover our ears and hold our breath. Guys who were gifted, with quick wits, or great wrists, or raw courage, or all of the above. Guys we thought were immortal, larger than life itself, who we would never forget.

Some we are grateful to still have, like Tommy Hinnershitz, Troy Ruttman, Foyt, Parnelli, Bobby Grim, Jerry Richert, Rollie Beale, Dick Gaines. Some we still miss, like Jud, Preacher, Don Branson, Johnny White, Gus Schrader, Ted Horn, Bryan, Hurtubise.

99

Then there were the men who built the cars, or owned them, or made them work, or laid out the money so it all could happen. They laughed when they won, and cursed when they didn't. Whatever the outcome, they always seemed to come back for more. Aggie, Speedy Bill Smith, Don Shepherd, Kuzma, Don Edmunds, Willie Davis, geniuses every one.

And the promoters, who put up the money. Officials, who broke up the fights. Writers and broadcasters, who recorded it all. J. Alexander Sloane, Frank Funk, Jack Gunn, Ralph Hankinson, Russ Clendenen, Al Sweeney, Dick Wallen, Chris Economaki, each building a great legacy.

There were countless more who made their mark on an era. It's time for their moment of glory, away from the field of conflict, away from the crowds. It will be a time to savor, to enjoy, to laugh and cry at the memories. It will be an impossible blend of joy and sadness, remembering the victories and those you saw go away.

They will probably find that this business meant more to them than they realized. Some spent the majority of their life pursuing a dream. Others gave their health and fortunes. It's a safe bet that during the June induction ceremonies most would say they would do it all again if they had the chance.

They did their part, now a nominating committee of fifty-five men must do theirs. It's an impossible task, really. When one considers the vast list of names which can be associated with greatness, it confuses the senses to try to trim the list to just sixteen. Finding those who qualify is easy, but separating those who are truly deserving of a first-ballot nomination is exceedingly difficult.

When the list is determined, and announced, we should quietly give a thank you to all of those named. They are the reason for our excitement in the springtime when we hear that rumble and the acrid methanol odor filters to our nostrils and the hair on the back of our neck stands tall. Finally, after all these years, the legends will live forever.

RALPHIE THE RACER COMES HOME

FEBRUARY 1990 - NATIONAL SPEED SPORT NEWS

It's a cold afternoon in Indiana, and Ralph Liguori has come home for his finest hour. Never mind that he was actually born in Brooklyn. Never mind that some of his greatest successes came at the wheel of a NASCAR stocker in the South. Never mind that today he lives in Florida. In his mind, in his heart, Ralph thinks of himself as a Hoosier.

Today, he's taking a step in that direction, as he and Kenny Schrader are inducted into the Hoosier Auto Racing Fans (HARF) Hall of Fame. They will join some well-known guys named Bettenhausen, Foyt, Andretti, Hurtubise, and Brawner. Pretty elite company, he'll tell you.

Throughout the ceremony, Liguori basks in the limelight; receiving congratulations from fans who remember watching him stand on the gas. His bright smile only makes his Florida tan look more bronze, and he is the picture of graciousness as he accepts the lavish praise offered. As he works easily through the crowd, it is obvious: if it takes class to get into the Hall of Fame, Ralphie the Racer was long overdue.

Well, there it is, that title. Ralphie the Racer. The nickname that's stayed with him all these years. It has been used in jest and in anger, in good times and bad. Ralphie the crasher, the wild man. He learned to live with the stigma, but still winces when it is spoken.

It's hard to figure exactly where he picked it up. When you get right down to it, he never should have been stuck with the label. He raced from 1949 to 1975 steadily, and still played with his sprint car occasionally through the mid-1980s. In all that, he can only recall seriously crashing a total of eight times. Some guys get on their head that many times in a season.

But Ralph made one major mistake. He crashed big when the TV cameras were rolling, focused on him.

In the late 1960's, ABC televised the Tony Hulman Classic for USAC sprint cars at Terre Haute, Indiana. The live shows were part of a Saturday afternoon segment of *Wide World of Sports*. Ralph pulled a spectacular shunt in 1969,

101

getting some major flight time, and ABC caught it all. This was long before you could shell out $50 for a videotape full of crashes. When something like this flickered across their TV screens, America paid attention.

The crash was so spectacular ABC added it to its regular Saturday afternoon *Wide World of Sports* intro. The music played, the skier went off the side of the jump, and there goes Ralph, end over end. Every Saturday.

To top it off, the following year, while Liguori was combing the garage area at Indy looking for a ride, the Hulman Classic was rained out. ABC was scheduled to carry the event again live, and with the rainout it replayed the previous year's show.

You guessed it. While America watched, thinking they were seeing a brand new live event, Ralph took his infamous header again. Geez, Ralph, every time I turn on the TV, you're crashing...

There went Indy; there went his last hope for a big-time ride. He appealed to ABC to please discontinue the use of the crash on the intro each week and it quickly complied, but the damage was done. Ralph was relegated to finishing his career in the cockpit of a sprint car.

Not that he's complaining. He says his career was as successful as he could have ever imagined. He raced with NASCAR during the early 1950s, winning some early Grand National events, before heading north to settle in with USAC. While most guys hated Langhorne, he did well there, earning $2,000 in 1957 when he set a world's one-mile record on the treacherous oval.

He was a gypsy, living from hand to mouth. It wasn't unusual to see Liguori and his young family sleeping in their car, or on the ground, because they didn't have enough money for a room. After a while, things got better, and Ralph began to do something most guys never think about: he started to prepare for tomorrow.

He began holding back small amounts of his winnings, and soon had enough to purchase some Florida property. His wisdom has been rewarded, as he now owns a fine home and a successful mobile home park near Tampa.

Through it all, the years have been kind to him. He looks much younger than sixty-three, and he and his lovely wife enjoy their "retirement" in the sunshine.

They have raised three happy sons, are financially secure, and have their health. Life could certainly be worse.

He didn't make Indy, and that still sticks in his gut. But he smiles when he talks about it. He made something much more important, he says, with a gleam in his eye. "I made friends," he smiles, gesturing around the crowded room.

Ralphie the Racer, no more. Ralph Liguori, Hall of Fame Member, forever. It's about time.

THE LIVING GOES ON

OCTOBER 1990 - NATIONAL SPEED SPORT NEWS

For Emily Vogler, the living goes on.

She spent nearly ten years loving a racing car driver, and on a warm July evening this past summer she watched helplessly as their life together ended. Now, she must look after their three children alone, and go on with the rest of her life.

The family faces a red-letter day this month, when an auction will be held at her husband's race shop near the family's Brownsburg, Indiana home. All the equipment—tools, race car parts, and related material—will be sold to the highest bidder.

For Emily, it is another face-to-face confrontation with reality, staring her squarely in the eye and not blinking.

"I guess you could say our whole year had been bad, and things culminated in the ultimate," she admits, not allowing bitterness or anger to enter her voice. "Sometimes it's still hard to believe."

Rich Vogler's shop was a well-equipped working facility, and he utilized it almost daily. Within a day of his death, Emily's family came to Indianapolis to help her through the crisis. A brother-in-law offered to clean up the shop, which was in the normal disorder that exists in the middle of another frantic season. A few days later, Emily ventured out to take a look.

"I remember looking around and thinking, `what in the world am I going to *do* with all this stuff?' I guess at the time I was pretty overwhelmed, but even then I knew that some of this stuff would just have to go. I mean, what am I going to do with a welder?"

She remembers a similar situation in 1981, when Rich's father Don was killed.

"When Don died Rich and his mother (Eleanor) talked about an auction, but we didn't get around to doing it, and most of Don's things just frittered away and eventually disappeared. Eleanor and I didn't want that to happen to Rich's shop."

Rich was a hands-on racer, with a lot of pride in his mechanical ability. His tools had become an extension of himself, much like a hand or foot. Seeing them go out the door will be a painful experience, but the cold, hard facts of life are very evident.

"I have no job and no job skills," Emily says matter-of-factly. "No matter what the circumstances, you find out that money spends pretty quickly. I have three children to look after, and I would rather not have to bus tables right away just to live. I hope to approach this by going after some sort of schooling to acquire some job skills, and that takes time."

The thirty-two year old widow is upbeat and readily admits that her situation could be much worse.

"Rich had a ton of life insurance, and anytime an offer for additional coverage came up he took it. I think because of what happened to his dad a few years ago, he realized what could happen. So I'm grateful he was thinking of us, although at the time this kind of thing doesn't really occur to you.

"Most of the reasons for the auction are logistical and financial," she points out. "It's really a matter of just being sensible. If I can move the equipment out, I won't have to heat the shop this winter. The kids are so small by the time they are old enough to use things like a welder and impact wrenches, these tools wouldn't be any good."

One item that has already been sold is Vogler's airplane; a six-seat Beechcraft Baron purchased by NASCAR racer Sterling Marlin.

Because some of the tools had earlier belonged to Don Vogler, Emily and Eleanor will share in the auction proceeds. Many items will be on the block, including a mill, parts washer, band saw, grinders, floor jacks, scales, high-pressure washer, and more. Race car parts include wheels, gears, torsion bars, shocks, hubs, oil coolers, radiators, and magnetos.

Additional memorabilia and miscellaneous items include a few driver uniforms, jackets, rifles, handguns, a motorcycle, and a lawn tractor.

Also, in what is undeniably a noble gesture, the Vogler's will share a portion of the auction proceeds with Shawn Snow, a seventeen year old Indianapolis youth suffering from a multitude of serious health problems. Shawn undergoes kidney dialysis three times weekly, and according to Emily, needs all the help he can get. She insists that sharing the proceeds with a needy party is a tradition she and Rich had practiced for years.

"I guess it's just a Christian upbringing, but we always believed you should share a portion of your earnings," she says. "We hope we get enough money from this to hold us over for a while, and we thought it would only be right to continue the way we've always done it, to share a portion.

"Rich had met Shawn earlier this year at the (Indianapolis) Speedway, when Shawn's health was really touch-and-go. The kid was in one of the suites, and they were trying to find a race driver who would come say hello to him. Rich went up and met him and tried to cheer him up, and after that we just kind of kept in touch."

So another chapter in the life of Rich Vogler will draw to a close. It is certain to carry some difficult moments for both Emily and Eleanor.

"Rich and I always handled things like a joint venture," Emily admits. "Now I feel like I'm on my own and that isn't easy. All you can do is make the best decision you can and follow it, and that's what we're doing with this auction.

"I'm not an emotional person," she says quietly, "but I got a little misty-eyed when I watched Rich's airplane fly away for the last time the other day."

Another minute ticks away, another hour goes by, another day of survival for Emily and her family. There will be many more to follow. The living goes on.

FUN WHILE IT LASTED

NOVEMBER 1990 - NATIONAL SPEED SPORT NEWS

It was fun while it lasted. For open-wheel fans in the Midwest, the last couple of years with Jeff Gordon have been memorable. Not only is he arguably one of the most talented sprint car and midget drivers around these parts, he is certainly the most popular.

Now, he tells us he is going away. The Busch Grand National series in the South is calling, and Gordon's career plan says it's time for a step up. It's kind of like watching your best friend drive off into the sunset, heading for a job he's always wanted. Of course you're happy, but deep down inside you know you're going to miss him.

It was six years ago that Gordon surfaced as a thirteen year old kid racing sprint cars in California. *SPRINT CARS!* Nobody believed he was for real. But slowly the word filtered back from people who knew the business, who had an eye for talent. This kid is something special, they said. He's going to make it and make it big.

For me, it was East Bay, Florida in February 1986. He started up front in the feature, and lined up a few spots back in a white No. 11 was a guy named Kinser, a guy whom you could describe as slightly on the competitive side. I figured it would be a lap, maybe two, and the kid would be history. But the gutsy youngster drove his heart out, and it took the King a lot of work and one of his slicker moves to get past. I was impressed with Gordon's savvy and intensity.

Around 1987 Gordon and his family moved to Pittsboro, Indiana to run midgets and sprints throughout the Midwest. In 1988 he was the sprint car champ at Bloomington, running the Friday-night winged show. His schedule gave area fans a chance to fall in love with him, and before long he had a large and vocal following. Then came his success on ESPN's coverage of midget and sprint competition, and Gordon became a bona fide national star. You couldn't have written a more exciting script.

His talent is obvious, but it is his attitude that makes this kid so likable. Here's a guy who went wheel to wheel with Kinser at fifteen; was a track champion at one of the toughest weekly sprint shows in the country; and became a nationally recognized TV racer, all before he graduated from high school. Through it all, instead of becoming an egomaniac, he has remained humble and unassuming. When writers toss acerbic questions at him in rapid-fire succession, he smiles innocently, and answers with surprising maturity.

On this day, after winning both the USAC sprint car and midget features at Winchester Speedway to close the 1990 season, he faced reporters in Winchester's press room. Across the room sat Bentley Warren, a veteran supermodified driver who has seen his share of wars. Warren was asked what advice he'd give the kid.

"Sounds to me like he's doing fine on his own," Warren sagely answered. "The guy's got his head wrapped up pretty tight."

Tight, indeed. As Gordon talked of the last few years, and how things have turned out, it was easy to forget that this is a teenage kid talking. He is articulate, honest, and so sincere he could probably talk you out of your ride home if he tried. Some examples:

"Five years ago I never would have dreamed it would turn out like this. Two years ago I didn't know if I had what it took to win a race at Winchester, and to come here and win both features is unbelievable. I'm really lucky, I've got good people helping me, telling me the right things, and I listen.

"Sometimes I still can't believe it, that success has come so quickly. If the Grand National deal would have come any earlier, I don't think I would have been ready. I'm definitely not ready for Winston Cup. I don't see any chance of being ready before 1993 there.

"The hardest thing has been me still needing to be a kid. My stepfather, John Bickford, has been helping me and pushing me which is great, but sometimes I have to tell everybody, 'hey, wait a minute, I still want to do some other things besides racing, I want to play.' So I'll go away for a while and just play around or whatever, and when I come back I'm ready to race again.

"I'm surprised at how comfortable I feel in the Grand National cars, so quickly. I know I'll be pushed around down there a little bit, and I know you can't be cocky and expect to fit in as a new guy. I'm prepared for that, and I'm committed that it's going to take some time to win. You've just got to be cool and patient. If it doesn't work out at first, you've got to keep trying. That's what we're going to do. We're going to keep trying until we get there."

He stares straight into your eyes, and you know that this is a kid who is either a tremendous actor or an absolutely straight shooter. Those in the know insist there is only one Jeff Gordon, the honest, hardworking guy, the kid who is sincere in everything he does, who is very confident in his ability without compromising his humble demeanor.

If you had a teen-aged daughter, you'd want this kid taking her to the prom. You can't get any more confident in his character than that.

Now, it's time to go. The press conference is over. Outside, the breeze has picked up and the temperature, as if on cue, is dropping dramatically. Tomorrow, winter awaits.

Gordon says his goodbyes, and assures us he'll still run a few open-wheel shows next year. However, he admits, it's got to be a weekend with no stock car conflicts. Somehow, you know it will never be the same, that the sight of Jeff Gordon climbing from a sprint car or midget is going to be a rarity in coming years. You're happy for the guy, but nearly everybody is sad to see him go.

Chapter one is over for Gordon. Future chapters are coming, rest assured. Someday, we'll boast that we witnessed the beginning of his book firsthand. It was fun while it lasted.

NOBODY SHOWED UP

NOVEMBER 1990 - NATIONAL SPEED SPORT NEWS

It was a quiet Sunday afternoon, and although the sunshine had pushed aside the grays of November, I stared at television most of the day. There, in bits and pieces between an old movie and a Browns game, I saw the Winston Cup title slip through Mark Martin's fingers, like so much sand. It made me remember a night not so long ago, when today's NASCAR superstar was just another guy with big dreams.

It was 1985, and the ASA series had come to Anderson for the Anderson 400, a long series pausing to bang around a very short track. Martin was in Jerry Gunderman's Thunderbird, which sported Miller Beer colors. He was revisiting ASA competition after suffering through a couple of tough years in the South, trying to break into Winston Cup racing, when we still called it Grand National racing.

I worked for Anderson Speedway as its publicity man, also cranking out racing stuff for the ANDERSON HERALD, the local morning daily. The Miller people decided to put together a hospitality party for the press the night before the Saturday night feature, and I was set for a grand old time.

Then nobody showed up.

I don't recall the exact details, but it seems as though the word got out late or some such problem, and I was the only press guy who showed up. The guy from Miller Beer, complete with a red face, was there; Martin and his crew were there; along with the late Leo Parrish, one of the owners of Anderson Speedway.

We all sat down, all seven of us, and had a party. Nobody seemed to mind that we were a small gathering in a large room, although I recall the Miller guy looking rather pale as he stared at all the food and refreshments.

I remembered Martin as the sensational kid who came along in the 1970s and helped put ASA on the map. He was young and fast, a lot of race driver in a small package. The pond was smaller then, but this guy qualified for big-fish honors. I wondered about his outlook, after having tried unsuccessfully to move to the big town.

Martin's crew really ribbed the Miller guy about the slim turnout, and it was obvious that these guys were not social wallflowers. It's been said that winners play harder than they work, so these guys must have worked very, very hard. They were quite fond of their sponsor's product.

Martin's crew chief was Jim Fennig, and Jim's brother Jeffrey was also a crew member. Jim, as I understand it, is today the crew chief with the team owned by Bobby Allison, where Jeff also works. Along with the Fennig brothers was another crew member, a rather husky chap named Mike.

Even though they ran a Thunderbird, these guys began razzing Leo mercilessly for his passion for Fords. Leo, after many rounds of refreshment, was bragging about a Falcon he had home in the barn, which he described as dreadfully fast. Jeff Fennig jumped to his feet, and while everyone shouted as if we were on the floor of the stock exchange, countered with a description of a Camaro he owned back in Wisconsin. It was a splendid conversation, among a bunch of car guys sitting around the carrot bowl.

Through all the shouting Martin seemed to be having a good time. We talked of his frustrating trip South in 1983, when he went from a guy who had won lots of races to being just another new guy trying to prove himself. He described the decision that carried him back to the North and ASA, even though he still believed he could get the job done in Winston Cup racing. He talked about a future that could possibly be limited to being the biggest fish in the small pond. Whether he knew it or not, he was squarely in the dues-paying phase of his career.

Those of us with small-town roots look at the stars and wonder if their success has spoiled them as a person. You look at the guy's picture with the kid in the wheelchair, but what's he *really* like, you know? When I sat down that night and looked across the table at the guy from Batesville, Arkansas, I had the same question. There weren't enough people for him to hide behind, or to distract either of us, or to fill the night with phony conversation. In a gathering that small, that informal, I knew I would get a look at what this dude was really all about.

Between the carrots and the refreshments and the laughter, I found Mark Martin to be a right pleasant guy with whom you could go fishing and enjoy the trip.

After a couple of hours, we decided to move the party to a popular lounge down the hall. The guy from Miller stared again at the refreshments and the munchies, still piled high, and turned another shade lighter.

The crowd in the lounge was young. Most, I'm sure, knew nothing about stock car racing, or anything about Anderson Speedway. But when we entered and the crowd buzzed about the Miller crew uniforms, I saw Martin's charisma rise to the occasion. He mingled with the crowd, shaking hands and smiling, and within minutes was seated at a table surrounded by curious patrons looking at the photograph cards he gave them and saying his name out loud. Soon, he was at the center of the dance floor, grinning and looking every bit at home.

That next night, after he dominated and won the 400, cameras, trophies, pretty girls, and an adoring crowd surrounded Martin. I wondered, now that he was back in his element, if he would acknowledge me, a guy he had met the night before, or if he had considered me just another cat he had to contend with as part of the job. I waited with other reporters for our chance to question Martin, as he was being interviewed on the PA. As he was talking, our eyes met, and he broke into a broad smile, and he winked. I realized that the guy I met was the same guy who drove the race car. It was a good memory.

Now, I watched TV as the cameras pressed in on Martin. He has established himself as one of the big fish again, and this time the pond is about as large as it gets. It wasn't hard to see the disappointment on his face, and even though his words were upbeat and positive, you knew at the moment his heart was breaking.

I suppose he has a right to become a different guy, to step up and assume the superstar role. Maybe he's already forgotten nights like those in Anderson, when he was mingling with us common folks. I wish I had been in Atlanta. It would be interesting to see if Mark Martin still winks at his friends.

QUITTING ISN'T AN OPTION

MARCH 1991 - NATIONAL SPEED SPORT NEWS

The next time you look at a serious challenge and question your ability to achieve success, think of Ray Fullen.

He is forty-seven years old, and is preparing to defend his late model division title at Anderson Speedway in Indiana. He has no sponsor, no financial backing other than himself.

And he has a broken back.

You don't suppose he would give up, would you? Not a chance.

"We'd like to come back this year and win some races," he says in his usual soft, quiet voice. "I've healed a little slower than I had hoped, and it's still gonna be a while before I feel really good. The doctor said it would take two years, so I've got to wear a brace this year."

When the horizon is darkest for Fullen, that's when he seems to shine the brightest. He began last season in a most humble manner, putting together enough of his own money to build a car, thinking he would run Saturday nights with Anderson Speedway late models. He had no financial backing of any sort. A friend built him a low-dollar, home-built engine.

"We only had one motor, but we had a lot of luck," he says.

With just a few guys helping out when they could, he and his crew figured they would have some fun. They really didn't know what to expect, considering the reality of going up against a Saturday-night crowd that includes Vic Hellis, Bob Fields, Jim Cooper, Bret Miles, and a number of guys who could easily be track champions elsewhere. When the season ended, he had earned the late model division title, edging Hellis in an extremely tight point battle that took the final feature to settle.

A few weeks later, when everything seemed rosy, he was running with the Magnum Oil series at Salem, Indiana. He was racing in a tightly bunched pack when they came upon a spun car. With nowhere to go, Fullen's impact caused his car to leave the ground momentarily, exposing the bottom of his car to oncoming traffic.

While Fullen was fully stretched in his harness, another car hit him from underneath. The impact, and angle of the blow, snapped his back like a twig.

So, while the rest of us spent the winter in more normal pursuits, Ray Fullen was in therapy.

"The back doesn't heal like anything else," he points out. "I thought it would be quicker, like the last accident."

"The last accident" was just five years ago. While most guys only face the prospect of a career-ending accident once, this is Fullen's second opportunity.

In late 1985 he tangled with another car during an open-competition event at Anderson, and his car was airborne momentarily before impacting the blunt corner of the track's pit entrance. In a split second, Fullen went from over 100 mph to zero. He suffered head injuries, internal injuries, and a badly crushed foot that took months of intense therapy to rehabilitate.

But the next season he simply got up, dusted himself off, and won his first late model division title at Anderson.

Quitting hasn't yet become an option. He does admit that the healing process is a bit slower now.

"The last time, it was just a matter of healing my foot up," he says. "Now, I think about what could happen if I had another crash, a large bump.

"The doctor doesn't want me to drive again. He's the same guy who treated me last time, so he knows what I do. We don't talk about it much; there really isn't much explaining to do. He just looks at me and kind of shakes his head."

Fullen once chased his dream down the road in the early days of the ASA when a wrecked Chevelle and some effort in the barn could produce a winning stock car. He's seen peaks such as winning the ASA Gran Marque series championship in 1988. He's also seen the valleys that can seem endless.

And in a quiet moment, he admits none of it makes any sense.

But in a few weeks, he's going to try again. He ran a very clean season last year, and didn't replace one body panel during his Anderson racing. He hopes for more of the same this year, because he doesn't have a big reserve of cash to replace bent and broken big-ticket items.

Maybe he'll be ready for the opener. Maybe not. But you hate to bet against him, because Fullen has this inner strength that always seems to bring him back with his desire turned up another notch or two.

When he does climb back into the car, his victory will be a quiet one. Perhaps he won't even be noticed the first time he fires the car and takes hot laps. That would be a shame, because the qualities that every great man seeks, like conviction, courage, ability, and desire, will all play a part in his return. Who said there are no more heroes?

LOOKING BLEAK FOR LONE STAR J.R.

MAY 1991 - NATIONAL SPEED SPORT NEWS

With each passing day, the clock is running out on Johnny Rutherford's Indy Car career.

He hasn't been in the Indy 500 since 1988, when he made his twenty-fourth start. And the three-time winner's phone isn't exactly ringing off the hook.

"I guess you could say it looks pretty bleak right now," he admits, trying valiantly to hide disappointment. "It's a bit of a shocker when you realize your talents don't mean anything anymore."

While it doesn't make him feel any better, Rutherford is in some pretty good company. Other guys who are standing idly in the unemployment line this month include Al Unser, Sr., Gordon Johncock, Tom Sneva, Roberto Guerrero, and Steve Chassey. Only Unser, who is rumored to be in line for a ride in one of A.J. Foyt's cars, is a likely Indy starter.

For Rutherford, who would dearly love to reach the twenty-five-start milestone, this period in his career comes as both a bitter disappointment and a surprise.

"I never envisioned this period," he says. "I never guessed I couldn't get a race car to drive at this stage. For twenty-eight years I could come to the track with my helmet bag in the trunk and get a ride, but that's not how it works anymore."

While his driving prospects are slim, his business prospects are looking up. He is busy working on developing the Johnny Rutherford Performance and Driving School that will offer courses at Texas World Speedway and the new speedway planned for the Dallas-Fort Worth area.

"I have to get it together and make a decision one way or another soon," he admits. "I'm involved in putting together the driving school, and that is going to take a full-time commitment to get going.

"I've been racing for thirty-one years, and I'd really like to do one or two more seasons under the right set of circumstances. This has presented itself at just the right time, and I think it would be very exciting. You hate the thought of not racing every year, but I guess there comes a time."

114

For Rutherford and many other drivers, "the right set of circumstances" really means Chevrolet. Because, three-time winner or not, the current state of Indy Car racing dictates that if you don't have a Chevy, you might as well be riding a jackass. And for drivers that are more than forty, people are quick to say they're over the hill if they show up at Indy with less-than-competitive rides. And top-flight Chevy rides are scarce these days.

"The sad thing about it is that guys will come up with just enough sponsorship to field a car that nobody could put in the race," Rutherford says. "And then when they can't put it in the show it makes them look bad, whether you're a veteran trying to stay on top or a young guy just getting started."

Rutherford also would like to stay involved in Indy Car racing with his son, twenty-two year old Johnny Rutherford IV, who would like to pursue a driving career.

"I would entertain thoughts of developing my own team, although I know it won't be easy. Few things are easy. It's really a matter of how hard you are willing to work to make it happen. What kind of racing? Well, I don't see anything other than Indy Cars, either that or Winston Cup. Sports cars, I don't think, will ever be what oval track racing is. Oval track racing is American. But that's just one man's opinion."

He and his son currently appear in a series of well-known Oldsmobile commercials, which continue to keep the Rutherford name in a high profile.

"They were doing auditions for that particular issue ("This is not your father's Oldsmobile"), and there were several parent-child combinations that tried out for the role. John and I were fortunate enough to be selected, and it has been really fun. We hope to get the opportunity to film more later this summer."

So he has a sizable commercial contract, prospects for a fledging performance driving business, numerous promotional deals in Indianapolis in May, a comfortable home in Fort Worth, and a few bucks in the bank. Still a star, but a star without a vehicle.

"Auto racing has been very, very good to me," he admits. "If I had to quit tomorrow, I've realized a lot of dreams that many drivers never will, so I certainly can't complain. I would not have quit any earlier, even if I knew that this period was coming. I would have driven right to it, just like I did."

115

Of all the modern-day drivers, Rutherford is probably the most visible in terms of his role as a statesman and ambassador for auto racing. Articulate and polished, he is as comfortable in front of a camera as behind the wheel. He realizes his role as a spokesman offers great visibility, and is careful not to present the image of sour grapes.

"I think things are getting ready to come to a screeching halt because of the state of the economy," he points out. "Many major sponsors are in for a two- or three-year deal with set budgets, and they aren't going to be bumped up just to cover the increasing costs of racing. That could leave several teams in an impossible spot.

"I honestly don't know what is going to solve the problem. It will take a while, and it's going to cost some money. There are not enough competitive engines, and they are just too expensive.

"I've been around it a long time, and I've seen lots of ups and downs, but I've never seen it down like this. But then, that's all just my opinion.

"I have always taken the attitude that I want to leave racing in just a little bit better shape than when I came along," he insists. "Now, today, with the current state of affairs, it's going to be mighty tough to do that."

A WIN TO REMEMBER

MAY 1991 - NATIONAL SPEED SPORT NEWS

The margin of victory was relatively small, but it was a huge victory for Jeff Bloom.

When the forty-one year old Bangor, Michigan driver took the checkered flag at the forty-third City of Anderson Little 500 at Anderson Speedway this month, it was a remarkable conclusion to an outstanding chapter of the short-track classic.

Perhaps never in the event's history had a field been so competitive. Bob Frey, the master who has claimed the last four straight Little 500s, took a pass this year to tend to his mortuary business in Arizona. That vacated the seat of what is arguably the most successful sprint car in America, Glen Niebel's Chevy V6. Niebel decided only the best would do, so he hired veteran supermodified ace Bentley Warren.

There were plenty of other guys who were also capable of winning, given the right set of circumstances. Jim Childers, Wayne Hammond, Frank Riddle, Doug Saunier, and Stan Butler all are top pavement shoes, and all were in strong equipment. Dark horses like Jack Hewitt, making his first Little 500 start; Ken Hamilton, strong in West Coast supers for years; Gene Lee Gibson, never afraid of a challenge; and Donnie Adams, a brilliant sprint car newcomer who nearly stole the pole in only his ninth start.

But nobody seemed to be talking about Bloom. Sure, there was plenty of talk about him making his fifteenth Little 500 start, an unprecedented number. Sure, he won here in 1972 and 1977, but that was a long time ago.

Bloom didn't mind the lack of attention. He is a low-buck guy who pulls his own way, using the same Shores chassis he has ran here the past several years. He says he's 125 horsepower down on most guys, because he lacks the funding to build the engine he wants.

If you lined up at the ticket window for this one, you couldn't have been disappointed. The first hundred laps were the Frank Riddle show, as the sixty-two year old two-time winner stormed from row three to lead with confidence. But he spun later in the race, ending his hopes for a third trophy.

Warren was five laps down at the halfway point, and decided it was showtime. The Niebel car looked like a scared pup as it slipped through traffic, running lines that normally don't exist on the Anderson banks. It was an example of what happens when you put a brilliant driver in an outstanding car. He made up the deficit and took the lead with a 125 laps to go, seemingly ready to cruise home.

Through it all, Bloom was there. He ran in the top five all night, and when Warren was thrilling the fans Bloom was quietly moving into second. It looked like a repeat of 1990, when he followed Frey to the checkered. But this time, Bloom's usually wretched luck rode with somebody else.

In making up the big deficit, Warren had abused his right rear tire. It blistered around lap 400, and suddenly he went from dazzling traffic moves to just hanging on for dear life through the corners. Bloom, who quickly closed on the leader, smoothly drove past as Warren waited on a caution.

Warren finally got the yellow he needed on lap 434, and the fans braced themselves for a thrilling finish as he set out to run down Bloom.

But Bloom was turning in a flawless performance on this night. He didn't flinch when Warren drove past to make up one lap of a three-lap deficit at the 449-lap mark, and Bloom was still poised when Warren slipped past again on lap 485. Bloom ran strong enough to protect his lead, without the panic that could have ended his quest for a third title, and took the checkered with Warren still in pursuit.

When he rumbled to a stop at the flag stand and cut the engine, it was an emotional scene. His wife, Linda, leaned into the cockpit for a kiss and some private words, and his crew embraced each other amid their tears. Bloom's face was black with dirt and sweat, and he slowly crawled up through the cage as the crowd cheered. Next to the car, in the midst of elation, Bloom's young daughter sobbed with uncontrolled joy as she watched her father turn and acknowledge the crowd.

It had been fourteen years since he had parked here. So long ago that many Little 500 fans had forgotten. This one, they will remember.

THROUGH THE EYES OF RETIREMENT

JULY 1991 - NATIONAL SPEED SPORT NEWS

Hwis big frame moves slowly through the concession line, and he soon wanders to a nearby bench to consume an elephant ear. In three hours the World of Outlaws will take the green flag at Kokomo Speedway, and Bill Lipkey will be watching through the eyes of retirement.

"Looks like lots of empty seats," he says, gesturing to the grandstand. "Gee, I hope Jim does okay tonight."

After thirty-nine years promoting the weekly show at Kokomo, Lipkey turned over the keys to his son Jim early this season. Like all men before him, and all who will follow, time has finally caught up with Lipkey.

"I got to thinking about my age this past winter, and I decided to just turn everything over to Jim," he admits, staring at his familiar surroundings. "I figured he should take it over while I'm still around to help him get started."

Like many men facing life's autumn, Lipkey is realistic that tomorrow is not guaranteed. Yet he is as active as most young men, hustling to maintain a pristine collection of old race cars, motorcycles, and whatnot.

Late last fall, just before his seventy-eighth birthday, Lipkey decided to visit his daughter in Washington, D.C. So he made the 1,200-mile trip alone, on his Harley-Davidson motorcycle.

"I like to stay at it," he shrugs.

He saw his first race in 1925, at the old Fort Wayne speedway, and soon watched the great Ted Hartley race in Huntington, Indiana. He soon discovered Winchester, and was hooked.

He bluffed his way into the pits, serving as a stooge on the car in which Al Cobb would later perish. The violent incident nearly cured his racing desire, but by 1946 he decided to try promoting a race at the old five-eighths-mile oval in Fort Wayne.

"I got the chance to promote this (Kokomo) speedway in 1952, and I wasn't sure if I wanted to at the time. I had a job working for an ice company, where I started out delivering ice from a horse-drawn wagon in 1932. I didn't miss one day of work in twenty years, but I decided to quit and try racing full-time."

Lipkey's oldest son Vic, after a brief stint at Purdue University, soon joined him in the business, and Lipkey remembers their efforts well. Sadly, Vic died of cancer in 1987.

"Vic's mother and I wanted him to be an engineer, but he had other ideas. We were also involved in the track in Lafayette, and Vic's help really made the difference back then.

"I remember when we introduced Figure 8 racing here in Kokomo in 1961," he says, a smile appearing on his lips. "We were worried about how many cars we'd get, so Vic and I built five of 'em. That first night, only three other cars showed up. Vic and I drove two of our cars, and by July 4th we had more than a hundred cars showing up every week."

Losing Vic was a very tough chapter in his life, Lipkey quietly admits. Not only did he lose a son, but a partner as well.

"When Vic died, I just about quit everything, racing included. But I figured, hell, Vic wouldn't want that. So I started doing both the watering and the grading here at the track, and it wasn't long before that was too much for me."

That's when younger son Jim stepped up and picked up the slack. Jim showed early promise as an artist, and in the late 1960s Lipkey sent his younger son to college. Uncle Sam, who provided an all-expense-paid trip to Vietnam, interrupted Jim's education. Luckily, it was a round-trip ticket.

"Jim came back from Vietnam and eventually opened up a sign painting business here in town. He is a really talented artist, but he'd probably just a soon letter an old race car as draw anything else.

"If it weren't for Jim, what the hell, I couldn't retire," admits Lipkey. "I think he'll do okay here, he seems to have a handle on things."

No other player in racing is an unappreciated as the promoter, and Lipkey is no exception.

"Promoting isn't as fun as it used to be. You never get to the point of not worrying, not in this business. Everybody thinks you get rich. Some years I've made money with racing, some years I haven't. It's been good to me, though."

While Kokomo has become known for its popular Sunday-night sprint show, it came about for one reason: Bill Lipkey put up the money every week, come hell or high water, with no guarantees. Without him, and a thousand other guys like him, we sit at home and stare at the tube every weekend.

"This race track has been real good to me, especially all the people who have been through here during all these years. I'm one of the luckiest guys around, I guess. I loved racing as a hobby, and it turned out I was able to make a living from it. That's more than most guys get the chance to do."

He is getting out of the business with his health intact, although he now hauls a pacemaker around. He admits people are surprised at his energy level.

"There's this one cardiologist who says all this racin' stuff, and the old cars, they're no good. But I like to keep busy. Really, it's like a lot of guys who have retired; I'm so busy now I don't know how I used to have any time to work. I've worked a long time for this, now I'm gonna enjoy myself. What the hell."

LARGER THAN LIFE

AUGUST 1991 - NATIONAL SPEED SPORT NEWS

It is quiet now. The sprint cars are parked; most of them loaded and ready to roll toward home. The line at the payoff window is nearly gone, and the cars creep like ants through the parking lot toward the exit onto U.S. 40. It is nearly midnight in Putnamville, Indiana and only the lingering few at Lincoln Park Speedway give the town any visible life.

Here, among the remnants of a local sprint car show on a beautiful Indiana summer night, stands a legend. It is a setting you could find at dozens, maybe hundreds, of tracks around America. But you could only find one Bob Kinser.

On August 21, he will celebrate his sixtieth birthday. If you are a schoolteacher, or truck driver, or coal miner, or shoe salesman, or a senator, sixty is not notable. If you are a sprint car driver, it is remarkable.

But it isn't age that distinguishes Bob Kinser. No, for he was remarkable at fifty, forty, maybe even thirty. It is something one cannot reduce to round numbers. It is character.

Bobby, as he is known to many of his loving fans, is one in a million. He is full of color, strength, wisdom, intensity, and honesty. Sometimes, some of his traits get out of hand. That's where the colorful part comes in.

For more than thirty-six years, he has bounced around the inside of a race car. When he first climbed in, he had two clear goals like all racers: win, and stay alive. He has been successful at both.

For those of us who were lucky enough to witness the Hoosier sprint car scene in the 1960s and 1970s, there was some heavy talent to write home about. It was a rough, raw era that saw the emergence of a new generation of Midwestern supermodified hillbillies, and their transformation into arguably America's finest sprint car drivers. The World of Outlaws, while drawing personalities from all over America, can easily trace a significant portion of its success to the sleepy hills of southern and central Indiana. Alive among those hills was Kinser.

He is just about the only remaining warrior from that period. Many, like Calvin Gilstrap, Stan Bowman, Ron Fisher, and Mike Johnson, are gone. Most others, like Dick Gaines, Butch Wilkerson, Bobby Black, Bernie Graybeal, Danny Bowlen, and Buzz Gregory, survived but elected to walk away while they could still walk.

Yet Kinser's luck held out. In all these years, he has never had an injury more serious than a broken hand. Legend has it he has been injured far worse in barroom brawls than any racing crash.

The brawler. It is a reputation that has stayed with Kinser, although he quietly insists he isn't nearly the wild man others make him out to be. But his appearance adds much to the notoriety. Just look at the guy, and you figure he's got to be mean as hell.

First, you notice the eyes. Steel blue and unblinking, his stare is frightening enough to make a wolf drop a fresh kill and run for cover. And his scowl. Strolling around the pits, with a cigar clamped tightly in his teeth, he looks as if nothing has gone right in sixty years. Then, there's the body. Honed by forty years of hard physical labor, he looks dead-on strong.

The reality? He is a kind man, with a good sense of humor, who enjoys talking to people. He isn't nearly as angry as he looks. He has a hell of a good time racing. He is proud of his kids. He loves his grandchildren. Not unlike any other man.

"I'm not nearly as bad as I'm made out," he says. His country dialect is spellbinding; with the words rolling from his tongue in such a fashion that one becomes transfixed in conversation. "Thing's ain't been near as rough as folks says they was, back through the years. Oh, yes, they was some fightin'. But not near as much as folks think."

He is, by any definition, a fine race car driver. His nearly thirty track championships, and more than four hundred career feature victories, prove that. His legend is so great today that many young drivers pale when he pulls alongside. Nobody ever clearly gives up, but it is sometimes obvious that many are reluctant to push hard alongside him for fear of the consequences. He is of the old school, and sometimes crosses over that edge and prefers to settle the score the old way, with a good tussle in the pits following the race.

Is that good? Probably not. But with Bobby, he is unflinchingly human. What you see is what you get. He hides nothing. When he is angry, when he feels he is wronged, when he believes a guy has intentionally put one on him, he reacts. Does he do so to send a message, or is it just plain anger?

"I guess it's a little of both," he admits. "I think today you've got more rough drivin' and crashin' than we had back then. Today, you got guys with sponsors they got to please, and a wing on the car, and they're young and strong, and they just drive 'em into the corner like they's no tomorrow. And that just don't get it.

"I've done things, in the heat of the moment, and I've hated myself for it later. That's probably just like anybody. But that's just part of it, you cain't take it back after it's all done. But I also have always believed that when a guy runs over you intentionally, if you don't take up for yourself, it'll happen pretty regular."

If age has eroded his talents, it is not visible. Tonight, in fact, he ran a strong second in the familiar Bayless Brothers No. 17 behind Jack Hewitt, outrunning some young guys who probably have an edge in hardware. But with time comes experience, and Kinser is perhaps most expert in getting the absolute most from what he's got.

"I reckon I'm not quite as sharp as I used to be," he admits. "But I figure as long as I can do a sprint car good, I'm a-gonna keep on racin'. Oh, I prob'ly don't have the hard desire I used to have, but I still have a good time."

He carries in his memory a vast storehouse of anecdotes and stories from yesterday: some sad, some happy, all interesting. He relates his most humiliating episode, the night very early in his career when he got upside down...in the pits.

"I was a-runnin' this old coupe, and something hadn't gone just right on the track, and I came haulin' 'er into the pits. I got to my pit and just pitched 'er sideways. A tow rig had spun his tires there earlier, and cut two grooves in the dirt. I dropped two wheels down in that groove and over she went.

"My dad helped me back then, and he kind of poked his head in the car and looked at me. I just told him, 'Git me turned back over afore somebody sees me!' I reckon it didn't hurt nothin', but it embarrassed the hell out of me."

Amid all his success, he never reached what many would call the big time. Indy was in his dreams, but when the opportunity arose he couldn't leave his job at the stone quarry to run the required fair dates that would put him in consideration for a championship ride. He was faced with a choice of priorities, and chose his family. He hasn't looked back, nor should he. His decision was rewarded with four good children who have never been distant from their father.

"I'm real proud of what I've done in racin' over the years. Boy, I've got to travel, and see the country, and I'd a-never done that without racin'. I ran the very first Western World out in Phoenix, ran Florida, East Coast, St. Paul, I've been all over.

"At the time, we didn't have nothin' like the World of Outlaws. I'm not sure I would've liked livin' on the road for a long period like those fellers do today, but I reckon I'll never know. But I sure got nuthin' to complain about.

"And the people I've met. My, some *great* people. Why, I go out East or somewheres, and I run across somebody I knowed when I was a-runnin' outlaw years ago. Folks still come around and say hello. I reckon that's been one of the best things about this deal."

Aside from everything he has personally accomplished, he has made a most significant contribution to sprint car racing with his legacy. He and his first wife Cora had four children, two girls and two boys, Steve and Randy.

If Steve Kinser is the King, Bobby is the Almighty. Both of his sons spent their youth watching their father, and both have grown to emulate him in many ways. They are immensely proud of their father. Although he was divorced from their mother when they were still in school, Bob made it a point to maintain a close relationship with all four children. Never mind all the success in racing; his efforts have rewarded him with a loyal, loving family.

It was Bob who first introduced his cousins Sheldon and Karl Kinser to oval racing, as they began hanging around watching him race when he was in his twenties and they were a few years younger. What would sprint car racing be today if Bob had never bought that first race car for $35? Not possible to imagine.

In a few days it will be time to blow out the candles and watch the sign that says "60" pass by. Mahala, his feisty wife of nearly twenty years, will likely see to it that this will be a birthday to remember.

Last year, Bobby said that 1991 would probably be his last season behind the wheel. That is not likely. Look for him to race the Bayless car again next season.

A friend recently described him in simple terms: "Bobby is just an 'ol hillbilly who never changed. He has never tried to be anything else, just the same simple man he was when he started. God, you've got to just love him to death for what he is."

"That's just how I'd want people to think of me," he says of the description. "I never wanted to be anybody but Bob Kinser. And I reckon I've succeeded right well."

Happy birthday, Bobby. May there be many more.

A WILD NIGHT AT LAWRENCEBURG

SEPTEMBER 1991 - NATIONAL SPEED SPORT NEWS

Rick Nichols walked slowly across the darkened pit at Lawrenceburg Speedway, and his head hung ever so slightly. He had just done what every racing official dreads: blown a call, and he knew it.

The All Star Circuit of Champions Competition Director has not had a good summer. He was run over by a sprinter a few weeks ago, and only the grace of God allowed him to escape with his life. His leg and foot injuries are healing, but the pain on his face at this moment has nothing to do with broken bones.

It had been a night of strange happenings, and maybe Nichols was just caught up in the weird mood. Earlier, in a bizarre modified heat, the leader developed mechanical trouble while idling around the track under caution. He headed for the pits, and apparently thinking the race was over, everyone but the guy running last followed him off the track. The astonished flagman waved the green, and one car drove the final two laps to the checkered.

Later, on the third lap of the Hoosier Fall Classic feature, Rocky Hodges broke his front suspension and drove into the infield. Unable to steer, and apparently out of brakes, Hodges missed All Star boss Bert Emick by a whisker as Emick leaped out of the way.

Now, Nichols had just had the unpleasant task of informing Sammy Swindell that he would be paid for twentieth and last position after finishing fourth in the feature.

"Sammy took the news in a gentlemanly way, very mature, very calm," said Nichols quietly. "He's very upset, and I know I'm going to eat crow on this one. But the decision has been made, and that's what we have to do."

It all began on lap eight of the feature, when Swindell had a flat while running fifth. Swindell slowed on the track to bring out the yellow, then flashed to the pits to change rubber.

Nichols checked the lineup, and after a very brief yellow, gave the one-lap signal. As the field moved down the backstretch for the restart, Swindell refired and headed for the track. An All Star official frantically waved him down as he headed up the pit entry road, but Swindell drove past and entered the track on the fourth turn as the field took the green.

He pulled alongside the field on the main straight, and paused briefly until every car had gone past. He then gassed the TMC No. 1 hard. The black flag was not waved.

"I saw Sammy come out, and he got on the tail, and I thought, 'Okay, he's on the tail, I'll give him a break and let him go.' Guys haul a long way to race with us, and no matter who they are, you try to give them a break and let 'em race.

"At the time I didn't know Sammy had driven right past my official in the pits, and came out anyway," Nichols continued. "When the race was over, and I found out about that, that really influenced the decision to score Sammy in last place. But we should have black flagged him right away."

So, there is Swindell, charging through the field, thinking he's racing for position. With one lap to go, he ducked under Jack Hewitt in turn two. His right rear banged hard into Hewitt's left front, sending Hewitt sliding over the banking before he recovered and got back on the gas. Swindell took the checkered in fourth.

But just because the race was over, the excitement was not.

Hewitt had already suffered through a particularly wretched night. He flipped in his heat, won the C-main, won the B-main, then stalled on lap eight in the feature while running sixth. He restarted on the tail, and worked his way back to fourth, only to watch Swindell muscle him out of a position with less than a lap to go. This time, Swindell had poked the wrong bear.

Hewitt caught up with Swindell as he slowed in the first turn after taking the checkered. He rammed the Murphy No. 23M into the rear of Swindell several times as they circled the track on the cool-down lap. On the main straight, as every eye watched, he shoved hard enough to nearly spin Swindell out. They headed for the pits, along with a multitude of people ready to see a fight.

As Nichols watched, it became apparent that all of this would have been avoided had he called for the black flag forty-two laps earlier. But it was too late. The next sixty unpleasant minutes would see him try to salvage what he could from the situation.

Swindell and Hewitt parked at their trailers, which were pitted just across from one another. Hewitt climbed from his car, pulled off his helmet and removed his uniform from the top half of his body, and began walking toward the TMC trailer.

Witnesses say one punch landed cleanly on Sammy's jaw, and that was the only punch thrown. Hewitt walked back to his trailer. Minutes later, as a large crowd stood around both pits, Nichols walked into Swindell's trailer and informed him he would not get credit for his drive from the tail. Do you suppose he greeted the news warmly?

"Sammy was very much a gentleman about the whole thing," Nichols related. "He was very calm, very rational, but he feels very strongly that he finished fourth."

After his talk with Swindell, Nichols walked across to Hewitt's trailer to discuss the after-race incident.

"I talked to Jack about whatever fighting might have gone on, but I was more upset about what happened on the track in front of all the people, because it makes the All Stars look bad.

"Absolutely nobody wins in this deal," he admitted. "Jack is very upset that we didn't do our job and get Sammy off the track, and in that respect he is correct. Sammy is upset he was penalized at all. I had a few seconds to make a decision, and it was not completely the right one. All I can do is try to do the right thing. That's all I can do.

"Sammy said he won't be back to race with us, and I hate that. I like Sammy, and I want him to always feel good about coming to race with us. But I know he means what he says, and that hurts me.

"Sammy said very clearly that if we're going to pay him for twentieth, he will not go to the payoff window. If we won't pay him for fourth, he doesn't want anything."

It was a hell of a spot, and at this moment nobody was more upset than Nichols. His guts were churning, although the professional, calm demeanor never cracked.

It will be a long, long time before he forgets this one. But the mark of a winner is not that he does not make mistakes; it is how he corrects those he does. Tonight, Nichols did his best. It's best to accept that and move on.

JUST GETTING STARTED

OCTOBER 1991 - NATIONAL SPEED SPORT NEWS

The leaves are on the ground, a chill is in the air, and the dirt tracks of Indiana are silent. Winter was the only thing that could slow Dave Darland this year.

It was sure fun while it lasted. Darland and his underfunded, overachieving team raced the weekly non-wing circuit in Indiana, arguably one of the most competitive in the nation, and won more than fifty percent of the features they started.

A lot of people looked around this year and began asking, "Who's Dave Darland?" Hardly an overnight sensation, Darland has paid for his success in advance, as he struggled over the past half-dozen seasons to pull his weight in a tough business. The smart money should have spotted his talents long ago, since he climbed into his first quarter-midget in 1971 at the age of five.

So he has proven he can race, and proven he can win. Now comes the hard part.

After winning nineteen features in thirty-six starts this year, Darland faces something of a dilemma. If he continues to race locally, he would be hard-pressed to repeat that kind of success. He also risks losing the recognition he has earned this past season, recognition that could prove valuable in helping him progress to the next level.

Yet, on the other hand, moving on to race with a group such as All Stars, USAC, or some such organization, is going to take money. Big money. While it's clear that talent isn't short in the Darland camp, money is.

A lot of people will read this and say winning nineteen races isn't really a big deal, because a few guys won many more this past season. But if you could see the way this bare-bones team gets by, you would understand.

"We've kind of done it the hard way," observes Darland, who just seems too quiet, too pleasant, and too polite to be a star. "We have tried to grow a little bit every year, tried to learn with every step, and gain what we could from every situation."

It hasn't been easy, but it has certainly been worthwhile. Darland's dad Bob owns and wrenches the car, and he is even more quiet than his son is. They are a low-profile group, the kind of good people from whom this sport draws much, yet often repays little.

Like most local racers, they have reinvested nearly every penny they win back into the car. Earlier this season they came up with a package consisting of a new reverse-tube Competition Welding chassis and a new Beachy-built engine from their hometown of Kokomo.

It worked. Watching Darland race was a fascinating exercise, as he drove past people on the inside. If that lane wasn't open, he might simply blow past on the outside. He is known as an aggressive racer who plays it clean, and he left a lot of fast people scratching their heads by the time the season ended.

As if to prove his talent isn't limited to non-wing racing, he climbed aboard Darryl Tate's winged car at Paragon late in the summer and won in his first and only start with Tate.

So he should head down to the bank and arrange a $100,000 loan to get his 1992 effort off the ground, right? Darland, twenty-five years old, has a wife and two kids, with another on the way. He works full-time in a Logansport meatpacking plant, where his arms are constantly sore from the intense and rigorous abuse of slicing very heavy sides of beef quickly enough to keep up with the line.

He isn't complaining, but it isn't exactly peaches and cream and soft music for this guy. If anyone has ever earned his share of success, here he is. For more than six years, he and his dad have hauled their yellow sprint car on their open trailer, getting a little bit better, making a little more money, finally stepping up to achieve their dream season.

Of course, they have their share of detractors. With the new Beachy mill this season, people were quick to whisper "big motor" every time Darland won. It came to an interesting conclusion at a USAC event at Kokomo in late August, when Darland finished third behind Tony Elliott and Jack Hewitt.

As the USAC tech inspectors walked over to pump the engine, a group of onlookers quickly gathered, smirking.

The comments were predictable. "He should have slowed down to finish fourth, they don't check fourth...now we'll see what this baby really is...no way it'll be under 410 (cubic inches)."

Minutes later, the USAC officials walked away, ruling it legal with no hesitation. Across the pit, Bob Kinser put it all in perspective.

"It ain't been just motor this year for Dave," he insisted. "The boy's just been hooked up. Lot's o' guys will complain, but the boy has just made it work."

So, Darland will spend the winter months awaiting the birth of a new baby, pondering what do with about 1992. Stay close to home, and hope to win like last year? Or step up to the plate and face a bigger, stronger, faster pitcher?

Somehow, it will work out for Darland and his family. Guys who play it right, with hard work, honesty, dedication, and desire, they always win. It's just a matter of deciding what you want to win. Stay tuned for 1992. He might be just getting started.

HOCKEY TONIGHT

MARCH 1992 - NATIONAL SPEED SPORT NEWS

Ladies and Gentlemen, your attention please," the voice of Jim Amstutz echoes through the Allen County Memorial Coliseum. "There is a black BMW, license number 'PRINCESS' that is rolling backward in the parking lot, blocking other cars. Princess, please go get your car."

It's Thursday in Fort Wayne, another night in the off-season for one of Indiana's busiest—and best—track announcers. In the summer, he calls more than sixty races at Kokomo, Avilla, and Baer Field Speedways. When the wind turns cold, Amstutz moves his microphone inside to become the announcer for the Fort Wayne Komets hockey team. It's a world far removed from auto racing.

Tonight, the Kalamazoo Wings roll (or is it skate?) into town. The Komets are part of the International Hockey League, what could be called minor league hockey. For a city the size of Fort Wayne, though, the Komets are a very big deal.

131

"This is a different challenge than calling a race," explains Amstutz as he lugs his electronic gear rinkside. "Here, I can be a fan, just like everybody else, cheering for the home team.

"At the races, there might be certain guys I like better than others, but I can't ever let that show. There is no home team in racing, you've got to stay neutral."

With that, Amstutz begins looking over the stack of announcements and promotions he must cover during the game. He called his first match here in 1982, when the regular announcer had pneumonia and they needed an emergency replacement. He tried a radically different style, introducing fast-moving music in place of the traditional organ tunes. It was a risk, and it worked.

He lays out at least thirty cassette tapes, all containing just a few seconds of music or sound effects used for the right effect at just the right moment.

Some of those sound bytes have landed Amstutz in hot water with the IHL office, especially when he used to play a few seconds from Alice Cooper's "Hey, Stoopid" when an opposing player headed for the penalty box.

"The league has a job to do, to look after the game," he explains. "But they also know this has to be entertainment. Sometimes, if they're hot about something, they'll tell me what the problem is, and we'll work with them. But you can't go over the line too often."

Komets General Manager David Franke says Amstutz is one of the best in the business.

"He's probably wittier than most, he comes up with quicker lines that entertain the crowd," he says as game time nears. "The music, and the announcer, they're almost as big a part of this as the players on the ice. Jim works the crowd really well; we like him a lot."

Amstutz' seat is literally on top of the ice, and when the puck hits the fiberglass boards in front of him during warmups it sounds like a bomb going off at your feet. A large glass wall is all that separates him from the action.

The game begins, and players chase the puck from the face-off at center ice to the boards in front of the booth. A Komets player gives an opponent a hard check, slamming him into the wall so hard it rocks back into the table where Amstutz sits. Tapes and papers fly everywhere, and the violence of the collision is startling. This is not a little girl's game.

At 6:24 of the first period, we get a good look at the vast difference between this type of sport and racing. Scott Gruhl of Fort Wayne breaks away with the puck toward the opposing goal, and is tripped from behind. This draws a rare penalty shot, where Gruhl has the chance to go one-on-one against the opposing goalie, kind of like a grudge race.

As the crowd of more than 5,000 rises, Gruhl takes the puck at center ice, skates in close, and flips the puck past the Kalamazoo goalie into the net. The roar of the crowd is instant, and hangs in the air as Amstutz hits a tape that makes a loud siren sound. The unison, the energy that the crowd delivers, is hard to match.

"When I call these games, I've got to try and get everybody pulling together for the home team. That's not possible in racing. A race can be just as exciting as any other sport, but you generally don't have the crowd all behind the same guy, at least not at the short-track level. Here, you get instant reactions when the home team does something exciting."

Amstutz has just a few seconds when there is a break in the action, and must have his music or message ready the split second the opening comes. Maybe it will be a few bars of a song, or a very quick announcement, or some sort of promotion. The moment play resumes, he must stop.

"We tried some of this stuff at Avilla, with the music and things, and it just didn't work," he admits. "I think lots of old-line race fans resisted the new ideas, like they originally resisted it here. But we stayed with it here, and we think it brought more fans. Look at this crowd tonight, more than five thousand, that's pretty good for a Thursday night. And this place really rocks; these people are entertained.

"Racing doesn't really lend itself to some of these things because of the open-air atmosphere, and because the breaks between races or during yellows are much longer. But racing needs to keep in mind that it all comes down to entertainment. It doesn't matter what sport, you've got to keep people's minds moving, you can't let them go to sleep."

Some of the most entertaining parts of the game have nothing to do with hockey. Several "side shows" are offered every night, and all are simply an outgrowth of an original zany idea that worked.

"We've got a high school kid that comes to all the games dressed like Elvis. We always play "Jailhouse Rock" for a minute or so, and this kid jumps from his seat, and runs down the aisle with his guitar to 'perform.' He's here every night, we don't pay him, he's just here to have fun. The crowd loves it, and it really adds a lot to the atmosphere. People love stuff like that."

The second period provides lots more fireworks, with several fights and penalties. This is when Amstutz shines, as he drops in just the right music for the occasion. Fights might call for "Superman," while an opposing player hears, "Walk Right In" as he heads for the penalty box.

Sometimes, Amstutz finds himself literally in the thick of things. His booth is located between the penalty boxes, where only the six-foot space separates the players. When guys haven't finished their dance on the ice, they take it up from the penalty boxes, giving Amstutz the opportunity to hear loads of profanity—in stereo.

"A few years back a couple of guys were hot enough that they climbed over the glass and fell down on the table here, fighting and rolling all over each other. Talk about having it in your lap. They busted up just about everything, but it made for a great excitement."

Late in the game, while the Komets have two players in the penalty box, the Wings are pressing. They get several shots at goal, but Komets goalie Sean Gauthier rejects them all, trying to kill off the penalty until Fort Wayne is back at full strength. With just seconds remaining, Amstutz cuts to "The Heat Is On," and the crowd rises to salute Gauthier. More electricity and emotion.

With the game tied at regulation, and tied again after an overtime period, the teams have a final "shootout" to determine the winner. Tonight the Komets are right on the money, burying three of its five shots to take the victory. As the final puck slips into the net, the crowd lets loose with a deafening roar as Amstutz implores them to salute the home team.

Then, in a matter or moments, the building begins to empty. Within minutes the scene has changed to one of quiet echoes, and Amstutz begins the task of unplugging his gear and packing it away in boxes which he will carry to his car in the parking lot.

Club President Mike Franke stops by and offers praise for his announcer.

"This guy is a magician, plain and simple," he says. "A magician. He really knows how to get 'em to rock and roll."

In a few weeks, his audience will be different. Maybe "rock and roll" isn't the right term. But he will be entertaining, no matter what. And he has to remember to sell lots of popcorn, too.

AFTER THE FIRE

APRIL 1992 - NATIONAL SPEED SPORT NEWS

It's only been a couple of weeks since the Kansas City fire. Already, I miss Doug Wolfgang.

He mends now, slowly, painfully, in the first few days of what will be a long and trying ordeal. It most certainly is the most difficult period he or his family will ever face. And all we can do is wait.

To define Wolfgang's career would be to define modern sprint car racing. A few years ago he was a scraggly kid with nerdy glasses, seen in a fading picture smiling proudly alongside car owner Bob Trostle after winning an early-1970s event in Alabama.

Outlaw sprint car racing was just that. No letters, no rules, no clear definition. Just a ragtag bunch of guys pulling open trailers loaded with iron that was usually beat up, bent, tired, and hopefully fast.

From that group emerged today's Outlaws, spelled with a capital letter, marketed and prominent, and Wolfie was the right player at the right time. The road was to become his home, and he would become a part of sprint car racing's big three: Steve (Kinser), Sammy (Swindell), and Doug.

Their show played to full houses, and to the fanatic following of sprint car fans, they were no less important than any rock star.

The road was their life, described perfectly in an old Bachman-Turner Overdrive song.

It's a hurried-up life
But it's the life I choose.
No use in askin' me to slow down,
Cause I got nothin' to lose
But time, and time is all I got

Sprint car racing needed the big three. These three became a dynasty in their own right, with personalities as diverse as the weather.

Steve Kinser is surrounded with such a powerful aura and intensity that many are intimidated to approach him. Sammy Swindell is similar, and so reserved and quiet that an attempt to draw conversation might be met with just a couple of words and a stare. Nothing wrong with their way; just sometimes difficult for people to relate to.

But Wolfie became the lunch-box hero. While he eventually lost the glasses (he says he got "gonked" on the head in a crash which corrected his eyesight), as the hairline receded he looked more and more like an everyday guy, one of us. He became the star everybody liked, period. No god-like status, just a normal guy trying to make a living.

When we come into a new town,
everybody's there
When we play our music,
hands are in the air
When the music's over,
you wonder where we are
I'm standin' in the silence,
With my old guitar.
Rock is my life, this is my song.

It wasn't an easy trip for Wolfgang; that journey from beat-up iron to first-class gear. He had been just about everywhere, and he saw the best and the worst the sport could offer. He saw five checkered flags at the Knoxville Nationals. He saw some of his best friends take their last rides. He endured.

It's a cryin' shame,
but some of us have not survived.
No use in askin' how it happened,
but very few are left alive.
I just want to keep on makin' music,
I gotta keep on keepin' on.
You're only as good as your last record,
I know that someday I'll be gone.

Wolfie has consistently been a class act in a sport that is often rough around the edges. In return, fans have made him perhaps the most universally popular driver in open-wheel racing today. Ever hear Wolfgang get booed? Not in this lifetime.

Some might say stardom shaped his personality, giving him the ability to be aggressive, yet relate well to fans. Maybe so, but his close friends say he would be a class act if he were a football player, a politician, or a coal miner.

Two strong images stand out in my mind today when I think about Doug Wolfgang. The first is a story that nearly every party would deny, but good authority confirms it indeed happened. Wolfie had been promised appearance money for a midweek sprint show in the Midwest. The promoter was trying something new, and was out on a limb. It was a cloudy, rainy night, and his grandstands were so empty it looked as though somebody had forgotten to open the front gate. A small smattering of sprint cars were parked in the pits, and it was clear Wolfgang was set for a cakewalk.

A guy from the sanction group went to the promoter and advised him to cancel. There's no sense in taking such a bath, he reasoned. But the promoter felt he would suffer more from the bad PR of a cancellation than losing a bundle on the show. He would run it.

Wolfie had it all set up. Guaranteed money, plus racing against a light field. But right before the feature, Wolfgang sought out the promoter. He told him if he won the feature, he would forget the appearance money. He then went out and dusted 'em off.

How many guys do you know who would give a guy a break out of his own pocket?

Another indelible image goes way back to the Eldora Nationals in the early 1980s. Steve Kinser was leading the Saturday-night feature, when Swindell slipped past. A lap or two later, a multicar crash in turn four brought out the red.

Kinser smoked into his pit, stopping and cutting the engine as car owner Karl Kinser and his crew went to work. Kinser pulled off his helmet and stared straight ahead. It was painfully quiet in the pits, and the tension was heavy.

"Karl!" Kinser barked, "anybody else runnin' with us?"

Karl bent behind the car with a tire gauge, working his magic. His gaze never wavered, and after a moment he spoke.

"Yeah, Doug's right on yore ass."

We need you, Wolfie. It doesn't matter if you drive, wrench, talk, work, walk, or just watch. There's a gaping hole in sprint car racing. We're holding your spot for you.

"ROCK IS MY LIFE, AND THIS IS MY SONG"
by Randy Bachman.
Copyright 1974
Ranbach Music/Top Soil Music - BMI

TEN THOU$AND REA$ON$

MAY 1992 - NATIONAL SPEED SPORT NEWS

The dust danced off the ground as Joe Roush idled back to his pit. They were waiting there, the throng of happy people, with their hands in the air. Above the crackling powerplant of Roush's sprinter, you could hear their cheers.

Mark one up for the little guy.

When Roush made the tow from Indianapolis to Brownstown Speedway, he thought of the ten thousand reasons he wanted to win the feature. Like all the Indiana guys on hand tonight, he hoped to take the CRA up on its $6,000 bonus in addition to the $4,000 first-place money for any in-state driver winning a "Tour of the Nineties" feature event.

Roush is a typical driver. He believes, deep down inside, that he can win any race in which he is competing.

The problem is, Roush doesn't have the same tools as most of the other guys. You could use the term "shoestring racer," but in Joe's case the shoestring is frayed on both ends with lots of knots in the middle.

As qualifying drew to a close, a reporter wandered over to the pit guardrail where Roush sat and watched the last cars time in.

"I don't feel too bad, with my old cast iron motor," he said. "I outqualified lots of those aluminum blocks."

Yeah, Joe, the reporter said, but what would you do, winning $10,000 in one show? You'd probably just waste it.

"Yeah, I would," he laughed. "But I'd have a hell of a time goin' through it, wouldn't I?"

Roush timed in tenth, which would put him in the middle of the pack if all the quicker qualifiers also made the main. He didn't make the feature through his heat, and although he was able to claim a transfer spot in the semi, he banged wheels hard enough with another car that he broke his front axle.

He and a couple of guys who help him out changed axles in the few minutes between races, and he was the last car pushed off for the main. Nearly everyone

139

else was already lined up. Two guys didn't make the show, and Roush moved up front on the pole.

Think about Roush's operation for a minute. He builds his own chassis, partly because he wants to, but mostly because he's got to save every single dollar he can.

The small dirt track was dry, slick, and treacherous. Roush took the lead and stayed on the bottom. A few guys tried the top, but it was hopeless. As the laps clicked off, Roush waited.

"I felt like I was going awful slow, and I figured somebody was gonna be there sooner or later. I figured, hell, I ain't gonna speed up and spin out or somethin'. So I just waited. It felt like we were running a hundred-lapper."

Kevin Thomas was right behind. Thomas is usually as aggressive as they come, but he's also smart enough to know what he can get done. He waited, behind Roush, and hoped Roush would slip. With eight laps to go, Frankie Kerr slipped, slid, and finally moved past Thomas on the high side for second.

The crowd began to sense that the impossible was about to happen. As Kerr closed, they began cheering, urging Roush to go, go, go.

With three laps left, Kerr made his run. The outside was hopeless, but Frankie doesn't need much. He pulled alongside, but Roush slammed the door as the entered the corner.

"Nobody ran with me for a long time," said Roush. "I knew we were close, with just a couple laps left, and somebody pulled up beside me, and I said 'You ain't gonna pass me now!' and I gassed it."

As Kerr slipped, Thomas moved up, and while Kerr defended his spot, Roush rolled under the checkered. The little guy had scored, and scored big.

It was pure, uninhibited joy in the Roush pit. Of course, nobody had any champagne, but there was lots of beer. Competitors came over to offer congratulations, and it was clear each was sincere.

You want to know something funny? Last year Joe Roush didn't make $10,000 for the whole season.

He showed up early in 1991 with a good-looking hauler and a decent trailer, and everybody figured he and his dad, Lafe, must have hit the lottery over the winter.

"We bought this gutted-out truck for \$350," he explained. "Me and Dad rebuilt it and fixed it up, and it's pretty nice now. This trailer was a drag racing buddy of mine who quit for a while, and he's just letting us use it."

That figures. If you spend less on your hauler, that's more for the race car.

"I need every cent back into the car," he admits.

Roush is a salty, outspoken guy whose blunt style has earned him some detractors. But like him or not, nobody races harder on less money than Joe Roush. He may not be spit-and-polish, and he may not swim in the same direction as the other fish, but racing needs guys like him, because they represent a gritty, underdog element that keeps a strange balance to this sometimes-ridiculous scene.

How long can he race on \$10,000?

"Oh, I'm sure I can go all the rest of this year on that, easily. With that, and winning a few bucks along the way, we should be okay now for a while."

Sure, it looked like a fluke. Sure, it was unlikely. But forget trying to make excuses. The fact is, this game is still unpredictable, and a nobody can become a somebody in about fifteen minutes. You only get one go-around in this deal. On this chilly night in Brownstown, Joe Roush seized the opportunity. Nobody was disappointed.

DEUCE

JULY 1992 - NATIONAL SPEED SPORT NEWS

The cars of the Kings Royal begin to fire again, after a few minutes of quiet.

The big man makes a few final adjustments on the red car, nodding to Terry Shepherd behind the wheel as the car is pushed away. He walks slowly toward the pits, the gait of a man who is confident and calm in the midst of chaos.

Deuce Turrill has seen these wars before.

He has traveled about a million miles along the way, with a lot of different faces peering from inside the helmet as he tweaked and tuned. For more than twenty years he has tried to find ways to make four wheels and some tubing go faster than the other guy.

So far, he's been pretty damned good.

This business has taken him to all corners and far away from his original home in northern Ohio. He once had a civilized, responsible job working in a BFGoodrich factory. After using every possible con job and excuse to get off work to go racing, he finally gave up and said goodbye to the mainstream life of nine-to-five many years ago. For most of the years since, his life was on the road.

Deuce doesn't live there anymore.

He has wrenched some of the best and brightest, and now his destiny has led him to Warsaw, Indiana where he works for a team which is somewhere between a serious All Star-caliber effort and that of a traveling World of Outlaws team.

"I was on my own after last season on the Wintermeyer team, and Terry Shepherd called me," he explains. "He was driving for Dee Chapman, and they needed a mechanic, a guy who could help manage the team.

"They seemed like good people, the kind who are decent to work with, so here I am."

Since the team races primarily within a few hundred miles of home, for one of the first times in his career Deuce is actually home most evenings.

"That's been the best part of all this," he admits. "I've seen just about everything the road can offer, and it gets old after a while. It's nice to spend time with your family, living something like normal."

So far, it's been a great match all around. Shepherd and Turrill have found themselves to be quite compatible, forging a good friendship as they got faster.

"Terry is a super guy, one of the nicest guys I've ever raced with, no kidding," says Deuce. "Dee has been supportive and allows me to run the team like I think it ought to be, and that's really important to me."

There is some adjustment to running at this level, however. Two years ago he and Doug Wolfgang won this race. Tonight, his team has a strong, reliable engine on board for the King's Royal, but it isn't a specialty one-race powerplant like the guys up front probably have. A top-ten tonight would be a good finish, he admits.

"Yeah, it's a little different, after you've raced to win here, then come back a little more conservative. But that's the reality of today. I knew that's what this deal was about when I took it.

"I've adjusted and kept my focus on my job of making this team faster each week. I still want to get us to the point of being right up front at any All Star show. We're not as consistent as we need to be yet, but we're gonna get there."

His ability makes him universally recognized as one of the top five mechanics in sprint car racing. He has impressed readers of his recent technical articles in OPEN WHEEL MAGAZINE; clearly written passages that tell a technical story in a fresh way.

That is the real genius of Deuce Turrill. He has that rare ability to talk to people who don't know nearly as much as he does without ever making them feel inadequate. He can be brilliant when he works and an everyday guy when he talks.

As brilliant as he might be, however, sprint car racing is still a challenge. Shepherd is starting near the back tonight, and Deuce works to help him move up. The red flag helped, as the car seems to be working better. Another stop for Dave Blaney's flip on lap five gives him another chance to tune, and a few more adjustments show promise.

But it's going to be a quick ending. On the restart a rock finds its way past the shield and hits Shepherd's visor perfectly dead center. The force popped the visor loose at both ends, dropping it in Shepherd's lap with no hope of repairs.

He slows on the backstretch, and coasts into the pits. If you can't see where you're going, it doesn't matter if your car is hooked up.

"He did the right thing," insists Turrill.

So they begin to load up, ready to race again tomorrow. Another chance to make the team just a little bit better.

As he works, people approach him to say hello. His broad grin lights up with each visitor, and after a few minutes it's obvious that Turrill is as comfortable with people as he is with race cars.

Terry Shepherd and Dee Chapman must be smiling like the Cheshire cat these days. They're going to go faster and have more fun than ever before. You can take that to the bank.

GREAT AMERICAN RACE?

FEBRUARY 1993 - NATIONAL SPEED SPORT NEWS

For the past few years, Ken Squire of CBS Television has referred to the Daytona 500 as "The Great American Race."

This past weekend, Jeff Gordon helped me understand what Squire was talking about: a young race driver who wants to be a superstar today is probably going to be in a Lumina, not a Lola.

Midwestern folks are cheering for a new star, and learning another lesson in the ongoing saga of what has happened to opportunity in American racing.

Gordon's impressive debut in Winston Cup racing at Daytona a few days ago didn't surprise those of us who watched him develop his skills at IRP, Winchester, and Kokomo. Frankly, many have felt Gordon's success wasn't a matter of *if*, but *when*.

I don't pretend to be an expert in Indy Car racing, or a NASCAR insider. Yet when you see all the talent heading out of town, it's obvious stock car racing is headed straight up, and is threatening to leave Indy Car racing in the dust.

Fact is, while the average person can still identify with a Winston Cup guy, he has a hard time pronouncing the names of most of today's Indy Car stars.

The obvious point: in Indy Cars, the focus is on the equipment, the technology. At Daytona, the media spent five percent of the time talking about race cars, and the rest of the time talking about race drivers.

Which do you suppose interests more people?

Visionaries such as Humpy Wheeler and Stew Reamer have tried to tell us for years that people don't really care how fast race cars go. It's *competition* they want.

There were more guys on the lead lap at the Daytona finish than at the start of some Indy Car races. Can you imagine the crowd at the Indianapolis 500 if you had eight or ten guys swapping the lead on the white-flag lap?

This is not a rap against Indy Car. Just a plea. Get rid of the rocket ships, guys, and put cars on the track that can draft and race each other. Nobody cares if the polesitter at Indy only runs 198; just give us some heroes, from places like Fenton, Missouri; Pittsboro, Indiana; and Bartlett, Tennessee.

Which leads us back to Gordon. No doubt the media focus on the kid this season is going to be unbearable, for both him and us. By the end of the season, we're probably going to be tired of hearing about him.

A couple of years ago, a small group was watching an ESPN "Saturday Night Thunder" highlight tape at a USAC trade show booth. Gordon tried a move in Rollie Helmling's midget that put his front end up in the air, climbing on the other guy in a shower of sparks. His front wheels came down, and he stayed on the gas without losing a spot.

Two of his sprint car rivals were watching. One turned to the other and said, "Did you see the move 'Ultra' just made?"

"Yeah, I knew it was him," his friend answered. "I could see his cape flapping through the roll cage."

There once was a fair amount of resentment about Gordon's overexposure, at least in the Midwest. But in defense of the kid, he never whined and begged for ink. The media came to him. He had people guiding him, leading him, but nobody had to be asked to cover him.

He looked good, he could talk, and he drove the guts out of a race car. The rest took care of itself.

He was, and still is, the perfect media darling. He's a great interview, and let's face it, we lazy media hacks love to take the easy story.

There was some complaining two years ago that Gordon was becoming the product of his handlers, and was becoming overrated as a driver.

Well, I leaned in close to my TV Sunday, and I couldn't see any PR guys riding in the race car with him.

He could have easily screwed up, maybe spun sideways at the start and took out half the field, and boy, would the story be different. But the fact is, the kid has had plenty of chances to step on it in front of a national audience, but he never has. He always seems to stand up and hit one over the fence. No matter what the media says, he's the one who has to swing the bat.

Now, he's on the team. Tryouts were this past weekend, and he's earned a spot, without a doubt. In fact, he could well be the star player before the season is over.

But as I watched him draft with Dale Earnhardt Sunday, an intriguing memory came to mind. It was 1986, at Florida's East Bay Raceway in February, and Gordon was fifteen years old. Late in the evening, he was leading the feature. Behind him was a No. 11 out of Bloomington, Indiana. Guy named Steve Kinser.

For several laps Gordon held off the King, until Steve made it look easy and blew past in traffic. I'll always remember how the kid stood on the gas, and how I figured this guy was going to be one of the very best sprint car drivers ever.

It seemed like not long after that he began racing with USAC, almost exclusively. When he did, a lot of people wrote him off saying the ultimate racing had the wings on top.

Maybe so. But people have different ideas of what "big time" is, and maybe it's a personal thing. Gordon set his sights unusually high, and he chose the path that included some pavement and lots of TV.

The result? There are many guys whom I consider to be great sprint car drivers. But only one of them got to race with Dale Jarrett at the finish on Sunday.

BREAKTHROUGH WIN

MAY 1993 - NATIONAL SPEED SPORT NEWS

Eric Gordon sat in his sprint car, sweat and grime dotting his face. He pulled a hat onto his head, and looked around as if in a daze. Photographers lined up ahead of his car, and Anderson Speedway track announcer Denny Adams' voice proclaimed that here was the first Indiana driver to win the Little 500 since Greg Leffler in 1981.

Gordon finally pushed himself through the top of his cage and sat on the back crossbar. As if they weighed two hundred pounds each, he raised his arms high in the air, and instantly dozens of flashes illuminated the night and recorded the moment forever as the sizable crowd cheered.

Behind him were five hundred neck-stretching, breath-holding, sweaty, vibrating, pulsating, electric circuits around this fabled quarter-mile. It was a $17,000 payoff and the biggest victory of his career.

What lies ahead? Gordon offered few answers but lots of hints. He was largely unemotional as he stood for picture after picture, interview after interview, struggling to come to grips with winning this impossible dream in just his second try.

There was that special moment, when right after climbing from his car he made his way past crew members toward the victory podium. He came face to face with his father, Fay, a man who always looks as though he has been awake for the past forty-eight hours rebuilding something on the race car.

They embraced briefly, and Fay could only pat his son lovingly on the back as he struggled for words that would not come. He blinked and in a moment Eric was gone, stepping up to the podium and waving to the cheering crowd. Anyone with a son would understand what such a moment does to a man's spirits.

What will come next to this star, who has been touted as one of the brightest on the USAC tour since finishing second in both the sprint car and Silver Crown divisions in 1990?

It was one year ago that he raced in the CRA event at Eldora, when he crashed hard and may well have set a new "Big E" altitude record. Since then, Gordon suffered through a disappointing 1992 season where both triumphs and earnings were well off their previous pace.

It's the CRA crash, some began to whisper; he hasn't been the same since Eldora. Maybe he's lost the fire, others hinted.

If he were ever gone, he's sure back now. He has help this year from Randy Steenbergen and Joe Matracia of Print Communications, and they have to be pleased with the effort and results so far in 1993.

Yet, at the pinnacle of winning this race, he insists he won't be here forever. He relaxes in a lawn chair after the race, still weary.

He describes a sticker on his car that says "Farewell Tour," hinting that next season we may well see Eric run, only somewhere else.

"I can't say much, but we're just about there," he admits, carefully choosing his words. Someone nearby laughs and says now, with this first place, he can buy "it," clearly suggesting he knows what the magic figure is.

"No matter what, if I stopped running sprints next year it's really special to win this race," he said, admitting that a victory here puts your name in the books forever.

Yes, winning here gets your name in the books. Maybe that's why people carry such a fire for this one, because it is so incredibly tough to win. There are a number of guys here who will tell you so.

Gordon's teammate Tray House knows. He's been trying since 1984, and last year suddenly became a genuine contender impossible to overlook. He was fast all week, and led this puppy for sixty-seven laps until a shunt with a lapped car set him back.

He hung in, and got back to third before he tested his belts—and his friendship—when he crashed with fellow local favorite Donnie Adams, who was running second at the time. Both were parked against the backstretch wall.

What happened? It led to the simplest and most elementary of all racing discussions: you screwed up and took me out; No, I was straight until you hit me and took us both out.

No matter, because another year is gone, another opportunity has passed. House and Adams will be back, and both will probably win this thing before they're through.

But not this year. This year belongs to Gordon, a man who is one of the few drivers equally proficient both dirt and pavement.

Maybe Gordon will head South to go stock car racing. That's the path that still seems open for guys who choose to go five hundred laps in a sprint car instead of writing a check for a nice, clean, pretty, rear-engine "development" division somewhere.

If he does, I hope he is successful. 8,000 people can join me in remembering a spring night at Anderson, when the kid had his program wrapped up nice and

148

tight. When he whipped this old place, when he cracked that tough nut that so many men finally give up on in frustration.

"Two hundred laps at Daytona?" he may say someday. "That's nuthin'...one time I went five hundred laps in a sprint car..."

CHRIS E.

JUNE 1993 - NATIONAL SPEED SPORT NEWS

He sits quietly on the warm Iowa afternoon, waiting his turn to be officially honored as a legend.

A New Jersey kid who did good, so it seems. Chris Economaki caught the racing bug early and has never recovered, and we all have benefited from his passion.

Like thousands of other depression-era kids, he sought to escape the hardscrabble life in 1932 when the roar of midgets beckoned him to Ho-Ho-Kus Speedway, located a couple of miles from his Ridgewood home. He peered through the fence and dreamed.

Within weeks the personable Greek boy soon was traveling the circuit with the team of Eastern champion Bob Sall, and it isn't difficult to imagine the twelve year old kid boldly walking into the pits and demanding to know the scoop.

He hasn't stopped asking questions since.

By the time he was fifteen, "By Chris Economaki" had appeared in the pages of the BERGEN HERALD's NATIONAL AUTO RACING NEWS, which would eventually become NATIONAL SPEED SPORT NEWS. He had chosen a path that brought him to this day, when he would be inducted into the National Sprint Car Hall of Fame. His career has so far spanned almost sixty years and touched millions of people.

He is now seventy-two, and his pace remains unmatched by much younger men. But it comes natural to the man who everyone knows simply as "Chris," because his enormous personality knows no visible boundaries. A banquet of a thousand people? No problem. Television audience of several million? No problem. Downshift during a dinner stop to a fast-food restaurant, and within minutes he is on a first-name basis with the girl at the counter, the cook, and most of the customers.

He became Editor of SPEED SPORT in 1950, by then already well known within the racing world as a persistent, inquisitive guy who always wanted the real story. But he had something more than the ability to collect the facts and write them down. In 1947 they discovered he also had the voice.

Ballyhoo, they called it. Sell those tickets, keep the promoter in business. Across the bustling midway at the county fair came Economaki's voice, hyping the scene in hopes of persuading fairgoers to part with some hard-earned money to watch the auto races just getting started. You only had a few moments, and you had to make them count.

"Ladies and gentlemen," he would begin, his voice rigid with tension, "this is the moment you've all been waiting for, all for the low price of just ten cents, ten Lincoln pennies...see these death-defying men in their racing machines as they roar to life...never before have you seen such incredible, dangerous action...just one thin dime, a tenth of a dollar, two small nickels...the seats are filling up fast, but a few choice spots remain...*OH, MY LORD!* Get that driver from his flaming machine, please...that's ten cents, ladies and gentlemen, and you will be thrilled beyond anything you have ever seen before..."

There have been many good days since those, but none he cherishes more. It forged his persona, his ability to light up a room with a few quick lines. It served him well when a television job came along in 1961, and his career in front of the cameras has made him arguably the most recognized motorsports personality in America.

His career has been marked by so many milestones and awards the list seems endless. In every sense, he is a celebrity. But it is very clear that the average person still relates to him as just another guy, as he strolls the pits and one onlooker after another stops him for a handshake and a quick hello.

The pits, that's where he is clearly in his element. That's where he began, where he signed on as a stooge for Duane Carter in the late 1930s. The salary was $15 a week, and he got paid maybe one week out of four. But it didn't

150

matter, because he was racing. Riding to the midget races in Carter's 1935 Chevy, hitting joints like Nutley, Paterson, Yellow Jacket, Hinchliffe, all over the East. He would bolt some parts on right, some wrong, but Carter kept him on. When Carter's wife later found out he was Greek, he had to ride in the race car up on the trailer.

Since then he went on to cover Indianapolis, Daytona, Le Mans, Formula One. They all are fine, but his love remains with the short tracks, where grass-roots racing is still strong and proud.

When Barney Oldfield rolled into Cedar Rapids, Iowa in 1910 and unloaded, he explains his car had a pointed tail, four open wheels, and a steering wheel in the middle of a single-seat cockpit. Today's sprint cars and midgets are the only throwback to that car.

He remains "Jersey" to the core, with his common greeting being "How-ahh-ya." But just up the road in Des Moines was where he made one of his best moves in 1944, when he met Tommye. She was a pretty young Iowa girl, and Chris a G.I. stationed nearby. They married in 1946, and remain devoted to one another forty-seven years later.

Now he has returned to Iowa, and soon takes his place at the podium. For the first time today the crowd rises to pay homage with an ovation. He has been honored many times before, but he talks of this being one of the proudest moments in his career.

He tells the audience that the real reason for his success are the writers and photographers who have contributed to the paper all these years, but nobody in the room seriously buys that idea. He stands on this podium for one reason: the passion in his heart for auto racing drove him to every length to succeed in the racing business.

In a little while, he will rush to Des Moines to catch a flight to Detroit for a Ford gala he is to emcee later tonight. Tomorrow, it's the Indy Car race. The next day, something else. Never-ending activity, with a pleasant pause like today in between.

It is fitting that also on today's list of inductees is Duane Carter, who died recently of cancer. It would have been nice to see them together again, one more time.

Carter's death reminds us that while the stories and memories are as interesting and sharp as ever, the subjects and characters are slowly fading away.

One more time, maybe they could load the old Chevy and go to Nutley. Risk their lives, hope to make a couple of bucks, and on down the road. Worry about tomorrow? Hell, there might not be a tomorrow.

Racing was a lifestyle that appeared to have no future, no future at all. But he has made it work. And he loves it so.

THE WILD CHILD

JULY 1993 - NATIONAL SPEED SPORT NEWS

Fifteen years ago Jac Haudenschild was a wild child running wide open when he found his way to the on-the-gas sprint car palace, Eldora Speedway. For many open-wheel fans, it was something of a religious experience.

Haudenschild still remembers that day all these years later, the images still fresh and vivid in his mind. Yet, only the memories have remained static, as nearly everything else in Haudenschild's life has changed from those early years.

It's hard to imagine that this wisp of a guy with the big smile is now thirty-five. The lifestyle has changed in recent years, and he has quietly tossed aside the fast living for the family life that seems to fit him quite well, his wife, Patty, and their young child nearby.

It is Saturday night at Eldora, where the big dogs have gathered for the tenth annual Kings Royal, a $52,000 departure from the World of Outlaws' confusing and confounding cross-country schedule. Haud remembers his first trip around these high banks, when he finished second behind a guy named Ferkel and ahead of an up-and-coming driver named Steve Kinser.

Haudenschild is enormously popular here at Eldora, partly because he grew up just a couple of hours northeast of here, but also because he is probably the most exciting guy to ever perform here.

He pauses to talk for a moment as the team readies the car for the feature. No, this really doesn't seem like home anymore, he admits, pointing out he doesn't race here any more often than the other World of Outlaws guys.

He is simply tired now, he explains. Tired of hauls from one track to another that take not just hours, but days. Everybody on this circuit has just about had it, he explains.

Yet, it is the only life he has known as an adult. He drove his first race in 1975 when he was sixteen, and in 1978 he found both sprint cars and Eldora. Since then he has lived for racing, never seriously thinking of a real job.

From the beginning, he has been thrilling. One recalls the night in 1983 when Fenton Gingrich hired Haudenschild to wheel his beautiful black No. 37 at the Indiana Sprint Week opener at Lincoln Park Speedway. It was a fast, fast car with a fast, fast driver, both full of excitement. They didn't make a lap in the feature, with Haud sailing end-over-end into the darkness of turn three, breaking his arm.

His racing has been focused on winged racing on dirt, which perhaps is just as well. The image of Haudenschild running wide open six inches from Winchester's outside wall is disturbing to say the least, perhaps more than one's heart should be subjected to.

Does he still feel like the wild child? Not really, he admits. All that stuff just seems like a long time ago. Believe it or not, he really wants to drive an Indy Car, and he's working on an Indy Lights program.

Indy Cars are not the deal tonight. He excuses himself and heads for his trailer to get ready for the feature. He feels good about this race, he says softly. Fast qualifier tonight. Starting sixth.

Soon, he is in his element. The cars are fired, and parade in front of a vast and vocal gathering of hard-core sprint fanatics. The car's engines sing as they pass by the grandstand on the final pace lap, growing in volume until all twenty-four are screaming, their tires digging the Ohio clay for traction.

He is fifth, and closing, as Dave Blaney races with leader Charlie Fisher when they soon encounter traffic. Blaney takes the lead and Haudenschild pursues Steve Kinser, closing fast when the King slips on the cushion on the tenth lap. A crash that flips Joey Saldana stops action on lap twelve, and men work feverishly on their cars.

Blaney roars onto the frontstretch on the restart, and Kinser seems to have the momentum to take the lead. Yet, Haudenschild is now running *very* close to Kinser, and the crowd is beside itself with adrenaline as the two nearly touch. Kinser hangs on, but on lap twenty-two Haud moves the Pennzoil car past for good, and everyone is on their feet.

Kinser hustles after him, and one lap later bounces his right rear against the concrete coming off turn two. On the next lap he hits harder on the turn-four wall, shredding his tire and coasting to a stop under the flagstand as the yellow lights flicker in every corner.

It was a curious scene. The King of the Outlaws, parked helplessly just a few feet in front of the grandstands. The guy who has won three of the previous nine Kings Royals, sitting in his car amid a puzzling roar of approval from a crowd delighted with his misfortune. Knowing there will be another night, he remains seated, eyes straight ahead, waiting for the tow truck to remove him from this inglorious position.

Blaney roars to a two-second advantage on the restart, and Haud soon whittles the lead to less than a second. They encounter traffic, and Haud is on him in a flash. With just eight laps to go, he tries the bottom. It works, and he emerges as the Kings Royal leader.

The roar of the crowd is actually louder than the race cars, and all eyes follow the leader. Blaney closes on lap thirty-seven, racing very close with Haud as they dance through lapped cars. He is right behind when Haudenschild moves through three and four to set up the white-flag lap. Haud's yellow machine rides too high off the corner, pounding the concrete as he fights to gather it up.

Blaney is ready, and as he tries to take advantage of the miscue, Haud is back on the gas. Out of nowhere appear a couple of lapped cars, and Haud is around them in a flash as Blaney falters. As he heads down the backstretch, it appears that Haud, a guy who had not won a feature this year, was going to win $52,000, and the atmosphere is truly electric.

But on this night, the racing gods were not smiling on Jac Haudenschild.

His car quit. Just like that, the story has a new ending. As he coasts through three and four, here comes Blaney. The Vivarin Ford roars past on the outside, as Haud's car slows. The checkered flag waves over Blaney, and in a few seconds Haudenschild's car rolls to a stop just a few feet past the finish line, a sad example of the toughest way in the world to finish second.

Blaney seems stunned in victory circle. The crowd seems lost in a blue funk, everyone asking the same question: What the hell happened?

The whispers are in the air. Ran out of fuel, everyone is saying. Blaney wipes the sweat from his face and says how badly he feels for Haud. Drove his heart out, Blaney says, only to lose like that.

Near Haudenschild's trailer, people stand and stare, eyes searching for the man in the yellow driver's uniform. Surely he is already gone, because nobody could be expected to face a crowd after such a finish.

But after just a moment, there he is. Standing in the side door of his trailer, he smiles and shakes hands, selling a few t-shirts and sipping a cold drink. He is light, happy, and gracious.

"You run out of gas?" yells a guy with no shirt.

"No, we broke a coil wire," Haudenschild explains, knowing he will be asked that same question for years to come.

The scene fades as the lights of Eldora disappear in the rear-view mirror, leaving the pitch black of the Darke County night and the memories of another Kings Royal.

They say nobody remembers who finished second. Not tonight, my friend. Almost is not enough for Jac Haudenschild. He will be back. Wide open.

STOCK CAR SAMMY

AUGUST 1993 - NATIONAL SPEED SPORT NEWS

Sammy Swindell leans in close to the Ford Thunderbird stock car and swings the rubber mallet, bringing it down hard against the inner fender. He is sweating in the afternoon sun, like the other dozen guys who toil alongside him.

He is far removed from the sprint car wars that shaped his life and his career, far away from the wild-and woolly dirt tracks where for the past ten years he has enjoyed superstar status.

Today he is on the pavement, making his first appearance at Indianapolis Raceway Park at the Kroger 200 for the NASCAR Busch Grand National division. He is making the transition to stock car racing, a transition many of his former competitors dream about.

He will be the first to tell you the adjustment has been difficult. This division is very, very competitive, with just a few tenths of a second separating a field of more than thirty cars. Yet he insists he is happy, and the gleam in his eye tells you he sincerely is.

"It is a challenge, but it is the challenge I needed," he admits. "It was just time to move on to something else, there was just so much about the sprint car deal that just wasn't enjoyable anymore. I wanted to try something I knew would be a challenge, and give myself something to aim for and try to get to the next level."

He is learning the ropes, and today the ropes are pretty tough. During the afternoon practice session for tonight's race, he backed into the turn one wall and put a big hurt on the left rear quarter. Now they hammer, weld, saw, and hope.

This is not the style to which he is accustomed. He and Harold Annett teamed up several years ago to race sprint cars, and both are meticulous professional people who like things to be very sharp. Although Annett is listed as the car owner, he and Swindell's relationship could more accurately be described as a partnership, since Sammy has a great deal of authority over the team.

They entered into this new arena earlier this year, knowing it was a big hill to climb. This is their fourth start, their best effort to date a nineteenth-place finish at Darlington.

Not an easy adjustment for a guy accustomed to winning more than forty features a year.

"I knew it would be a different world," says Swindell. "This division is so tough, and you've got to change so much of your style. Everything is different."

There are a lot of reasons he made this move, reasons that are as much personal as professional.

While sprint car racing was good to him, it was certainly not all wine and roses. Sammy is a quiet, intense guy who is very aggressive on the track. Yet, because he was not a talkative, effusive person, many think he is aloof or snobbish. That carried over from year to year, and the more he won, the louder the boos.

Although he says that didn't bother him, a guy can only take so much without it beginning to wear on him. He has had people stand in line for long periods of time to get an autograph, and then after he accommodates them, they wad the paper up and throw it on the ground and laugh in his face. His wife and family have been insulted and verbally abused, and despite any logic for such behavior, after a while one would understandably have a belly full.

So, here he is, somewhat anonymous, driving the black Ford with the familiar TMC colors, along with sponsorship from Bull and Hannah Meat Snacks. It doesn't bother him that there isn't a vast sea of people standing around his pits watching him work.

But one of the real motivations for his career change is travel. In 1992 he raced more than ninety times. To do a full Busch season you're racing less than half that number. That translates into more time at home.

"Sammy works as hard now as he ever has," says his wife Amy, standing nearby. "But he's working at the shop near home, not out on the road. For me, that's the real benefit of this type of racing. We actually have a life at home."

She stares at young son Kevin, now four years old.

"We've got a little one who wants to go to Sunday school, and play baseball, like other kids. It's not fair to drag him all over the country and keep him from all the things other kids do."

The team is making progress, and this weekend they are joined by Rick Ren, a veteran crew chief with more than a hundred BGN starts to his credit. It's a one-race deal, each feeling the other out, and Ren says it could be a promising relationship.

"I've known about Sammy, known who he was, for many years now," he explains. "I've talked with him and Harold, trying to help them here and there, and we thought we could try to work together.

"Sammy is very smart. He is a winner. He has a lot of the qualities it takes to win in this series, and he will be there sooner or later. I'm told he's the type of guy who, when something gets him down, he won't rest until he beats it. I can see that."

So they keep hammering on the Ford, hoping to make the field. NASCAR officials offer help, bringing tech equipment over to make sure repairs conform to their specs. Other teams offer assistance, ranging from manpower, to tools, to spare parts.

They gut it out, and finally fire the car in time to take a provisional starting spot on the tail. Where they finish, says Ren, isn't as important as starting the feature.

"When people see you quit, not try to make the race, they won't take you seriously," he explains. "It's important that people see you are willing to keep fighting. It's a matter of respect."

So Sammy is out under the lights at Indianapolis Raceway Park, with the smooth pavement rolling under his Goodyear tires. He lasts just eleven laps, because his suspension is bent to the point that he isn't sure exactly where his car will be going at any given moment. Rather than take somebody else out, it's time to park.

Later, after Tracy Leslie won the race, Sammy and Amy stand nearby as the crew loads the car into the hauler. Right behind them, Larry Pearson's crew works on a badly crashed race car that looks like it caught the losing end of a train.

At least yours rolls right into the trailer, someone tells Sammy. He laughs.

"Well, mine would actually even go around the track. Not very fast, but it would go."

Everything you've heard about the man in black being a bad guy seems out of place here. Fans begin to filter in, and a guy in an IMCA modified t-shirt stops to chat. Swindell is quiet, but he shakes the guy's hand and talks with him a few minutes.

So it's home to Memphis, then to Michigan International Speedway in two weeks. There's plenty of work to do in between, but that's okay.

"I like it," says Swindell. "This has turned out to be exactly the challenge I've needed at just the right time."

So the black TMC rig hits the road, headed for home, where most of the sprint car stuff has been sold. There really isn't any looking back, at least by Sammy and his family. But sooner or later, at some dirt track where the sprint cars are stirring it up, someone will finally admit it: sprint car racing will miss him.

NIGHTS IN THE HOTEL SILVERADO

OCTOBER 1993 - NATIONAL SPEED SPORT NEWS

The rising sun peeks over the horizon at Eldora Speedway, the chill of an autumn morning enveloping the infield. Inside the gray Chevy truck, wrapped in musty blankets and blinking away the dust of last night's racing, Tray House awakens.

Sleeping in the truck again.

When he was sixteen, he dreamed of this life. Racing, racing, racing, that's all there has ever been. His dreams have slowly, quietly come true, and today he is a reserved, shy person who is an underrated talent in sprint car racing.

When he begins next season, he will be turning thirty years old. It seems like a long time ago that a fresh-faced young boy appeared at Kokomo Speedway, eager to go right to the top, despite wheeling a tired iron box that was hopelessly out of date.

It has not been an easy road, but it is his road nonetheless. House was introduced to this business by his dad, Kermit, a fiery, stubborn, strong-willed sprint car warrior who carried ten tons of desire in his back pocket. Tray is indeed his father's son.

He has had a good year, now holding a virtual lock on second in the USAC sprint car standings. Next year, he says, they will race knowing they have the ability to win the title.

As the team prepares for today's feature, car owner Bill Frampton walks in the trailer. Frampton is an engine man who is a hands-on owner, although

159

Greg Mahoney and Chuck Castor handle most of the car preparation. Frampton owned stock cars for many years, running weekly at Anderson Speedway until getting the sprint car bug in 1986.

"I'm real happy with this whole bunch," he says, describing the group as just a collection of friends who want to race. "I can count on one hand the number of dollar bills I've taken from the car this year," he laughs, explaining that every penny goes back to the car just to keep going.

"This is what it's supposed to be," he says. "This is having fun."

Nearby, House walks around the car, studying every angle, every adjustment. He and Mahoney stroke the car, both aware that Tray starts the feature today from the pole position, in an event that pays $10,000 to the winner. These guys could race for a long time on that kind of money.

Tray remembers the cars with which he started his career, and admits that, yeah, he wishes things could have been a little different.

"It took me five years to get to the level of equipment where most guys start out," he says. "Steel all over the race car, truck rear ends, 305-inch motors, manual steering, it took a long time. Nobody starts out like that anymore."

It was Kermit who kept him going, along with grocery owner Don Murphy, who has since fielded some winning entries with Jack Hewitt. Tray bagged groceries down at Murphy's market, talking his boss into putting some money into sprint car racing. Neither has been the same since.

While it was not an easy beginning, it seems to have forged a work ethic that is today an integral part of this man's character. During the week, to support his family, he toils as an apprentice brick mason. He is a hod carrier, a backbreaking, tough task that starts early and goes till late in the day. After that, you'll find him thrashing on a race car till late, then back to the mud buckets the next morning.

"It keeps you in shape," he laughs. "I work all week to earn money for the wife and kids, then I take a little bit of that and add it to what the car makes, and keep racing. That's how it goes."

This year has been better; the team received some sponsorship help from Print Express. But the fact remains that House often lines up next to guys whose spare stuff is newer than his primary equipment.

He soon suits up for the feature, and battles with Jack Hewitt and Tony Elliott before settling into third. Hewitt crashes heavily with just three laps to go, but Tray is unable to challenge Elliott for the victory.

A bit later, he climbed into David LeFevre's Silver Crown car, taking it from fourteenth to sixth. Just another journeyman effort.

He is a versatile racer, as he has won on pavement and dirt, with and without a wing. He admits the team really doesn't have the engines they need to race with wings on a regular basis, but holds out hope that, well, maybe next year.

His pavement skills have grown as he has moved into faster cars. He led the Little 500 this past year before crashing, and nobody should bet against him someday winning the event.

He remains a quiet man, and when people tell him he needs a glitzier image, he smiles and nods, soon retreating to the car to work on it some more.

He can still turn into a ball of fire, never hesitating to get in your face when the intensity level rises. Maybe that's a throwback to his days as a high school wrestler.

He admits he likes to race with USAC.

"They're good people, and they've been pretty good to me," he explains. "I wish they had more races, I'd like to travel with them. I'd go anywhere they want to go."

It's good to watch him, because those of us who saw him in the beginning know he is a testament to determination and hard work.

Maybe the most remarkable thing is his consistency. There have been plenty of nights in his career when his team was down on power, or off on the setup, or out of tires. But there has never, ever been a night when their driver didn't give it all in the car.

Finally it is evening, and the crew loads their gear and hitches up the "Hotel Silverado" to the long blue hauler. Tray stows his gear and prepares for the ninety minute ride home to Chesterfield, Indiana. Just one more USAC race at Winchester, and then we can talk about next year.

There is a good year waiting on this guy. There has to be. Maybe they'll hit a couple of big ones, and get a motorhome. That damned truck sure does get stuffy.

THE BUTLER HANGS IT UP

NOVEMBER 1993 - NATIONAL SPEED SPORT NEWS

His sprint car career lasted just twelve years, but he sure scored some points while he was at it.

Steve Butler said last week that it was over; at age thirty-seven he's going to be a spectator like the rest of us. While it's always much more desirable to say goodbye to people while they're still living, it's tough to think about sprint car racing without the soft-spoken, hard-driving man from Kokomo, Indiana.

To describe this guy is to try and piece together a puzzle that doesn't seem to make sense at first glance. He is as aggressive as anybody you'll see in this hardcore business, yet personally he is kind, gentle, well mannered, and pleasant in virtually any situation.

As usual, Butler was articulate and straightforward as he described his reasons for quitting. He is clearly motivated at the thought of returning to school to complete his education and earn a degree, and it's obvious that spending more time with his wife, Thomasa, and two young kids is a big factor.

He spoke of desire, and how it has slowly gone away. He has been at the top, and knows the level of commitment it takes to be successful in a sprint car. And he knows when that commitment isn't there anymore.

It's odd that a guy like Butler talks about lacking the desire to return to championship form, because it was sheer desire that got him there in the first place.

He graduated from high school and took a job flipping burgers at a local drive-in to earn enough to buy a buddy's racing motorcycle for $500, making weekly payments of $25. He eventually moved to a bigger, more expensive bike, and paid the price in a tough game, averaging a broken bone a year.

He wiped out big in 1977 when he smacked a guardrail on a Michigan course, spending a month in the hospital and picking up a permanent limp in the process. By 1980 he had discovered sprint cars and Thomasa, both just the right tickets to move him up the ladder. She was his girlfriend at the time, and she borrowed against her house to lend him money for a sprint car. Maybe he figured any girl willing to finance a guy's racing career was a keeper.

He was on the gas from the start, and guys around Kokomo said he'd either be a winner or dead. He stayed alive and made their predictions come true.

In 1983 Butler made his first USAC start at Paragon, and just one lap into his career got some serious flight time when he crashed while qualifying. But he hung in, and the next year won five USAC main events. Then he got a call from Phil "Jock" Poor, who was putting his first solo sprint car deal together.

It looked like it would be a weird relationship, with Jock being so crusty, tough, and firm, and Butler being the wild young racer. But it worked. Jock proved he could wrench a sprint car as well as anybody, and Butler proved he had the right stuff to go to the front. Their title run in a low-buck, hard-working operation over Rick Hood in 1986 was a memorable effort that proved both Jock and Butler the real thing.

People will remember Butler as a USAC star, but there was also another dimension. When he ran winged races consistently, he was always competitive. He set fast time at several World of Outlaws meets, and drove from the back of the field to finish fourth at the 1987 Kings Royal. If he would have elected to run wings consistently, there's no doubt he would have been a contender in that arena as well.

This past season was tough on Butler, more than most people will ever realize. Being suspended by the same organization with which you had won six championships would be hard for anyone to swallow. But that fateful day at Terre Haute on July 10 will be remembered as the day the ugly, dark side of sport rose to the surface, when Butler came close to losing his hide to irate onlookers after he and Billy Rose crashed.

I talked to him the day after, and it was obvious he was shaken. But he discussed the issues with class and dignity, never calling anyone names or swearing. He was a class act throughout the entire ordeal.

Anytime a young guy says he's quitting racing, you can usually take that with a grain of salt. After all, once the smell of methanol and the rush of adrenaline have gotten in a guy's blood, it seems to be tough to quit. But I think Steve is serious. I would be surprised if he drives again.

I'll miss him, seeing the mild-mannered guy rock the joint when he got 'er up on two wheels. I'll miss his straightforward, honest explanations, and I'll miss knowing that no matter what happened, he would offer the story exactly as he saw it, without verbally ripping the other guy's guts out.

He leaves a void that seems to be growing. Jack Hewitt is hurting, Robbie Stanley and Eric Gordon want to join Jeff Gordon in the South, Rich Vogler and Sheldon Kinser are gone, Rick Hood and Kenny Schrader moved on, Larry Rice retired, and now Butler joins him.

There will always be new faces at the top, but it's going to be interesting to see who takes the place of the disappearing heroes in USAC sprint car racing. Whoever they might be, they may want to bring some extra feet. Because Steve Butler leaves another pair of big shoes to fill.

WINTER OF DISCONTENT

JANUARY 1994 - NATIONAL SPEED SPORT NEWS

Jack Hewitt stares at the sweeping grayness of the cold January sky, and thinks about the toughest winter of his life.

It has been a winter of discontent, of healing, and personal loss, and introspect that forces a person to look within to find out what they are really made of.

For nearly all his life he has raced sprint cars, developing skills and making a secure living in an insecure business. Although he has put his neck on the chopping block a considerable number of times, he has enjoyed a career almost completely devoid of serious injury.

But it all changed that October afternoon at Eldora Speedway a few months ago, when a careening sprint car crashed down on Hewitt's roll cage. He had just won a $10,000 midget race, and in another handful of laps would have collected another $10,000. What should have been a day of legend instead became a day of fear, heartache, and hurting.

Like so often in his career, Hewitt refused to yield to his situation. He is healing nicely and it is apparent we will soon see the old war horse in full battle dress once again, doing the only thing he has ever been interested in: standing on the gas.

Amidst the satisfaction of an encouraging recovery, however, came the heartbreaking loss last month of his very dear friend, J.W. Hunt.

Jack Hewitt is as tough as they come. He has refused to allow a devastating injury to break his will or his spirit. All the same, losing Mr. Hunt made it a time for tears in Ohio.

"At first Mr. Hunt was my sponsor, then he became my buddy, then I guess it just became a family," says Hewitt, who began his relationship with Hunt six years ago. "He was just a great guy, he and his family, his wife Mimi, everyone was always so good to us. It was way beyond just somebody giving you money to race with, Mr. Hunt truly wanted to help people because he loved them."

J.W. Hunt could well be the most universally beloved person in the modern era of sprint car racing. To many, he was a rich guy who liked to pass out money, who liked to keep a high profile.

But for Hewitt, and others close to Hunt, it was far beyond the issue of economics. Hewitt insists that the financial contributions of Hunt were only a small indication of his love for sprint car racing. Despite their thirty-two year age difference, perhaps that love for the sport was the foundation of their powerful friendship.

"Mr. Hunt had some money, and he loved to get in the spotlight a little bit and help guys out," explains Hewitt. "But he never had to buy anyone's friendship. Anyone—and I mean anyone—who ever met him figured out real quick that he loved racing, and winning, and the money was just a small part of that."

Perhaps another reason Hewitt and Hunt forged such a close relationship was that they were alike in one key respect: each lived every day, every minute, like it was the most important moment of their lives. A zest for life that means real *living*, not just putting in your time.

Hewitt is popular not just because he can go fast in a sprint car. He is outspoken, outrageous, always doing it *his* way, and you can't help smiling when he's around.

165

He has punched and been punched, tangled with some of the best ever, yet you can't find a guy in the pits with whom he isn't on pretty good terms.

Maybe that's what drew he and Hunt together. Hunt was a hardworking guy who knew strawberries and people. He made some money with the berries and spent his life with the people.

In death, just like in life, Hunt couldn't escape Jack Hewitt's incomparable wit and sense of humor.

"I'm a sentimental guy, and I probably cried more than anybody at the funeral," admits Hewitt. "I told Jimmy (Hunt's son), 'Gee, Jimmy, you're gonna kill me. I leaned over into the casket to give Mr. Hunt a kiss, and I got snot all over the side of his face.'

"The next day, I was sitting behind Mr. Hunt's desk when Jimmy came in, and I drummed my fingers on the desk and said, 'I'll tell you, by God, there's gonna be some changes around here now. And I mean big changes.' Jimmy just looked at me and walked around the desk and gave he a hug and said, 'Don't you ever change.'"

Like most who have suffered the loss of someone close, the strength of family was what delivered Hewitt from his grief.

"We (Jodi, his wife) went to Florida to help Mimi and Jimmy, but I think they were the ones who helped us," he explains. "It was like therapy, going down there to share our tears, and we came home feeling stronger than before."

The last couple of visits from Hunt came when Hewitt was hospitalized. Two days after his crash, Hunt flew to Dayton to stay at Hewitt's bedside, and later after his transfer to Methodist Hospital in Indianapolis, Hunt again came north to spend some time with his friend.

Those will be cherished memories for Hewitt, amidst the cloudy recollections of the most severe crash of his life. He was entering the first turn at Eldora, when ahead of him the lapped car of Mike Mann jumped the cushion and hit the wall, flipping high into the air.

"I remember (Mann) hitting the wall, and I remember turning down toward the bottom to miss him," says Hewitt. "Right after that, my lights went out."

Out for what could easily have been forever. Mann's car came down on top of Hewitt's, knocking Hewitt unconscious and breaking his neck and right arm. When his neck was broken, it blocked his air passage and he could not breathe.

Medical personnel restored Hewitt's breathing at the scene, and he can remember bits and pieces of the helicopter ride from a nearby hospital to Dayton. The neck injury was his most serious, and he has continued to slowly recover after wearing a steel "halo" to hold his neck in place as it healed.

(Those who know Hewitt insist it be referred to as an "orthopedic device," because "halo" and "Jack Hewitt" don't work in the same sentence.)

He spent five weeks in the hospital after the accident, struggling with throat paralysis that wouldn't allow him to swallow, not to mention his damaged arm, nerve damage in his right eye, and a serious bout with pneumonia.

Finally, he went home with Jodi to their son, Cody, where he continues to recover, looking toward the USAC season opener in late March where he insists he will mark his return behind the wheel of a sprint car.

"I'm getting better every day," he explains. "I've started going to the spa to exercise and build my strength, I'm a little sore but I feel like it's getting better."

Like most injured racers, Hewitt was moved by the outpouring from fans and competitors from across the country.

"The cards coming in, seeing the people saying 'Get well' on TV, it all helped," he insists. "You can't believe how much better that makes you feel. Our recovery was really pretty good, and I think it was partly because we had a lot of moral support."

Despite the misery of days on end in a lonely hospital bed, despite the pain of body parts that wouldn't work properly, despite the knowledge that a race car had inflicted this hurt on his body, there was never a moment when he thought he might not race again. More than anything else, that is the essence of Jack Hewitt.

"I knew that as long as I was still alive, I would race again," he says with absolute resolution. "There was never, not one second, when I doubted. Racing is all I know. It is all I want to do. That, to me, is living."

And there again is that link to his old friend, Mr. Hunt. Each deeply respected the other, and Hewitt speaks with admiration of the old man's style.

"Probably the thing that helps me accept (Hunt's) loss more than anything is the way he went out. He crammed a hundred years of living into seventy-four. Those last five or six years, man, he did a lot of living. He went out like a rodeo rider: he jumped on that old bull, hung on through all the bumps and jumps, kept his hand high in the air, and he rode it all the way to the buzzer."

Living all the way to the buzzer. Just like a guy named Hewitt.

ANDY GOES SOUTH

FEBRUARY 1994 - NATIONAL SPEED SPORT NEWS

Someday, when Andy Hillenburg tells his grandchildren how he made his way into stock car racing, he'll need a couple of witnesses to back up his story.

Because it is just too far-fetched to be true, the kind of stuff only Hollywood considers believable.

The thirty-year-old native Hoosier was a rising open wheel star four years ago when he chucked everything and moved to Charlotte, hoping to find that elusive key to the next level. It has been a very tough road, but he may well have finally turned the corner.

Hillenburg grew up in Danville, Indiana not far from the far-reaching shadows of the Indianapolis Motor Speedway. As a kid, his dreams had nothing to do with Cale Yarborough, Richard Petty, or David Pearson. He looked to guys like A.J. Foyt, Bobby Unser, and Mario Andretti for his legends.

Hillenburg dreamed of racing open wheel cars, and winning the Indy 500. In school, he gazed out the window, reciting in his mind the finishing order of, oh, say, the 1954 Indy 500, the familiar names rolling through his mind more easily than Social Studies or Math.

There were two things he was sure of: he would drive a race car, and it would not have doors.

But life can hold some surprises, can't it?

He became a pretty good sprint car racer, bouncing around Midwest short tracks, following a trail that is supposed to lead to the Promised Land. He won some races, and the equipment and competition continued to get better.

Like most open wheel guys today, Hillenburg was beginning to wonder why he hadn't gotten a shot at an Indy Car ride. He raced clean, he was fast, and kept his private life on the up-and-up. He did all the things a race driver is supposed to do; yet nobody seemed to notice. For the first time in his career, he began to question: Was this going to be it? Was he to be a sprint car driver for the rest of his life?

Finally in 1990, he thought he had an Indy Car ride. He was signed to drive a tired old machine, and the press release said he would make his debut at the Indy 500. But the car never showed up, so he wound up just another would-be star, wandering through Indy's Gasoline Alley and struggling to pronounce the names of all the rookie wanna-be race drivers.

The disappointment was huge, but those close to him told him not to give up. Maybe, some began to suggest, you have the right idea but the wrong direction. His friend Bill Simpson put him through the Fast Track driving school in Charlotte, then during the summer of 1990 he took Hillenburg to a Busch Grand National race at Hickory, North Carolina.

His eyes were opened. Very wide.

"That's when I made up my mind," he admits. "I could see right away that the chances of making it into this league were so much more realistic than getting an Indy Car deal together. But I had only driven a stock car once."

That was actually an E-Mod modified at IRP in 1989, which was ahh, a limited success to say the least. On the last lap, Hillenburg, who had never raced with anyone in the field before, was going for the lead. He and the leader tangled, and Hillenburg came home the winner. But a crowd with tire irons and clenched fists came looking for him in victory lane; it was not a pretty sight.

"The police wouldn't let me leave by myself," he remembers with a chuckle. "A buddy of mine drove my car down to the Clark station on (State Road) 136, and the police drove me down there to get away from the mob."

By late 1990 he knew his future lay South, but he needed to finish the season with his sprint car and USAC Silver Crown rides.

Then, in September, came a defining moment in the life of Andy Hillenburg.

He suited up on a hot afternoon at the mile dirt oval at the Indiana State Fairgrounds in Indianapolis for the Hoosier Hundred, perhaps the most prestigious race on the Silver Crown circuit. It was a race Hillenburg had dreamed of winning since he was a small child.

He took the lead early, pulling away from the field. As laps clicked by, he knew he could win it. His supporters and friends held their breath, knowing how much winning the race would mean to the guy.

Three laps from the end, his right rear tire popped. He gathered it up and held on, as Gary Hieber flashed past to take the lead. What was a sure thing had exploded like the dark rubber ribbons flapping on the right-side wheel, as he limped around the track until the checkered waved.

"Just past the start/finish line I parked the car, and just sat there," he recalls. "I climbed out, and got a standing ovation from the crowd, and that picked me up a little bit. Gary Bettenhausen came over and handed me a beer, and said, 'Kid, I know just how you feel, you drove a hell of a race.'"

As Hillenburg walked toward the finish line, reporters surrounded him. He looked up and saw Hieber, alone in victory circle. He told the reporters to follow him, and he grabbed Hieber's right hand, raising it majestically in the air as the crowd roared their approval. After a fleeting, magic moment, he quickly left Hieber alone in his glory. It was a telling episode.

Two weeks later, Hillenburg finished the Silver Crown season at Milwaukee. He borrowed $100 from his friend John Fisher, and drove nonstop to Charlotte, loaded with a helmet bag and one suitcase.

"I had zero connections here," he admits. "I was an acquaintance of Kenny Schrader, but didn't know him that well. The first few nights I slept in my car at the speedway parking lot. During the day I drove around, figuring out where the race shops were, getting my bearings.

"I bumped into Schrader after a few days, and he let me stay at his Busch shop. I worked for him as a janitor, emptied the trash, whatever I could. I did that at night, and bounced around race shops during the day to meet people and learn."

He knew the Fast Track guys, who said they needed some help, so Hillenburg finally had a job. It was a great opportunity, because it allowed him to get to know key people in the sport while remaining hands-on with a race car every day.

"Things just kind of clicked after that. They were going to put a sportsman car together, and we went and tested a car, and I tested within two miles an hour of the Winston Cup speed. They said to heck with the sportsman, let's try to put you in a Winston Cup car. So I ran the spring Rockingham and Atlanta races.

"We blew an engine at Rockingham, the motor had about fifteen schools on it (3,000 miles), we lost it after six laps. In Atlanta we ran all day, broke a wheel and lost a few laps but finished thirty-second."

He then bought a Busch car from Schrader and ran two races, then ran the Charlotte Winston Cup race. Later, he tested a car for the Hendricks team at Talladega. He kept building for his own team, and eventually in 1993 got hooked up with the Budget Gourmet Entrees people.

"We had hoped we could run ten to fifteen races this year, but then they stepped up and now we can run the entire season."

While this is just a start, Hillenburg is more confident than ever that he made the right move nearly four years ago.

"The people and the tracks down here, the racing is really good. It's like the month of May in Indy, only it's year-round here. It's that big in Charlotte. May was always fun, but after the race was over you didn't hear anything about it till April. Here it's nonstop.

"It's tough, because the competition to get into one of these cars is incredible. But there are more good rides to look for. There are thirty Winston Cup teams that can win. If you can get into one of those cars, you have a shot."

During his darkest days, he also found salvation in his partner and soulmate, Michelle, whom he married in 1991. Their daughter Ashley joined them a year later and Hillenburg now admits that something more powerful than racing is the major focus of his life.

"It's kind of funny, when I was growing up, all I ever thought about was running Indianapolis, winning three in a row, four-time winner, all the things a kid can think of. By the time I was twenty-three or twenty-four, I realized that wasn't going to work out, and I accepted it. I moved here and realized I might never race again, and I accepted that, too. So it's really not just too good to be true...sometimes your life works out way better than you expect it to."

As he prepares for his first full season in Busch racing, he can look back at that hot day under the Indiana sun, when a right rear tire came between him and a lifelong dream. He is philosophical about that day.

"I was always saying how I was saving my luck. After I blew the tire at Indianapolis, I said that. I really wish I would have won that race, but it didn't happen. But by not winning, it helped me come here and make it a total commitment. And really, that's the level of commitment that it takes to make it here.

"You really have to understand the rules before you begin to play the game. The way I started, at the very bottom, that's given me some longevity, and it's starting to pay off."

The American dream could be defined as taking nothing and building a success for yourself with hard work and desire. Andy Hillenburg proved he's not afraid to risk it all to go for it. It's good to see him get the chance.

GIVING IT A GOOD RIDE

MAY 1994 - NATIONAL SPEED SPORT NEWS

He lined up ninth, a chilly Indiana spring evening under the lights at Terre Haute, Indiana. There were plenty of heavyweights ahead, and some big dogs behind him as well. But Gary Fisher cinched up the straps and gave it a good ride. He will always give it a good ride.

For many years he has traveled from his Kokomo home aboard the overachieving rig of Kent Evans. They have struck a bond, he and Evans, two blue-collar guys who like to mix it up against bigger and better stuff.

Always clean and shiny, wearing No. 79, always lettered with *Evans Bottle Shop* on the cowl, the team proudly pulls its open trailer down the highway, with the entire world to see what a sprint car looks like.

Evans is the master of doing more with less. He is cagey and wise, and knows how to buy used equipment and make it work like new. It isn't that Evans is poor, but he seems to get a kick out of taking secondhand stuff and beating guys with it.

They qualified well tonight, but missed their heat transfer. So Fisher started patiently in the semi, picking off cars until he was out front, pitching his sprinter delicately across the Action Track clay with finesse. He sets a twelve-lap record in the process, but is thinking more of the main event, the Tony Hulman Classic, which follows.

He gets a good start, moving to the top four in just a few of laps. Robbie Stanley is strong in the Hoffman sprint car, but when they line up for a lap eight restart, Fisher is right behind. The green flag is waved and they race to the first turn. Fisher tiptoes inside Stanley, gets a nice bite coming off, and Fisher leads lap nine.

It really isn't a big deal, I suppose, that he's leading. He is a good racer, with a load of experience, and although Evans likes to put a car together within a reasonable budget, he and his crew always have a competitive car under Fisher.

Yet, one can't help but notice that the guy with the little open trailer, the guy who spent less this year on a new car than many of the other guys have in their tow rigs, is out front. The underdog is winning. If that doesn't appeal to you, perhaps my idea of the meaning of sport is a little bit different than yours.

Fisher begins to pull away slightly, and behind him is a catfight for nearly every position. Cars race side by side nearly all the way back, snarling, clawing, biting, and banging for a yard, a foot, an inch. Stanley is challenged by Cary Faas, the exciting California driver who on this night has landed in Steve Chrisman's black No. 25.

Their war carries them to the rear bumper of Fisher, and the three duel. Stanley and Faas on the outside, feeling for the cushion and slipping within inches of one another, Fisher working the bottom groove to perfection. With nine laps to go Stanley challenges for the lead, as Fisher's left rear tire begins to lose pressure.

Stanley gets a great run off turn two to rocket past, and one lap later Faas slips by Fisher for second. They slow for Derek Davidson's yellow,

173

and on the restart Faas and Stanley make a gutsy plunge into the first turn in a test of nerve and ability.

Stanley holds off Faas and stays out front, and appears to be headed for his second straight USAC victory. But as he comes off turn four on lap twenty-nine, he sees not the checkered, but the yellow. Davidson has again stalled in turn one. As the heat fades from Stanley's right rear tire, Faas pulls close behind, licking his chops for the restart.

He pokes his nose under Stanley as they roar turn one, hanging by a thread to the lower groove. Fisher watches from third as Faas pulls off the corner into the lead, finally taking the checkered by a narrow margin.

It's a happy night all around, at least within the top five. Faas brings Chrisman a big trophy that is so long overdue. Stanley, who really doesn't like to lose, takes it like a man, smiling and biting his tongue at the same time, showing that character really is a part of the package. Bryan Hayden comes home fourth in a good effort, and Dave Darland tops everyone with a magnificent, brilliant drive from eighteenth to fifth in a borrowed car.

And third belongs to Fisher. It's always a satisfying sight to see a car sitting behind an open trailer getting its engine checked by the technical inspectors.

Evans talks about the team's "new" car, explaining he sold all his chassis stuff this past winter to buy a year-old car from Maxim Chassis. The previous owner, he admitted, said the damned thing just wouldn't work. Maybe not, but Fisher sure did a good job of faking it tonight.

The engine pumps within the legal limit, and they roll the car onto the trailer, tie it down, count their money, and head home to Kokomo for another working man's Monday morning.

Outside the grandstand, as the crowd was filing toward their cars, a man in a Knoxville Nationals sweatshirt clutched his cooler as he moved through the exit. He grinned like a child and turned to his buddy right behind.

"Them non-wing sprints are sure different, ain't they?" he said, with both nodding in wide-eyed agreement.

Not really different, friend. Sometimes just a little less horsepower and a little more driver, that's all. And Kent Evans always brings a full load of driver.

OHIO SPEEDWEAK, ER, SPEEDWEEK

JULY 1994 - NATIONAL SPEED SPORT NEWS

The sign on the marquee one night earlier at Fremont Speedway perhaps said it best: "Welcome - Ohio Speedweak Fans."

After seven days and nights of motels, cheeseburgers, car washes, coolers, muddy shoes, beer, laughter, laundry mats, and racing, racing, racing, Ohio Speedweek was almost over. The tow rigs had rolled to a stop in the middle of Earl Baltes' sprawling Eldora Speedway complex, ready for the final round at what some argue has become the pearl of Ohio racing venues.

Bert Emick and the All Star Circuit of Champions have developed quite a following after all these years; a curious bunch who look and act more like outlaws than the Outlaws who use a capital O. They aren't as polished, they aren't as rich, they aren't as far from home, and they aren't as famous. But they race like hell.

Tonight's event pays $10,000 to the winner, a nice round figure that always gets your attention. As tired as the racers may be, nobody has forgotten about the $10,000.

In 1993, the All Stars fired them up for sixty-four races. After the last race, two guys were tied for the championship, the same two guys who have developed a fierce and friendly rivalry since each arrived to chase this circuit in 1990. They are interesting, these two.

Kevin Huntley, racing from the sprint-rich hills of Bloomington, Indiana; the smiling, excited guy who looks like he's always ready to race. He is aggressive, full of youth and intensity, and doesn't like to get passed, not ever. He has, on occasion, shown the ability to be shockingly fast, making his competitors look almost anemic as they pursue.

Frankie Kerr, the precise, focused driver from Fremont, Ohio who seems to explode when given a smooth, consistent race track. His goal, it seems, is to always make this lap just a little bit better than the last. He sneaks up on you, getting stronger all the time, until—BOOM!—the orange car is leading.

They are, as usual, at the top of the current All Star standings. They are also both in the hunt for the Speedweek title, with Kerr holding the edge, and Ed Lynch, Jr. second.

Sitting in a lawn chair next to his hauler, Huntley appears pensive, or perhaps bored. "We're decent," he says, "but we're not great." He nods his head toward Kerr and Lynch, parked nearby. They are going good, he explains, but "Tonight they start behind me."

Down the way, Lynch changes and tweaks. If he can do well, and Kerr has trouble, he's going to be the winner. One week ago, he finished second in the Pennsylvania Speedweek. He would really like to win this, he says. He really, really would. He turns to his car and stares. More changes. More tweaking.

One spot over is the imposing orange No. 23 owned by Stan Shoff and driven by Kerr, who is right in the thick of things, making sure the car is just right. He likes this place. He knows he can go fast here. He thinks about the $10,000, and the title. He doesn't smile.

Soon it is time to line up. They are strapped in and they fire. They take their positions. They wave at the fans. They move down the backstretch, and in an instant they are all on the throttle.

Byron Reed leads. Huntley has followed him from outside row two to hold second. Kerr rides fourth, with Lynch right behind. The field slows for a lap-seven caution, but are soon right back at it.

Reed hangs on, running a fast line on an open track. But right behind, the gold No. 1 of Huntley is coming like a scalded dog. He draws up to Reed, pulls alongside, and then simply drives away. As the field behind him fights and flings themselves past one another, Huntley takes it to another level.

He chases the cushion higher and higher, inching closer to the imposing concrete wall. The race reaches its late stages, and Huntley wisely becomes more conservative in traffic. His nearest threat, Bobby Allen, is more than a quarter-lap back and shows no sign of challenging. Soon, Huntley races past the checkered flag and looks for a place to park.

Huntley is soon standing next to his car, with Berneice and Earl Baltes to his right, and Ohio Speedweek promoter Jean Lynch and the trophy girl to his left. He's holding a mock check for $10,000, a big trophy is waiting, and the

176

checkered flag is held over his head. Photographers flashes blaze away, and his car owner, Jim Wahlie, is one happy man.

It doesn't matter if it's Indy, Le Mans, Daytona, or Eldora; it doesn't get any sweeter than this.

Minutes later, he begins to talk. Mike Cooley, he insists, is making the difference. Cooley signed on with the team a short while back as chief mechanic, and they seem to be headed in the right direction.

That cushion, someone pointed out, sure looked like it was getting close to the wall...

"It had another foot or so," Huntley says. "I like it even closer than that. *Real* close. 'Cause then most of the other guys won't run up there."

Four feet away, Frankie Kerr is interviewed. He is the overall Speedweek champion, beating Lynch by a handful of points. Another title, another good night. He is smiling now.

Huntley looks over at his friend and rival as Kerr faces the media. Huntley is asked, "Do you ever get tired of that guy?"

"Only when he's beating me," he says.

With these two, that might be tomorrow night, or the next.

Load the haulers and grab the kids. It's time to go home. Speedweek—or is it Speedweak?—is finally over.

THE RETURN OF GARY B.

AUGUST 1994 - NATIONAL SPEED SPORT NEWS

The news, it was good. Like a cool breeze on a summer day, it brought a smile.

Gary Bettenhausen is going to run the Hoosier Hundred.

He is fifty-two years old, and there will be those who will wince at the thought of the living legend climbing into an open wheel race car on the daunting Hoosier mile. There are probably a million reasons why Bettenhausen, whose ten career USAC Silver Crown victories rank him third all-time, should be content to race only Indy and perhaps a few Winston Cup events, enjoying his life with relative good health.

But those million reasons don't equal the one that draws him back to the scene, over and over and over again: he loves to race.

There are business reasons behind his decision to spend Labor Day weekend chasing a few dollars and a trophy through the heat, the dust, and the sweat. But it is about passion, as well. He has limited his efforts the past three years to running Indianapolis, which if you haven't noticed leaves quite a few weekends open.

He still has the mind of a race driver: that is, if it's the weekend, I'm supposed to be driving something, somewhere. He still has that drive, that fever, that addiction. He's still a race junkie.

To understand Gary Bettenhausen is to understand heartache, and pain, and tragedy, and triumph. This racing game, which has been kind to many people, has been something of a roller coaster to he and his family. It has tempted them with opportunity, and teased them with rewards of money and fame, then taken it all away as the world crashed down around them, forcing them to start all over again.

He grew up the son of a racer, watching his dad Tony, who seemed to race anything, anywhere, from midgets to stock cars to championship cars. Tony, one of the greatest drivers in an era rich with talent, died in a tragic accident at Indy in 1961.

Despite that tragedy, within a few years young Gary was ready to give it a go.

He has become a journeyman racer, talented and versatile, understanding this dangerous game enough to survive and make a living. Make no mistake about it, though; racing has tried its best to shake this kid off the trail. He has been beaten, battered, and burned, but no matter what, he refuses to give up.

His friend and former rival, Larry Dickson, once said of Bettenhausen, "He's just a tough old stubborn German."

In 1974, he headed East for some July 4th racing, and a rock broke his nose at Reading on July 3. No matter, just blink the pain away, and keep racing. The next day, he was aboard a champ dirt car that had a mind of its own. On its very first hot lap, the car wanted to push to the fence. No you're not, Bettenhausen must have been saying to the car, gritting his teeth. You're going to get into this corner like you're supposed to, whether you like it or not.

He didn't win that battle. The car caught a rut and jumped into the air, slamming end over end across the clay of the Syracuse, New York mile. It leaped the fence, punched a hole in the roof of a concession stand, and landed tail-first on the race track. Its battered length came to rest standing straight up against the fence, with Bettenhausen's limp body dangling outside the cockpit, as if the car were saying: there, you SOB, I've beaten you.

But nothing has ever beaten Gary Bettenhausen.

His arm was seriously damaged, with long-term injuries that to this day cling doggedly to him. Yet, within a year, he raced. And won.

Indy has never been good to this man. Suffice to say the desire and the effort were there, but a victory just hasn't happened. He found his greatest success in the Silver Crown cars, with their long, fine bodies gleaming on the mile ovals, venues rich in history and heritage: DuQuoin, Sacramento, Springfield, Indianapolis.

Interestingly enough, his Syracuse accident might have actually contributed to his success, as his arm injury forced him to effectively drive with one arm. While others would wrestle the wheel like they were driving a truck through traffic, Bettenhausen just tickled the steering wheel, gently prodding the car through the corners. He was silky smooth, and hooked up. He began to go faster, then began to win races, and finally began to win championships.

It was a great run, from the mid-1970s to 1990, in the car of Tim Delrose and Dale Holt. The name "Terre Haute First National Bank" was proudly emblazoned on the cowling, one of the most enduring sponsorships in Silver Crown history. Bob Galas was there with his wrenches, and together they earned two USAC Silver Crown titles (1980, 1983), and finished second twice (1978, 1984).

Now Galas owns the car, a new Magnum chassis that promises to be competitive, and brings with him a commitment to run the entire Silver Crown series. In an interesting and wonderful reunion, Terre Haute First National

Bank is once again on board, with its proud name boasting from the hood of the car. Like all of us, the THFNB folks still love the legend.

It is fitting Bettenhausen chose the Hoosier Hundred for his return, a race he won in 1980. Second only to the Indy 500, this was once the big daddy of all races, carrying a huge purse and loads of prestige. There are those who quickly point out that it has fallen far from its lofty perch, but a more reasonable argument might be that modern racing, with its many big purses and new household names, has simply grown up around it.

Now another legend, A.J. Foyt, is one of the race promoters. He insists he will bring the shine back to the Hoosier Hundred, and the Indiana State Fairgrounds, and he appears to be headed in the right direction. Crowds are up, interest is up, and moving the event to the evening under cooler skies has helped provide a better show.

The Hoosier Hundred cars are officially referred to as USAC Silver Crown cars, but most everyone still calls them by their honest and correct name: dirt cars. These cars, on the mile, have their own special magic. They look big and bulky, with their oversized tail tanks loaded with fuel for a hundred-mile grind. They sound heavenly, winding impossibly tight down the long straightaways, until the driver lifts his right foot and teases the steering wheel to the left, sending off a loud retort from the engine. He blurps the throttle, sliding across the surface, setting the car into a controlled slide that will within moments have it going the other direction down the backstretch. All this on a crowded race track, on a Saturday night, under the lights, with the scent of methanol hanging in the air. Yessss!

Four years ago, Bettenhausen walked away from this magic, when he crashed heavily on the first lap at the CalExpo mile in Sacramento in 1990. Once again, a dirt car tried to pound the life from his body, and burned him with flaming methanol as well. He was badly hurt, and during his recovery decided to focus on his Indy career, which was surging with his association with John Menard and his Buick-powered Indy program.

This year, he missed Indy after teaming with brother Tony. It was a major disappointment, and there was more disappointment earlier this month when he failed to qualify for the Brickyard 400.

But he's still a race driver. And what do race drivers do? They climb into the car and they race.

"I never really retired from the Silver Crown cars," he says, as if to offer some reasoning for his return. Of course, there isn't anything logical about racing, so it's easier to look at it from the perspective of passion: he's still in love, and the old girl is calling him, pleading with him to return. It'll be just like before, she promises.

It will probably take him a few races to get back into form, and it's unfair to expect instant success in a very, very competitive division. But just the sight of Gary B. sailing down the frontstretch, foot into the throttle, the engine singing its high-pitched song, brings a little more of the magic home to all of us.

Dirt cars and dust, methanol and Gary B., together on a Saturday night. Yessss!

Author's note: Gary ultimately missed the show at the Hoosier Hundred, but finished seventh at the Silver Crown event at DuQuoin, Illinois on September 10, 1994. He has since retired from driving.

GOODBYE TO THE OLD OUTLAW

MARCH 1995 - NATIONAL SPEED SPORT NEWS

He was a real outlaw.

Dick Fraizer died the other day, taking his final breaths in the home in which he was born seventy-six years ago. Unless you're fifty-plus years old and from the Midwest, you probably have no idea who he was or what he did. That's a pity.

To me, he represented what short-track racing was all about fifty years ago. His show had already long closed before I came along, but through his clear, sharp memory, he could make it all come to life again.

He would tell stories, and I would sit completely transfixed, enjoying every word. But no matter how carefully he explained things, I could never truly understand his old world. Not really.

How could anybody, in the context of today, understand the realities of what yesterday was to guys like Dick Fraizer? So much of his world has disappeared that it's nearly invisible today.

If you grew up as a race fan around central Indiana, you knew about Dick Fraizer. For many people in this area, he was a genuine hero, one of the greatest of the greats of that time.

He began racing before the war, and the blossoming roaring roadster craze caught his eye around 1939. He raced with the Mutual Racing Association at tracks such as Muncie's Steeplechase Speedway (yes, it really was a steeplechase track) and Mt. Lawn Speedway near his New Castle home, against rivals that included Red Renner, Kenny Eaton, Avery McAdams, Bob Beeson, George Tichenor, and Sam Skinner.

It was a rough and tough scene, and it's hard to imagine how a gentle, polite farm kid like Fraizer fit in. But racing was the only thing he really got excited about, and soon it had consumed him.

He won the Mutual title in 1942, then like everyone else waited until the conclusion of World War II to resume racing. After the 1947 season, he went to work on a new car, a car that would change the way a lot of people looked at roadster racing.

With the help of area mechanics Hack Winninger and Floyd Johnson (according to Don Radbruch's fabulous book, "Roaring Roadsters"), he built a car that was lighter and sleeker than most others. He turned to noted mechanic Clay Smith to craft a Mercury flathead engine. When he was finished, Fraizer handed him $900, and Smith gave Fraizer a piece of history.

"Smith could build a hell of an engine," he once told me. "I really didn't understand what he was doing to the damned thing, I just told him I wanted something strong and new."

The car was fast right away, dominating with both Mutual and Andy Granatelli's Hurricane Racing Association near Chicago. Most roadster engines were six cylinders, of the big, long-stroke variety. But Smith knew what he was doing, and Fraizer quickly figured out he had a dynamite race car on his hands.

"Smith told us to really turn the motor, that we wouldn't hurt it," he laughed. "We'd turn that thing over 5,000 rpm, sometimes over 5,500. God, I can't believe it didn't fly apart. But, the car was light and handled just great, and with Smith's motor, hell, they just couldn't hardly keep up with us."

He won seventy-two races in ninety-six starts from 1948 to 1950, an incredible run. As Mutual's gifted press man Dutch Hurst cranked out the PR on Fraizer's sensational runs, many AAA people sniffed that, since he was just another hot-rodder, he couldn't possibly be all that good.

On June 20, 1948, Fraizer cut a lap at Winchester of 21.37 seconds, setting a world record for a half-mile track. The event was especially notable because it erased the old mark set by either Duke Nalon or Ted Horn (there are conflicting records), both AAA stalwarts.

As Fraizer began to concentrate on AAA midget racing in 1949 and 1950, other drivers raced his potent roadster. Everett Burton was aboard at Anderson in 1950 when the car hopped a wheel and literally sailed over the wall. As the car rolled over in the air, Burton unbuckled his safety belt and leaped from the car. It landed upside down, and had Burton remained in the cockpit he would have certainly been crushed. Later, Burton would relate to other drivers, "When she gets upside down, boys, get that belt off." But old No. 32 was history until it was restored by Don Anderson in his Dayton, Ohio shop before being displayed at the Smithsonian Institute in Washington, D.C.

Fraizer is usually remembered as an outlaw, and aside from a few successful runs with AAA in the midgets (he won the first race ever held at Anderson Speedway in 1948), he was never able to take his game to the next level. But he proved his mettle when he raced with Hurricane, holding his own against talented racers such as Jim and Dick Rathmann, Don Freeland, Red Amick, Pat Flaherty, and later back in Indiana, Pat O'Connor.

He was part of a curious development back in 1953, as roadster racing was dying in the Midwest, replaced primarily by stock cars. Bill France of NASCAR developed an open wheel series called the Speedway Division, featuring cars very much like roadsters.

Joe Walls of Redkey had successfully campaigned Hudson-powered cars in the Midwest, and was hungry for more action. When he learned of France's new division, Walls began building a brand new car and hired Fraizer. On the day he finished the car, they rolled it right onto the trailer and headed for Hickory, N.C.

"We hadn't even ran the car, and there we were driving all night to a race," remembers Walls, now a clear-minded eight-five years old. "Dick just about begged me to test the car first, but I told him it would run all right.

"We got to Hickory and they had a bunch of cars, a really good-looking field. We were really put off by that, we didn't think we could even run with those guys. So we towed around back of the race track, and just laid down to take a nap, and gave up on the idea of racing that day."

But France apparently needed their car, so he sent a man back to wake them, promising $250 tow money if they would try to qualify. Fraizer suited up, and the flagman explained he'd allow some warm-up laps to let Fraizer get used to the new car and the new track.

"Hold up your arm when you're ready," he was told.

After just two laps, Walls was shocked to see Fraizer's hand lift as he came off turn four, his foot planted deep into the old Hudson.

"On his first lap he broke the track record," Walls recalls, "and on his next lap he was quicker. His third and final lap was exactly the same as his first one."

There they were, a couple of local yokels from Indiana, a long way from home, a little scared and a little hungry. But Fraizer, on this day, was *the man.* For the rest of his life his eyes would glow as he told that story, and it never changed over the years.

"When I came off that corner after I broke the record, that whole damned grandstand was on their feet," he would recall. "Everybody a-clappin' and wavin', it was the most exciting thing I've ever seen."

"In our heat race, and in the feature, why, nobody could even get close to us," says Walls.

But the Speedway division was short-lived, and soon Fraizer was back home, done with racing. As he farmed the old homestead, calendars came and went and one day he was just another old racer, enjoying days when he would sit with other old racers and talk like young men again.

Sometimes, when I sit in such gatherings, I wonder if I look foolish, a relative youngster sitting with the legends. I wonder if anyone else cares about these old racers, guys like Dick Fraizer, heroes and villains who were really just ordinary people doing extraordinary things.

With Dick's passing, it pains me to see another link to the past slip away. Racing, for the most part, surely must be one of the least documented sports, and as guys like Dick leave us, I'm afraid our history is leaving us as well.

He must have been a helluva racer. He was certainly a helluva guy.

STEVE KINSER COMES HOME

APRIL 1995 - NATIONAL SPEED SPORT NEWS

It was the middle of a workday, a Monday that seems far removed from the coming weekend. The phone rang, and the caller was brief.

Steve Kinser was now between jobs, the caller said.

The news of the King's departure from Kenny Bernstein's team left big ripples, at least around the world of short-track racing. Disappointment reigns, for a variety of reasons, yet perhaps this is one of those situations that will turn out over the long haul to be not all that important after all.

But phones were ringing all week, wires buzzing with rumors, questions, and opinions. It was as if all of this was permanent.

Some of the questions? Was Kinser fired or did he quit (does it matter?); was he the problem, or the scapegoat (we'll know based on how his replacement does); does this mean he is overrated as a race driver (get real); will he get another shot at Winston Cup (probably, but only if a team is smart enough to give it a legitimate, long-term effort); is it true that every sprint car owner in the world called to offer

185

him a ride (probably, with one exception); and, in the meantime, will he be a force in sprint car racing on his own (yes).

This much is obvious: this experience has made Steve Kinser a wiser, more mature man. Consider this fact: in almost twenty years of racing, he had *never* been fired from a ride until April 10. Yet, he has handled this situation very professionally, graciously, and with a lot of maturity.

Some will now boast that they knew it all along, that these open wheel guys are overrated, with no business rubbing fenders with the stars of Winston Cup racing.

Racing is a lot like church: many attend, but few understand.

Where did we get this ridiculous notion that a guy who consistently runs in the back in Winston Cup racing, a guy who has never won a Cup race, has more talent than someone like Kinser, who can whip the finest in his field several dozen times a year?

There are guys who know how to drive a race car; and there are racers. Many Winston Cup drivers qualify well, seem to be reasonably close every week, season after season, but for some curious reason then never, ever win. They are smart, good talkers, and upstanding citizens. It could be said, perhaps, that they race from their brain.

Racers do it from the heart. Something seems to click when the race is on the line, and they become instinctive. Foyt raced from the heart, as does Earnhardt. Mario, Darrell Waltrip, Little Al, Cale Yarborough, Bobby Allison, Emmo, they've all been in close races where their sheer desire and will made the difference.

Trust me on this one: Steve Kinser is a dead-on, game-faced, hard core, race-drivin' fool, and he comes at you from as deep in the heart as it gets.

To look at seven Winston Cup races and decide he isn't cut out to be a stock car driver conveniently ignores all the facts. The Bernstein team has won one race in ten years; is struggling with a Thunderbird; and has had major turmoil and turnover since last fall. Yet, because the car didn't go fast, it must be the driver, right?

It has been said Kinser's firing was a kick to the shins of all open wheel drivers, because conventional wisdom now says they aren't stock car material. This ignores, of course, Jeff Gordon and Kenny Schrader, as well as Kinser's IROC victory last season. Besides, if a guy really wants to go Winston Cup racing, wants it more than anything in his life, he can absolutely make it happen.

If it takes one year, five years, ten years; whatever happened to Kinser or fifty other guys won't bother the man who wants it badly enough. That's always been the case, and it will remain so.

This entire issue of classifying race drivers based on the type of car they've driven is certainly a narrow form of thinking, ignoring some of the most interesting transitions in our history: Foyt and Andretti at Daytona; Allison and Yarborough at Indy. If Ricky Craven isn't ultimately a Winston Cup star, will that mean drivers from the Northeast are no longer worth a look?

All of this speculation is meaningless, at least to one person: Steve Kinser. Through all of the developments of the past six months, he has been calm, rational, and realistic, while everyone else acted as if his Winston Cup effort was of epic and profound importance. As if the future of the world rested on how well he made the transition.

"I don't feel I had anything to prove," he said last week. "I went (Winston Cup racing) mainly for my own curiosity."

Indeed, last fall at Terre Haute, in what was thought to be his final Indiana sprint car start, Kinser was the focus of a vast amount of attention. Yet, he downplayed the significance of his move, the only person saying publicly what everyone knew: nothing is certain in this business.

Getting fired happens a lot in the business world. You see it regularly: a successful, highly regarded exec with a great track record takes a new position with a struggling company, and after a few months either resigns or gets fired, and relatively few people know about it. But in Kinser's case, as a public figure, his career is scrutinized by hundreds of thousands of people.

Most of us wouldn't like that very much. But Kinser doesn't seem to be a bit worried about what others think. He's decided to move forward, smile, and do what he does best: race.

"I don't want anybody feeling sorry for me," he insisted last week. "Racing has been wonderful to me, and I have no complaints at all."

So the King will return to his roots. Soon, his name will begin to appear in the World of Outlaws standings, and more people than ever will follow his progress on the short tracks. Many will see. Few will understand.

HILL ON WHEELS

JUNE 1995 - NATIONAL SPEED SPORT NEWS

Bill Hill sits pensively, waiting his turn to walk to the podium. It is his big day, a day when he will take his place among a hundred other men who are regarded as the greatest in the history of sprint car racing and inducted into the National Sprint Car Hall of Fame at Knoxville, Iowa.

He is humble, saying he isn't really sure why he is here, saying there are others who should go before him. That is poppycock; he is here because the fifty-eight voters on the National Induction Committee say he deserves it. And they are right.

One of the difficulties in describing Bill Hill's career in racing is simply finding a place to begin. He was a great announcer, a PR man without peer, and a very respected writer. He was a salesman, a promoter, a schmoozer, and a friend to countless racers and hangers-on.

The remarkable thing is that, over all these years, he has not lost one ounce of ability to continue to do all those things; only the desire has faded somewhat.

"I'm starting to feel all those years," he laughs, preparing to face his sixty-fifth birthday later this year. He was a tough guy from a tough generation, a paratrooper who found the courage to make forty-six jumps during the Korean conflict, including two over white-hot war zones filled with fear and death. It was a toughness that never left him.

He saw his first race prior to World War II, near his boyhood home in Colorado. It sparked a passion that continues to burn after seven decades, a ferocious belief that racing is the greatest sport on earth.

That conviction led him to his greatest calling, that of a PR man. He worked for the best of them: J.C. Agajanian, Don Smith, USAC, BCRA, and the Rocky Mountain Midgets. He would grab a box of fliers and hit the road, calling on newspapers and television and radio stations within a hundred miles of an upcoming race. Call it sales skills, chutzpah, or just plain persistence; nobody in the history of the business generated more publicity for racing than Bill.

Some people are in racing for the money, some for the ego, and some because they are too lazy or dumb to do anything else. But Bill was in it for the simple love of the sport, and the lines on his face reveal the tremendous hours and stress he's endured simply because he wanted it done right.

In 1961, a guy he knew won a midget race out in Colorado. Hill thought the guy deserved some publicity, and wrote a results story and sent it to NATIONAL SPEED SPORT NEWS. It began a writing career that continued uninterrupted until 1994, when he decided it was time to take some time off and catch his breath.

He became far more than a writer; rather, he was a participant, as much as the guys driving the cars. He befriended nearly everyone along the way, drinking beer and standing alongside them through thick and thin, victory and grief, elation and poverty.

His "Hill on Wheels" column became a classic, and it will be a legacy that stands long after he is gone. When historians poke around for something thirty years from now, their review of SPEED SPORT pages will reveal Hill's revealing work, week after week, year after year.

It was a fast-paced life with a fast-paced crowd, and he led the way. Raising hell, drinking and having fun, he was immersed. He talks quietly of that period, sometimes leading a story with, "Well, that was when I drank a Budweiser or two."

The stories! From California to Florida, the Midwest to Mexico, he was there for all the good stuff. He laughed and loved, and in between was never afraid to mix it up when the opportunity arose. He has brawled over women, seats in the grandstand, and anything else that seemed worth fighting about at the time. He once punched Waylon Jennings in a bar fight after the singer accused Hill of flirting with his girl.

He is embarrassed by these stories today, but he shouldn't be. He was never a redneck or a bully, and he never tangled with anyone who wasn't as willing as he was. Besides, when you are living at a hundred miles an hour, you are bound to trade some paint along the way.

But that was all before Ruby. She sits beside him today, gentle and pretty in her yellow outfit. If he had not met Ruby, Bill would probably be inducted posthumously today. One day some years ago, he began to realize that he couldn't go on like this, as he took a job at Tulsa Speedway in 1980. He had three children from an earlier marriage and had lived a wandering lifestyle for nearly twenty years.

Ruby worked at Tulsa. She liked the new man, and he liked her pretty well, too. They were married in May 1981, and in the time since Bill became a Christian, stopped drinking, and actually bought a house.

Today, he remains an account executive with K&K Insurance, helping track promoters with insurance issues. He will retire later this year, and isn't sure what he will do. You can bet, though, that he will not disappear from the sport.

He has amassed a breathtaking collection of memorabilia, and talks of writing a book. He would like to spend more time with Ruby. He wants to see more of his eleven grandkids.

Today, he looks around this room and realizes he's had one hell of a career, one that certainly isn't over. He talks of being a writer and PR man, and admits it was the only thing in racing he could do.

"I tried being a driver, a mechanic, and a car owner," he says, "and that was a disaster."

Actually, it's a good thing. If he had won that first race, he would have never been the greatest PR man in the business. And we would have never read "Hill on Wheels."

Now that, you see, would have been a disaster.

REMEMBERING THE ARIZONA COWBOY

JUNE 1995 - NATIONAL SPEED SPORT NEWS

He lived large.

Thirty-five years ago this month, the hereafter received Jimmy Bryan. He was just a few months past his thirty-fourth birthday; he has now been gone more years than he was alive.

But among racing people, especially those with a love for open wheel cars, his legend lives on. From Skagit to East Bay, from Bakersfield to Flemington, people can't seem to forget the big man from Phoenix. Nor should they.

Was he a great race driver? Yes, but so were other men. What seems to inspire the Bryan legend, and make it arguably the most enduring in the history of the sport, was his extraordinary personality.

It is difficult to imagine Jimmy Bryan in the midst of championship racing today. His practical jokes would be considered politically incorrect; his cigars disgracefully blue-collar; his crew cut dreadfully out of fashion; and his incomparable dirt-track skills totally wasted.

In a way, many who still grieve for Bryan believe he embodied what they loved about racing's days gone by: wide open, fun loving, pitching it sideways through life come hell or high water. There were never any apologies, never any regrets, and a day without a practical joke was simply a missed opportunity.

He was a big fellow, Arizona rugged at 6-foot, 200 pounds. He was handsome, and carried with him enough charisma to charm a squirrel down out of a tree. Virtually everyone he met would remember the occasion. He never knew a stranger.

Bryan elevated practical jokes to a fine art. He carried firecrackers with him at all times, dropping them at an unsuspecting person's feet and laughing as they danced. Pity the poor guy in the phone booth, or the tollbooth, as Bryan left their ears ringing.

At Indianapolis, where racers were thrown together for several weeks with plenty of time to kill, he was at his peak. Entering the track in his passenger car, he would gently knock over portable toilets by sideswiping them, giving us an indelible mental picture of some poor soul having a tussle when he undoubtedly least expected it.

He watched for delivery trucks entering Gasoline Alley, and when the driver left the truck to make his delivery, Bryan used a floor jack to raise the rear wheels about an inch off the ground. When the unsuspecting driver hopped back in, he was puzzled why the truck wouldn't move. As he gunned the engine impatiently, Bryan would drop the jack, sending the truck lurching and squealing until the terrified driver slammed on the brakes.

At Sacramento, Bryan and Tony Bettenhausen were walking across the lobby of their hotel one night when Bryan noticed a man sitting in a chair reading a newspaper. As the elevator doors opened and Bettenhausen stepped in, Bryan used his lighter to set the man's newspaper on fire before jumping on the elevator as Bettenhausen howled.

Playing cards, drinking whiskey, staying out all night, it was all part of the Bryan legend. It is interesting that despite his imposing size, there are few, if any, stories of Bryan punching anyone out. Certainly it happened; it was a way of life not just in racing, but also in society during that era. But it is easy to speculate that Bryan was simply too fun-loving to hurt anyone. The pranks and jokes were never mean-spirited.

But the light, humorous side of Jimmy Bryan was just one facet of his life. The other is a clear, vivid image to all who saw it: the big, muscular man, sitting upright in the cockpit, using his large frame to manhandle the car through the ruts, like nobody before or since.

He raced roadsters and midgets in the West during the 1940s, and came east and missed the 1951 Indianapolis 500. He left Indy that May so flat broke that he had to collect pop bottles to get home. But in no time he was back East, landing in the Leitenberger Offy to run the AAA eastern sprint car schedule.

Late that year Bryan found himself among the greatest of the sport at the Ted Horn Memorial race at Williams Grove. Tommy Hinnershitz, Ottis Stine, Duane Carter, "Bronco" Bill Schindler, and Ernie McCoy were all suited up, and Bryan was the unknown kid from the west.

That day, Bryan did something that remains awe-inspiring, even though more than forty years have passed. Hinnershitz was fast, but Bryan just a bit faster. Finding his line, Bryan pushed the Leitenberger car and made his move past Hinnershitz: on the *outside*!

It was remarkable on two counts: one, that he tried it; and two, that it worked. It is said that Bryan became a race driver that day; but really, he was already a race driver, and that was the day it became apparent.

His champ car magic began in 1953, when he paired with Clint Brawner in the Dean Van Lines car. Irascible, tough, stern, fiery, Brawner was all of that. But he and Bryan became close, close friends, and together they won a lot of races.

When Bryan quit Brawner to jump aboard George Salih's layover roadster at the end of the 1957 season, Brawner was furious. But even he couldn't stay mad at the big guy for long. Besides, that was the ride that propelled Bryan to true greatness, winning the 1958 Indy 500.

Looking back, it almost seems that winning Indianapolis was Bryan's undoing. He cut back on his racing, having fun and living the good life. But he just couldn't stay away, and he was frustrated by not having driven one of his beloved dirt cars in months, then years, and the fire still burned.

By 1960, he was clearly restless. There was a date at Langhorne coming in June, and Bryan asked A.J. Watson if he could drive the Leader Card machine, since Watson's regular driver (Rodger Ward) had long ago lost his desire to race at Langhorne.

On the first lap, starting alongside Don Branson on the outside of the front row, Bryan chased it deep into a first-turn area called "puke hollow." He never emerged alive. His car caught a rut and flipped violently, end over end, snuffing the life of the big man who had not yet seen thirty-five years on earth.

They say rock 'n' roll was never the same after Buddy Holly died, and, in a way, the same could be said for racing and Jimmy Bryan. Oh, sure, racing went on, and there were new heroes, but for many, many people, June 19, 1960, was the day the music died.

Yet, his legend lives on. That is remarkable, when one considers that his life took place completely outside the generation of most contemporary race fans. Perhaps that is evidence of Bryan's greatness, because the greatest challenge is not in becoming famous, but in staying famous.

At that, Jimmy Bryan was vastly successful.

LUKE WARMWATER WAS PRETTY HOT

JULY 1995 - NATIONAL SPEED SPORT NEWS

The bright Indiana sunshine bathes Jimmy Sills, and he is quiet for a moment amid the busy Sumar Classic pit area at Terre Haute Action Track.

Six months ago, he stood in an Indianapolis hotel ballroom and accepted the championship awards for the USAC True Value Silver Crown series. Today he is in the midst of one of those seasons, when everything that can go wrong does. Three championship events have been run, and he hasn't finished any of them.

But Sills is a survivor, and has been around this business long enough to know that this is simply a valley, while another peak may be right around the corner.

The years have been good to Jimmy Sills. He's beat around this game for more than twenty years, on just about every significant sprint car circuit in the country. Outlaws, USAC, Pennsylvania, midgets, dirt cars, he's done it all. Very well.

There was a time when all Sills wanted to do was race. Breakfast, lunch, and dinner, with racing packed tightly around all three, every day. It was the middle of the 1980s, and he was a fixture on the World of Outlaws circuit, racing with teams such as Marks and Kepler and Lenard McCarl. From there he went to central Pennsylvania, running Bob Weikert's car 116 times a season.

"That was okay then," says Sills, "when racing was everything. Today, there are other things."

There is Stephanie, his twelve year old daughter back home in Placerville, California and she serves as his link to the normalcy known to millions of Americans. School functions, volleyball games, quiet chats over dinner, those are some of the other things that today are important in Sills' life.

But make no mistake about it; there is one thing that gets this man's heart really pumping. Surrounded by a race car, competitors on both sides, that's when he is at his best.

He approaches driving race cars as a science. He knows what goes where, and how, on the race car, and knows what a driver must do to utilize the machine. But more than do, he also teaches at his driving school near his home.

"That's been very rewarding," he admits. "It's one thing to go out and drive the race car and do well. But it's a different challenge to help someone else do well. It's a good feeling."

One day a few years ago, things didn't feel good any more, and Jimmy Sills walked away from race cars, saying he had seen enough. Like a lot of major decisions, there were many factors that had piled up until they could no longer be ignored. One major influence came on a summer night in Ohio, when his friend Brad Doty was badly hurt at the 1988 Kings Royal.

"I went to see Brad several times when he was in the hospital," remembers Sills. "I looked at him, all beat up like that, and began to ask, 'Is all of this worth it?' And all of a sudden, it wasn't."

So Jimmy Sills retired. He was thirty-five years old, and he began to do the things normal people do.

"I'd go dancing, or to parties, or just stay home," he says. "I took a job as a rep for Carrera shocks, so I still went to some of the races. I figured that was it, I was really serious about it."

But a funny thing happened. After a few months away, he found there was still something missing.

"I discovered that normal people lead boring lives," he laughs. So in 1989, it was time for another long, hard look at his life.

"When I was retired, I really thought about life, and risks, and rewards, and I finally decided, that, yes, it *is* worth it. All the risks in racing, and the work and challenge, it *is* worth it. It can be so rewarding that it overcomes all the negative stuff."

Here is where we meet Luke Warmwater. Sills had insisted to friends he was serious about retiring, and yet after just a few months he was ready to go racing. With the thoughts of a thousand people in unison shouting "I told you so," he raced under the name Luke Warmwater.

"The first race back I won, and they announced Luke's name when I pulled up at the starting line," Sills laughs. "But I pulled off my helmet and somebody in the crowd yelled, 'Hey, that's Sills!' But I kept the name for a little while, until I was really sure I was ready to come back.

"Luke was pretty hot, though," insists Sills. "He won three of his first five races, then he retired."

There is another name, though, even more familiar. One day years ago, when Sills grew his tightly curled hair long, he walked into the shop and a crewman looked up at him. "Hey, it's Buckwheat!" he yelled.

"I thought, 'Oh, God, please don't let that stick,'" Sills moans. "But it did. I hate that name."

In 1989, his friend Jack Hewitt told him the USAC Silver Crown series offered the most fun in all of racing. So Sills gave it a try, and agreed. He was the 1989 series rookie of the year and the 1990 champion. He was second in 1991, then third in 1992. Sills then hooked up with bright, introspective Gary Stanton, and they have been both happy and effective together ever since.

"I like the series, the bigger cars, the longer races," he says as he begins to walk toward the starting grid on the Terre Haute half-mile. "It's been really good, Gary is a great guy to race with, and I'm having fun."

He walks along the front straightaway, and a voice from the crowd booms, "Hey, Buckwheat!!" Sills winces and waves, and admits, "Well, I guess a few people still call me that." Moments later, another fan calls, "go get 'em, Buckwheat!"

"There's another one," says Sills softly. "Damn, I hate that name."

In a moment, he is strapped into the car, and all thoughts of nicknames have vanished. It is time for business, all hundred laps of it. It has not been an easy night so far, as Sills missed nearly all the hot-lap sessions with oiling problems. He then went out last after forty-plus cars and posted an impressive third-quick qualifying time.

Soon, his engine is fired, and he is away. Crews scurry across the track as other cars behind them roar to life and get under way, their engines bubbling and snarling. Methanol fumes hang heavy in the night air. Jimmy Sills is now on duty.

The green flag waves, and going into turn one polesitter Robby Flock executes a slow spin in front of the field. Sills narrowly misses him, and soon everyone is back underway. Kevin Thomas sets the pace, with Sills riding sixth.

Sills has Stanton's machine glued to the bottom, as others try varying lines on the legendary Terre Haute surface. By lap forty-one he moves past Thomas, who had slipped to third. Sills looks strong, but behind him the cars of Kenny Irwin and Dave Darland appear to be closing.

At lap fifty-six he still holds third, a straightaway back from leader Donnie Beechler and Jack Hewitt. The bottom groove is still working, but fifteen laps later Sills decides to try the top. He pushes the No. 75 to the outside, clawing and scratching to try and gain some ground on the leaders. Soon he is back on the bottom.

A yellow on lap ninety-five gives Sills hope. He draws up behind a lapped car on the restart, looking ahead to the tail of Hewitt's machine, wondering if there is enough left to pick up another spot. But Hewitt hangs on, and Sills flashes under the checkered a second back from Hewitt, four seconds behind the winning car of Beechler.

He pulls to a stop on the main straight, and in moments it is quiet. A low-key third-place finish, nothing spectacular or wild, but exactly what the situation would offer him. Not a bad night, all things considered.

"The car could have been tighter," he says, wiping the sweat from his face. "I tried the top there later, and even though it felt like it was faster, it really wasn't. So I went back to the bottom and felt like I was gaining a little bit. But we just didn't have enough."

He moves to the podium, talks to reporters, and is interviewed by Mike King on the track's public address system. Things he has done a dozen times before.

After a couple of hours of sleep tonight, he will arise early in the morning to catch a flight to California, where he will run a sprint car at Chico tomorrow night.

He smiles and shakes hands with well-wishers, soon disappearing into the quieting pit area. Luke Warmwater seems like a long time ago. But Jimmy Sills is alive and well. And going strong.

HARD ON THE THROTTLE

JULY 1995 - NATIONAL SPEED SPORT NEWS

Five years ago, on a stormy Saturday night, Rich Vogler stood on the gas for the last time.

There is some truth, it seems, to the adage that the brightest stars burn most brief. In thirty-nine years Vogler managed to reach the pinnacle of open wheel racing establishing himself as an unforgettable icon on the USAC scene.

He was cheered and booed, loved and hated, a winner of races and a crasher. All those things he did in exactly the manner he set forth; nobody called the shots but Vogler.

His career was marked with great highs, spent standing in front of the cameras amid the elation of victory; and the miserable, torturous lows of crashing and damaging his body.

It is still, years later, very difficult to put the career of Rich Vogler into perspective. He was a complex, intense man who defied simple description. His legacy in USAC racing is this: despite the strong offering of talent today, nobody has yet matched Vogler in terms of sheer excitement.

There are a lot of ways to establish a successful racing career. Some guys are rich, and some are loaded with natural ability. Whether Vogler had any of these gifts would not have mattered, because he was going to be a great race driver simply because he had an unwavering belief that he could be.

He came from a Chicago racing family, and watched his father race midgets throughout the Midwest. Don Vogler was probably not an easy man to have for a father; tough, demanding, and impatient, he had grown up as a hardened Depression kid with nowhere to go but up. But despite his father's hard nature, Rich grew up with a far gentler, more optimistic outlook on life.

At nine years old, Rich began racing quarter midgets. It is an amusing picture to imagine, that of a pint-sized Rich Vogler intimidating another little kid into giving him a lane. When he was nineteen, he began running his father's midget on occasion.

There was no turning back at that point, and although Vogler learned carpentry as a trade, it was only a matter of time before racing would be his life.

Doug Caruthers had clashed and raised hell with Vogler during the 1970s, finally hiring Rich to drive his midget in 1978. They dominated the USAC circuit, winning the title just months before Caruthers lost a long bout with cancer.

It was that kind of life for Vogler. A great high, followed by heartache and pain. Win a title, then deal with sadness. Consider 1980-1981: Vogler became the first man in the history of USAC to win the sprint and midget title in the same year in 1980, then just months later lost his father to a violent crash at Indianapolis Speedrome in May 1981.

Later that year, Vogler nearly did himself in. He was racing on a rutty, treacherous surface at Terre Haute at the Hut Hundred, on an afternoon that saw ten race cars upside down. Across the ruts charged Vogler, refusing to give up, pushing closer to the edge every lap.

Finally, his number came up, and he crashed very hard between the third and fourth turn. Somewhere, as he rode the flipping, spiraling midget, he suffered a devastating head injury, one that required months of rehabilitation.

If there was one thing Vogler did not know how to do, it was quit.

He eventually raced on, winning races in just about every type of car. Midgets, sprint cars, champ dirt cars, it didn't matter. Give him a decent car, and you knew he would be in the hunt.

In his heyday, he heard his share of boos and jeers. It was only natural, because he was focused on winning, no matter what. It seems he had that rare ability to come out on top when the banging began, whether he started it or not. Soon, he had a reputation, and if he was anywhere near someone who spun, many just assumed he must have been the culprit, even when he was innocent.

Some say he was abnormally brave. A more reasonable definition of his style is that he was so confident of his own ability, he may have believed he was capable of doing virtually anything with a race car. Sometimes it worked, sometimes it didn't.

One night he was fast and smooth, another night he may have looked wild and ragged. Perhaps a major factor was that he drove a multitude of different race cars. There he was, sitting in a race car for the first time, insisting on a particular setup with which the car owner might be completely unfamiliar. But this guy Vogler is a champion, so he must know the quick setup, right? So before the night was over, here comes Vogler, trying to find the handle on a car, often carrying it on sheer will and desire.

If he was booed on Saturday night, he certainly was cheered one weekend a year. He was one of the few guys who managed to make it to Indy, ultimately making five starts there. Despite any feelings many fans held for him, they universally cheered his success at Indy. He was a hero, one of the dwindling few who could forge his way to the next level, yet never losing his love for short-track racing.

There is, and was, considerable speculation surrounding the events of the night of July 21, 1990. We do know this: it was a Saturday night USAC sprint race at Salem, one of the first night races there. Vogler was driving the Hoffman Racing car, leading the feature with just a handful of laps to go. It was the car he had driven to the USAC championship the prior year.

As he came through turns three and four, preparing to take the white flag, Vogler encountered traffic. In the split-second chaos of sprint car racing, he somehow touched wheels and was sent flying into the outside wall. He was pronounced dead at a nearby hospital.

Now, five years later, finding fault in that instance seems a cruel and needless exercise, because no amount of rehashing will bring Vogler back. Rich Vogler died that night because men made real-time decisions in a split-second, and there was an accident. That is the cruel nature of our sport, of our life.

In the final tally, Vogler posted some impressive numbers. Two USAC sprint titles, five USAC midget titles, member of the National Sprint Car Hall of Fame, and the AAA/USAC National Midget Auto Racing Hall of Fame. His 134 USAC victories rank him second only to A.J. Foyt in career victories.

Today, he most certainly leaves a legacy. He had his detractors, yes, but he also left behind legions of adoring fans who miss his wide open, exciting style. USAC misses him dearly, as one of its great champions, always willing to hit the road to generate publicity for an upcoming event.

His widow, Emily, dealt with her grief over time and eventually married Jimmy White, a well-known racer and fabricator. Together, they continue to raise three children born to Rich and Emily, boys now ten, eight, and six. They are a loving, happy family living in California, far from the wilds of Midwestern open-wheel racing.

The Rich Vogler Scholarship Fund has helped educate a number of young people, and with a bit more work it will become self-perpetuating. Can there be a better memorial to a man than to help others, even after he has gone?

Perhaps the most heartbreaking story in all of this is Eleanor, Rich's mother. She spent a large part of her life immersed in racing, first following Don, then Rich, virtually the only person in the world who referred to them as "Donald" and "Richard." She lost her husband, then just nine years later, her only son.

Today, she is tireless in her quest to help others remember Rich, working hard on the scholarship fund. Soon, she says, she will leave Indianapolis and return to Chicago to live near her daughter. She has absolutely no bitterness toward racing.

Five years have gone by since Vogler's death. For most of us, the grief of the moment has passed, but the pain has not. Still, you can smile when picturing the real Rich Vogler, the one we all knew. Hard on the throttle, eyes front, grinning widely as he crawled from the car in victory circle.

That's a good memory to keep with you. Forever.

ZIGGY AND OZ

SEPTEMBER 1995 - NATIONAL SPEED SPORT NEWS

He sits quietly in the long black race car, amid the dust and furor of Hoosier Hundred. He has been here before, and knows what it takes to get around the four storied corners of the Indiana State Fairgrounds mile oval in Indianapolis.

George Snider is a quiet man. In today's media-is-everything atmosphere, he might be considered a tough interview. He isn't hard to get along with, nor unfriendly; he just doesn't have much to say.

He is tough, candid, frank, and very strongminded. Ziggy, as he is affectionately called, probably hasn't been to charm school. But over the past thirty years, you'd have a hard time finding anyone who has driven the guts out of it more passionately than George Snider.

He has seen victory and adulation, strife and pain. Through it all, he soldiered on and today, at fifty-four, is the war horse of what is likely America's most pure and most traditional open wheel racing series, the True Value USAC Silver Crown Series.

In a few moments, he will attempt to qualify for his 113th Silver Crown event, more than any driver in history. He has struggled a bit over the past couple of seasons, but tonight is optimistic.

"I got my old mechanic back," he says, finally allowing a hint of a smile to play upon his face.

Yes, his old mechanic. Nearby stands Lee Osborne, a former sprint car great who walked away from the sport nearly ten years ago. Oz is extremely knowledgeable about race cars, very wise about life, and is absolutely one of the few people connected with racing who still has fun.

He and Ziggy go way back, and each carries a deep trust and respect for the other. They have many things in common, but one trait is especially strong tonight: they both want so badly to win they can hardly stand it.

Osborne wrenched Snider's car several years ago, before "retiring" once again to his hot rod shop in Jamestown, a few miles west of Indianapolis. But Snider needed a wrench a few weeks ago, and at Springfield, Illinois, Oz rolled into town to help his old buddy.

Tonight, they choose a tire with a hard compound, and moments after Snider rolls onto the track Osborne is pleased. Ziggy is third quick. He rolls into the pits a happy man, but you wouldn't know it by his expression.

While his crew and everyone else enjoy a bowl of stew inside his nearby hauler, Snider is concerned about race setup. He flits about the pit, as Osborne methodically prepares the car. With the addition of seventy-five gallons of fuel in the huge tail tank, they must loosen the car for the start of the race.

Within minutes, Osborne's work is finished. But Snider and other crew members stand around the car, debating the setup.

"Maybe we should change the stagger," says one.

"I'm not sure we've got the right gear in," says Snider.

"How about changing tires?" asks another.

Osborne looks around and shakes his head.

"I think we should go back in the trailer and eat some more stew and leave it alone," he says.

But Snider grabs a wrench, and soon they pull a spark plug. It looks as though the engine, built in partner A.J. Foyt's Houston shop, might be a bit too lean.

So Osborne and Snider stand side by side over the toolbox, fiddling with the fuel setup. Soon, all is well, and Snider now must while away the time while two qualifying races drag on.

He looks around, and thinks a little bit about what might have been, remembering a twenty-four year old kid from Bakersfield, California who took the big step so long ago.

"Sometimes I think I was born about ten years too late," he says. "When I came east in 1965 and ran the Speedway, the Indy car deal was changing a lot. I ran the rear engine cars pretty well, but these cars...the big upright cars...they were my deal.

"I never liked Indy much. I would have liked to run the old roadsters. That's what I figured I did best, anyway."

Coming from George Snider, that is a remarkable comment. From 1965 to 1987 he qualified for twenty-two Indianapolis 500s. His best finish was eighth, in 1978. What the records won't tell is the real story, of the many late-Sunday banzai runs in somebody's backup car, which Ziggy would somehow put into the show. Time after time.

There has never been anyone more competent on Sunday evening's Bump Day at Indianapolis, when the pressure was incredibly high and the quality of equipment sometimes incredibly low. But Snider is a journeyman race driver, and when he sits down to go to work, he performs. Give him a couple of warm-up laps, and he's ready. He has an uncanny ability to wring every possible ounce of performance from a car, no matter how tired it might be.

But race cars have not always been kind to Snider. In 1981, he suffered severe burns to his lower legs in a Silver Crown accident. And in 1975, on a hot August afternoon at Winchester, the world thought they had seen the last of Ziggy.

He was leading the USAC sprint points that day, when he locked wheels with a spinning Darl Harrison. Snider's car flipped hard onto its cage, then sailed over the daunting Winchester wall. Amid the shock and chaos of the violent accident, nearly everyone assumed Snider was dead.

Of course, Ziggy fooled them all. He was unconscious for several days, and both arms were terribly broken. To this day, he struggles with limited use of his right hand.

1975 seems like a lifetime ago, but in another way, it was only yesterday. Injuries or not, Snider pressed on, and today he is just as fierce a racer as he was a long time ago.

Soon, it is time to race. The car is pushed onto the grid, where he will line up inside row four. His crew tends to him, giving him one more gulp of water before the hundred-mile grind. He is strapped in, the helmet is on, and he asks Osborne to give his belts one final pull.

If you think a man who is fifty-four years old might be here just to have a little fun and stay out of the way, you didn't see the eyes of George Snider at this moment. Riveted and steely, he isn't thinking about how many races he has started. With every ounce of his being, he intends to win this race.

The command is given, and Osborne gently presses the button on the hand-held electric starter. The engine rumbles to life, and a crewman raises his hand. All around, the air is filled with the rich methanol fumes of shuddering, rasping race cars, each singing its own song: rappa-rappa-rappa-blaaata! After just a moment, they are away. Now, it is Ziggy against the world.

He runs well at the outset, and is sixth, then fifth, then sixth again. Standing on the hauler, his wife Debbie writes lap times and communicates with Snider by radio. He is struggling with some brake difficulties, but uses the onboard equalizer to fix the problem.

At the halfway point, he fights with Tony Elliott for fifth. There is a yellow on lap fifty-two, and several of the faster cars have used up their too-soft right-rear tires. Snider tells Debbie he wants to come in and change as well. But the flagman shows the field the furled green flag, and he cannot make the change now.

Nine laps later, there is another caution. Debbie leaves the hauler and finds Osborne standing on the inside of the track, and tells him of Snider's desire to stop to change the right-rear tire. Osborne is calm, and his eyes study the black car as it rolls slowly past under caution.

"The tire is fine," says Osborne. "Debbie, tell him we're real good right now. We're real good."

A few laps later, Elliott pits. Then, Chuck Gurney stops as well. As quick as a wink, Snider finds himself riding in second behind Dave Darland.

There is another caution, this time with just over ten laps to go. Snider brings his machine up directly behind Darland, but on the restart he can only watch as Darland powers Galen Fox's car into a comfortable lead. At the end Darland is several lengths in front as they flash under the checkered flag.

Snider drives back to the hauler, shutting the fuel off as his elated crew surrounds him. He unbuckles and stands in the car, and they help him remove his helmet. He is sweaty and hot, but does not look tired.

"I just didn't have anything for him," he says of Darland, as he swigs large gulps of water. Osborne leans in and slaps him on the back.

He is happy when he learns he is now the series point leader, by just one marker over Darland.

"I'd like to win this thing one more time," he says quietly. He isn't sure how much longer he will want to do this, but shrugs and says that "at least for a couple more years" Ziggy will be a part of this scene.

So there he stands, sipping water and shaking hands, Ziggy in his element. In 100 years, 100 PR men could not create another like him. An American original who does things his way, who will, like all of us, someday fade from the scene.

But not yet. Ziggy and Oz, they're still in there swinging. It has been a good Saturday night. There will likely be more to come.

ON THE BRINK OF STARDOM

SEPTEMBER 1995 - NATIONAL SPEED SPORT NEWS

His hands quietly fiddle with the shiny helmet, as he stands in the near-darkness of the hauler. Outside, crews prepare a couple of his rides on this night, the Eldora "4-Crown Nationals."

Tony Stewart is poised on the brink of real stardom. Last year he was the USAC midget champion, and this year he is in the running for an amazing three USAC titles: Silver Crown, sprint car, and midget.

He thinks about that and smiles. He's still seems like a kid, having seen just twenty-four birthdays. Old enough to race like a man, but too young, really, to understand the meaning of what is within striking distance. No driver has ever won three USAC titles in the same year. Only one—Pancho Carter, perhaps the most exalted star in USAC history—has won all three titles in his entire *career*.

It's surprising, really, when you consider how quickly Stewart has ascended to the top here in the Midwest. A go-kart star as a kid, he didn't run his first TQ midget until he had graduated from high school. In 1991 he drove his first midget, and in less than three seasons was the USAC national midget champion.

But it has not all been wine and roses. He is intense and sometimes immature, and that combination has caused some problems. Like a lot of kids, he doesn't have stress; he gives it.

"I know I still have some growing up to do," he admits, looking up as he adds tear-offs to his visor. "I get mad sometimes, and I throw fits, but it's only because I want to win so bad. What really is a problem for me is when I feel like other people around me don't have the same desire I have. That just drives me crazy."

His midget title last year came aboard Ralph Potter's midget, and all looked rosy at last year's USAC banquet. But earlier this season, as they were trying to engineer a repeat, Stewart abruptly left the team, landing in Steve Lewis' Performance Racing Beast house car. There were rumors Stewart was fired because he was difficult to work with, but he insists it was a mutual parting.

"It was a frustrating deal because we just weren't on the same wavelength any more," he says. "The car would break and the guys sometimes didn't act like they were in a hurry to get it fixed, it just seemed like they weren't motivated at times. So I would wind up yelling and everything, and it wasn't a good situation.

"You've got to remember, Ralph (Potter) had had heart surgery some months before, and up to that point he had been doing all the pavement setups. So they were trying to regroup a little bit, and it was a difficult time. So we just felt like we'd both be better if we split."

Aside from his headstrong nature, Stewart appears to have all the tools. He can be fast, smooth, and aggressive, and as he matures is beginning to understand which is the proper mode at the proper time. Part of the maturing process this year has come from two key mentors, Bob East and Glen Niebel.

East has become one of the most successful car builders in short-track history, and also prepares Steve Lewis' midgets. He has a strong background both as a driver and a mechanic. Both he and Niebel know how to get inside a guy's head to help him. Stewart recognizes how important they have been.

"Every race, both of those guys have put a great car under me," he insists. "I've tried to be a better listener, and be more patient, because I realize both of those guys can help me. A lot.

"One key thing is that both Glen and Bob, and their whole crew, have as much desire as I do. They are always focused on getting the job done, every night."

Niebel is a USAC warrior with thirty seasons under his belt. He has seen good ones come and go, a lot of them spending time in his race car. For the past several seasons, he ran only USAC pavement shows, last season with Mike Bliss in the car. They were very successful, but at the conclusion of the season it was obvious to Niebel that Bliss would be moving on to other venues.

So when Niebel looked for a new shoe, he thought of Stewart, who last season ran the 6R Racing sprint car when he wasn't midget racing. Niebel had also this season teamed with car dealer Willie Boles to field a new Silver Crown car, and when they rolled out of the trailer at Phoenix at this year's opener Stewart qualified terribly, starting the feature near the back. But he drove a spectacular race to finish third, probably prompting Niebel and Boles to share a bottle of Maalox.

"I've never had any doubt about Tony's ability," insists Niebel, who for the first time in many years elected to run the full USAC season. "But the biggest problem I have sometimes is that he's great one minute, and the next minute he might do something you'd expect from a twelve-year-old. But he is really a good kid, and he's come a long way just in this season.

"The thing is with Tony, he's got everything he needs to be a very, very good race driver. If he will listen to the right people, and keep his head on straight, he could do great things, absolutely. But he's a typical kid, and he can make you crazy sometimes."

But the results appear to have been well worth the effort. Stewart has clinched the sprint car title already (Niebel's first ever), and has regained the midget point lead with five races remaining. When the Silver Crown series arrives in Sacramento for the finale next month, Stewart is a challenging 155 points behind Dave Darland and Jack Hewitt, with only two hundred points available.

"He's a helluva race driver," says Kenny Irwin, Jr., himself a young, aggressive lion who has dueled heatedly with Stewart in all three divisions. "I feel like I have more desire to win than anyone, but I'm beginning to see that Tony has as much desire as I do. We've had some great, great races, right down to the last inch, this year.

"It's really hard, when you want something so badly, and the guy next to you wants it just as much. It can create a lot of problems, but Tony and I have raced it clean and hard."

Stewart is single and lives alone in an apartment on the west side of Indianapolis. Racing's financial realities are becoming clear to him, however, and he realizes his professional future will likely need to grow beyond sprint cars.

"I can support myself right now with what I'm doing, but it would be just about impossible for me to support a family with racing alone," he admits. "But I never really looked at midget or sprint cars as a steppingstone, I just always wanted to drive them because they are so exciting."

There is talk of an IRL test, of a Busch ride, etc., etc. But Stewart says he really isn't sure where the next chapter begins.

"Do I want to drive an Indy car or a stock car? Really, I don't know, because I haven't been in either one," he says. "Sure, I would like to grow, but I'm trying hard to find the right long-term opportunity. I can't really tell you much right now, other than to say I've got several things working, and we'll just have to see."

He finishes with his helmet, and soon it is time to race. As he slides into the seat of the Silver Crown car, it is striking that he looks almost like a small boy sitting in the cockpit. He proceeds to win the midget and sprint features, and finished second behind Hewitt in the Silver Crown race. His winnings are about $25,000. Not a bad night.

The future belongs to Tony Stewart. Now, the question is, what will he do with it? It will be an interesting winter.

Author's note: Shortly after this column was written, Tony Stewart clinched the USAC Triple Crown. He has since raced both Indy Racing cars and with the Winston Cup series.

PAPA BEAR SPEAKS

OCTOBER 1995 - NATIONAL SPEED SPORT NEWS

He stands high atop the grandstands, looking over the Toledo Speedway infield. A brisk wind snaps the flags and blows hats off spectators as they wait patiently for race time.

Rex Robbins sighs, and ponders a question about where the sport of stock car racing is headed. For more than twenty years, his American Speed Association has been on the leading edge of this business, and when this man begins to talk about the future, one would be wise to shut up and listen.

ASA isn't the biggest stock car organization in the land; some folks in Daytona Beach obviously have that honor. But way up in Pendleton, Indiana Robbins and his people have quietly put together what is arguably the most attractive and marketable—not to mention *fun*—series today.

Like any business, there is a largely unseen core of people who make ASA work. But Robbins is the glue that holds them all together, presiding over his baby like Papa Bear.

He has seen times of great success, and has lived through lean days when tomorrow looked like nothing more than a distant dream. But, through it all, Robbins did something many men seem incapable of: he learned from his mistakes, and each "next time" was a little bit better than the one before.

Tweaking, tuning, pushing, prodding; he has been at the forefront of so many stock car developments and trends they are beyond counting. But he is the true pioneer, with a few arrows in his chest and a growing legion of followers clamoring to keep up.

In the early 1980s, he watched his series suffer as engine costs throughout racing soared. While a lot of others stood and wrung their hands (and they continue to this day), Robbins was one of the first to try a limited-compression engine formula. Others in the business laughed at him. But the ASA made it work, and...POOF!...suddenly the 9:1 engine looked like a good idea after all.

Before that, he had seen his racers go through tires faster than the government spends money, and knew that meant trouble. He worked with Goodyear to develop a hard-compound tire, and...POOF!...suddenly a one-tire series looked like a good idea after all.

There are talkers and dreamers and wishers and wanters; Rex Robbins is one of the few people who are willing to choose a strategy and then make it happen, even when everyone else says it will never work.

He is nearly sixty now, and the pioneer has surrounded himself with people who will take some of the load off and guarantee the series will see a tomorrow. His son Brian is an obvious successor when the time comes, and if he and his colleagues are wise they will sit Rex Robbins down and drain from him every little snippet of experience and use it carefully.

He can, right out of his back pocket, conceptualize the past twenty-seven years and figure out the direction of the next few, then put it into words that anybody can understand. Let's listen:

"It's just so hectic now, it's changed a bunch over the last five years, just dramatically. I'll take some of the blame, or credit, whatever. The difference for us

210

has been the sponsor, having ACDelco on board just gives you instant credibility and the ability to grow. I don't care what kind of business you're talking about; you've got to have a strong foundation if you want to grow today.

"Television has probably put a new perspective on everybody. All of a sudden you're in a world where you do everything differently. Is that good? I don't know, but you can't go back once it changes you. And it will probably change again in the next five years.

"Probably the perfect motorsports broadcast would have no commercials, but then it would be worthless to the network. Where is that line between that and an infomercial? But the viewer says, yes, they will tolerate some of those commercials. "The thing that makes (ASA) different is this: a guy running a weekly race track who wants to move up, when he looks around, he might say...'trucks!' But those numbers aren't very different than running Winston Cup. And putting together a Busch deal, that's still a ton of money. But that guy can say 'ASA!' and he can run our series for $350,000 to $500,000, compared to $1.5 million for the truck series or the Busch series. No matter what direction they choose, they've got to go find some sponsor support. Now, are there more companies that could do $300,000 versus $1.5 million? I'd say yes.

"The reason you can still race with us for $300,000 is our tire cost is $100 per tire, versus $330 each. Our fiberglass body is about $2,000, but a sheet metal body is going to be $10,000, plus take a really skilled guy to do it.

"People might say we're a 'niche' series, but I guess I don't know how to define 'niche.' Our goal is to run on a variety of tracks in front of as many people as possible and the largest television audience possible, I guess that's our niche.

"What none of us can control—and I'm talking NASCAR, CART, everybody—is that man sitting at home in front of the television on Sunday holding a remote control. We can't control him. We're in the entertainment business, no more or no less. I guess that's why we run a 'competition yellow.' Because if you let a race get boring, the guy at home or in the bleachers, you'll lose him. I mean, five hours of racing at Dover? There is a limited amount of attention span for everyone, and we've got to be absolutely aware of that.

"The reason I know I'm right is that NASCAR is going in that direction. Why didn't they run the Brickyard 500? Because they know that's too long. It's silly to do things when spectators are telling you otherwise. We try to fit a two-hour television window, plus thirty minutes for starting and finish. So you look at how long it takes to go around that track, plus some time for yellows, and that's the package you put together.

"Gearheads have no place in racing. When you sit with a guy and he talks about carburetors, tires, springs, get away from that guy. Write your rules away from that guy, write them to keep costs down and keep entertainment in the mix. You have to watch your tech, and have your people calling it even.

"Because this isn't *about* gears and springs and tires. It's about real people, working on the car and driving the car and making it happen. You can't let the technology become your series, because you'll have a very boring, predictable situation where the fans aren't interested and your racers are going broke.

"Costs? Engines are still at the top of the list. Our (9:1) engines aren't cheaper, but the maintenance is much cheaper. Our guys can get 1,500 to 2,000 laps out of our engines. If we would make another rule change, it would probably be to put some more limits on the engines, maybe a rev limiter. Guys today are just shortening the life of the engine, and there's just no need to do this, some of our guys are turning 8,000 rpm, I think we should keep it around 7,800.

"I laugh at the guys in the truck series, all those guys are spending thousands of dollars blowing (9:1) engines, trying to make them work, when the technology for that engine is sitting in a notebook in Detroit right now. All they have to do is use what's already been learned about that engine. But they have to justify their position that they are the engine geniuses, and they just keep blowing the money.

"The first race we ran (in 1968), we paid $200 to win out of a total purse of $1,200. Today, my budget just to move officials and equipment to the race is $10,000. This money issue, that's what I don't have the answer for. How much is too much? A crew chief in Winston Cup wanting $300,000 a year? An F-1 driver asking for $25 million? Come on.

"It's important that my drivers up front don't go broke. But it's just as important to take care of fifth through twenty-fifth, because your top five, they sure can't just race with one another.

"The cheating today in the sport, money controls that. But I feel like maybe you've got to just zero a guy out for the entire weekend before you begin to make an impression. A fine isn't the answer, because that's just an excuse to go back to the sponsor to say you spent money trying to get competitive.

"We did sixteen races this year, and that will grow next year. We'll do twenty dates in 1996, that seems like the magic number. We'll have to look somewhere toward the South for our opener to catch some warmer weather, say somewhere along in February to April.

"Our drivers are as good as any in the country, period. If one of our guys goes through a road race school and a Winston Cup guy is in the same group, we ask the school which is better, they say no difference. A man is a man is a man. A race driver is the same, it doesn't really matter where you come from, some guys just have it.

"We look back at some of the guys who grew up in our series, and they were pretty damn good race drivers. Alan Kulwicki, Dick Trickle, Rusty Wallace, Ted Musgrave, Mark Martin, it's a good feeling to see their success. But I know we've got a group of guys today with a load of talent, there isn't any doubt in my mind.

"I know there will come a time when I'll want to leave the hornet's nest, who knows when. But all you can do is get the right people around you, and then there isn't any doubt the business will go on. That's what we're doing right now, we're trying to hire good people and get them into the right role here. We're growing, and I can't do anything about that.

"I was laughing with someone the other day, about when we had a typewriter and carbon paper, and that's what you ran your business on. Motorsports has changed, many of the traditions have to change with it. Sometimes I think the whole world, every area, that we change too fast. We forget traditional values, things like that. But, like I said before, you've got to change with the times. Or they will leave you behind. Quickly."

Rex Robbins steps into the official's booth, and prepares to go racing. Papa Bear has spoken.

213

HAIL THE NEW KING

OCTOBER 1995 - NATIONAL SPEED SPORT NEWS

The fall air is cool this night, and the lights of the pit area shine brightly on the blue Vivarin Ford transport. A man walks outside to stand on the ramp, waiting to hot lap.

Hail, the new King has arrived.

After several years of trying, Dave Blaney is finally going to face the crowded banquet hall in October as the World of Outlaws champion.

It has been a long time coming. Only once since 1987 has Blaney failed to finish among the top ten in Outlaws points. In 1993 and 1994, he finished second to Steve Kinser. He's had his best season ever in 1995, winning twelve World of Outlaws "A" features.

He survived a season-long duel with Ohio buddy Jac Haudenschild, winning with the Blaney trademark: consistency.

There are those who make their living racing; and there are those who make it their life. You can define Dave Blaney with just three words: racer, racer, and racer. A race track brat born thirty-two years ago, he grew up watching his father, Lou, race modifieds and sprint cars in Pennsylvania and their home state of Ohio. The time he spends racing is when he's most happy; the other time, well, that's just passing time until the next outing.

He has raced with this team, owned by Casey Luna and wrenched by Kenny Woodruff, for three years. Three years isn't very long for most people to stay with a partner; but here on the Outlaws circuit, three years is a long, long time. But Blaney is a mature, thoughtful man, one who knows how to get along with others.

In this endless life of night-after-night racing, it would seem to be difficult to get along with your competitors for any length of time. But among fellow World of Outlaws drivers, you'll never hear a derogatory word about Dave Blaney.

"He's a smooth, good race driver," insists Jeff Swindell, who has raced against Blaney for at least ten years. "He's got the right mix of being aggressive yet not doing stupid things. You can race any time with him and you never have to worry about him taking you out.

214

"Now, if he sees a spot, he'll take it, don't get me wrong. But I'm not afraid to rub wheels with him. He's a clean racer and a clean guy."

Everyone says nice things about him except, well, Dave Blaney. He is uncomfortable talking about himself or about his career. He is polite and friendly, but just doesn't have a whole lot to say.

Likes to do his talking with the race car, you know.

He was just a kid when he began to realize little things about life, things like being nice to people and taking care of the race car and don't run over the guy beside you. He learned it from good old Lou, his race driver dad, his hero, his mentor.

Those lessons stuck pretty well, and today he talks of Lou with obvious respect and affection.

"He is a special racer," Dave says. "I mean, every kid would think their dad is the best, but it wasn't just that he won races, he was clean and he did it right. That's what it's all about, doing it right."

So that's how Blaney goes about it, with the idea of doing it right. No prima donna, his typical day sees him working with Woodruff and crewman Dwayne Krieger on the race car for several hours prior to race time.

"I think it's important to know how the car works," he explains. "Out here, you've got to be a team, with everybody understanding what's going on and what needs to change to go faster. You can't just show up and drive the car. It doesn't work that way."

Since the late 1980s, Luna has used Ford engines in his sprint car. What was once called "The Penalty Box" now boasts big, big horsepower. Just how much stronger they are than most of the conventional GM powerplants is a subject of debate today.

"The Ford is real good right now," says Blaney.

They've had a great year, this team. Outlaws title, at least twelve features, the Kings Royal; a good year. Yet, Blaney's title will undoubtedly be cheapened by some who insist that since Steve and Mark Kinser didn't run the full circuit this season, well...

"I don't argue with that because it's true," says Blaney, staring you right in the eye. "Steve is just the best ever. If he had run the whole season with us, I don't know if we'd have beat him, we'll never know. But it's silly to argue about something like that. I try to not worry with stuff like that."

Now that Blaney is the new Outlaws champion, he's the subject of rumors about his future. Will he stay with Luna? Will he go stock car racing? Will he test an Indy car? What's up?

"I don't really know for sure about next year," he admits. "I'm sure I'll be racing here with the Outlaws. It might be fun to race a Busch car, but for me, it would almost be a step down.

"I mean, you look at the year I had this year, and my financial situation, and I can't imagine there's anybody in the Busch series that's done any better. So why would I want to drop all of this to go run with a struggling team on the Busch circuit?"

He remembers Steve Kinser's Winston Cup experience earlier this year, and smiles.

"Steve's deal this year really kicked my butt," he says. "When he went down there and was testing really well, I got a call from a team that flew me down there, tested me, and I thought they were going to put me in the car on the spot.

"Now that Steve is gone, I don't think they even remember my name," he laughs.

Besides, he says, racing just once a week would be a drag.

"I'd probably race every day if I could," he admits. "Oh, you know, I need a vacation every now and then just like anybody else, but after a few days I start getting impatient and pretty soon I'm itching to get back at it.

"In the winter I usually build a car with Dad, that keeps me occupied. Then when the season starts I'm usually pretty well ready."

So it's been another year of endless miles in the motor home, with his wife Lisa and children Emma (five) and Ryan (two). Another race track brat?

"Oh, yeah," he says when asked if he'd want his kid to race. "Sure, if he wants to. I mean, there's nothing wrong with this business. I sure wouldn't discourage him."

In a few days in Dallas, a nervous Dave Blaney will step before the crowd at the Outlaws banquet and tell everyone thanks, that he's proud to be the champion. He will smile for photographers and shake everyone's hand as his name is written into the sprint car history books.

Next February, we start all over again. But that's another story. For now, we should smile and shake the hand of the man everyone respects. Hail to the new King.

THE MAN WHO GOT IT RIGHT

NOVEMBER 1995 - NATIONAL SPEED SPORT NEWS

Calling him a historian is so...inadequate. A historian is someone who recites mere facts and figures, dates and times of nearly forgotten episodes from black-and-white yesterdays.

No, he was much more than that. Bob Laycock was, in this point-and-click world of instant information, a vibrant, clear channel that spanned eight decades of auto racing. An insightful, correct man whose vision through time cut through countless errors, omissions, and exaggerations, allowing the past to leap out onto the table in bold, bright color, time after time.

He died last week, his passing noted in a brief obituary in the local newspaper. It's odd, isn't it, that a man's entire life can be reduced to just a few paragraphs when he is laid to rest?

Bob was more than just a few paragraphs. In fact, of the countless volumes written over the past forty years about championship racing and the Indianapolis 500, Bob's work can be found in each and every edition, because his work laid the foundation for every writer and broadcaster who has stepped up to tell the story.

Officially, he will be remembered as the Historian of the Indianapolis Motor Speedway. But a big, important title was never a big deal to Bob. He was into something else: Accuracy. Cold, hard, indisputable facts. If he is remembered for nothing else, Bob was obsessed with getting it right.

"Who told you that?" he would say, his eyes boring through you after you had asked him if such-and-such had happened to so-and-so. "Dammit, that isn't right," he would sneer, and off he would go, to search through his archives for the real deal. If it took a minute, an hour, a day, it didn't matter: dammit, it was going to be *right*.

Of course, no man is correct 100 percent of the time. But if we based the past forty-some years on percentages, I'll bet Bob Laycock could put up impressive numbers. And nobody was in much of a position to argue with him about Indy, because nobody else had his depth.

He liked to talk of his first trip to the Speedway in 1914. He was there, he laughed, but, you know, he wasn't really *there*. His mother was still expecting him, he would explain, but technically....

In 1920 he began an incredible string that saw him witness every Indianapolis 500 until 1994, when his health began to slip. Think about that for a moment, and try to grasp it: his eyes saw Gaston Chevrolet in the Frontenac, all the way to Emerson Fittipaldi in the Penske chassis.

But he didn't just *see* racing. He lived it.

By 1950, he was an assistant in the IMS Press Room, working for Snappy Ford. When Ford died in 1953, Laycock was an obvious replacement, stepping up to the official title of Press Liaison. His assistant, by the way, was a fresh young kid named Bill Marvel.

During his run at IMS, he proofread lists, stories, summaries, anything related to Indy 500 data. The joke around the office at times was that you hated to show your work to Bob; he always found those embarrassing, pesky mistakes. But his review made any document more secure, because he could always back up his facts.

He scored USAC sprint car races for years, venturing from the vast expanse of Indianapolis Motor Speedway to half-mile haunts with a few thousand patrons sitting in the Sunday afternoon sun.

His passion, of course, will outlive him. Earlier this year, climbing into the USAC wagon for a ride to a Terre Haute sprint car race, there was Josh Laycock, grandson of the master, traveling to the fabled half-mile as a USAC scorer.

It will be noted that, at age eighty-one, Bob Laycock put fifty-one hours on the IMS time clock the week prior to his death. He drove from the Speedway the last time Friday afternoon, and his health faded quickly during the weekend. He had, over the past eight years, fought through cancer, diabetes, and the loss of his beloved Virginia. It was time to stop fighting, that's all.

In the mid-1950s, Laycock was a player in forming three organizations that remain vibrant and important forty years later. The American Auto Racing Writers and Broadcasters Association (AARWBA); The Indy 500 Oldtimers Club; and the Hoosier Auto Race Fans (HARF). Bob helped build the houses; we will live in them for years to come.

A man's work should be about more than just making a living. It should be viewed as a message he is sending to a time he will never see. In that regard, Bob Laycock's impeccable, precise legacy will live on forever.

He got it *right*.

SILLY LITTLE CARS

DECEMBER 1995 - NATIONAL SPEED SPORT NEWS

These silly little cars are not going to go away.

Legends, they call the beasts, and they seem like birds; you never see just one. Open up the RCA Dome in the middle of December, and the little boogers come from everywhere, until they fill the floor.

Someone once said, when describing the difficulty of driving a sprint car, that "when it gets to where anybody can do it, it isn't racing anymore."

But for eighty-some guys here Saturday night in Indianapolis, it was as close as it needs to be. From all over the country they came to John Stiles' second annual Race in the Dome, everyday guys who are also honest-to-goodness race drivers.

They ranged from rich to not so well-to-do. Some were veteran racers; others were taking their first ride. Some were very able mechanics, and others hardly knew the front of the car from the back.

But they had fun. Does the deal need any further qualification?

Bruce Walkup knows what fun is. An accomplished sprint car veteran, he long ago made his last start in the fire-breathers. But he's suited up tonight, wearing a big grin.

"My son and I each have one of these things, and I can't tell you how much fun it's been," he says, leaning on his brightly colored race car. "It doesn't take much money, or time, and it's still a great thrill to get in here and get it on.

"There are guys here who are really serious about winning, and there's a lot of guys who just do it just because they like the thrill. You see just about everything. But it doesn't have to be serious at all, you can just relax and have a good time."

The key here is something absent in short-track racing: it doesn't cost a guy his entire income to go racing.

The cars are five-eighths-scale replicas of 1937-1940 coupes and sedans, and every one is sharply painted and lettered. There are actually two classes of cars today: Legends and Dwarf cars. Legends are marketed exclusively through 600 Racing in Charlotte, and are extremely tight "spec" cars using 1,200cc Yamaha motorcycle engines. Dwarf cars, promoted and sanctioned by a completely separate organization, are a bit more loose in terms of modifications and equipment, and on certain tracks will be much faster than Legends.

The cars can and have run all types of tracks and surfaces, but according to Walkup, "it's best to keep them on a three-eighths-mile or less. You can get them on a half, but you're really haulin', and you're talking about some guys with not much experience, and you worry about getting somebody hurt. So they race best on the smaller ovals."

The cars run on spec BFGoodrich street tires, and a racer standing nearby admits he's run on the same tires for almost two full seasons.

"It's just about impossible to hook up all your horsepower to the race track," says Walkup, "so it's pointless to go out and spend a bunch of money on a special engine. So, it keeps everybody pretty much even."

The drivers are all suited up and within minutes will fire their cars for the fifty-lap feature. Nearby is Tony George, an enthusiastic Legends racer who also happens to be chairman of the board of the Indianapolis Motor Speedway. He paces, perhaps pensive before the race, where he will line up sixth.

In front of Walkup's car is the machine of Dane Carter, a wisp of a boy and the son of USAC great Pancho Carter. Looking like the schoolboy he is, he gets last-minute instructions from dad as he prepares to strap in.

"I've been trying to get Pancho in one of these, but he says he isn't old enough yet," laughs Walkup. "He says when he hits fifty, he'll be ready."

Soon, the command is given, and drivers enter their cars, ready to take to the floor. They fire their engines in the pit building, go outside and reenter the Dome itself. They sing their high-revving song, and anyone who has ever aggressively ridden a late-model Japanese motorcycle can relate to the feeling the engine gives when it hits its high-end torque curve.

They are quickly lined up, thirty-three cars on the flat, tight indoor course. They receive the command to fire, and soon—zoom, zoom, zoom—they take the green flag, the little cars all tiptoeing into the first turn, their combined sound roaring and reverberating inside the huge building.

Now, remember, these are just silly little cars, right? Not real race cars, not at all. But when you look around at the crowd, at all the moms and dads and kids and drunks and ladies and old farts who bought a ticket, a funny thing has happened: at this moment, they are watching a real race.

Nobody cares about specs, or rules, or how much these cars cost. It has all been reduced to a very simple issue, the exact same question that got it all started a hundred years ago: I wonder which car will win?

George is very strong at the start, and a couple of laps into the fray challenges Legends veteran Larry Fritz for fifth. By lap six, he is second. Two laps later, he rockets past Ken Rice to take the lead. His white car runs about a half-groove off the inside pole, and soon he is shadowed by the car of Steve Mendenhall, a national Legends champion with a load of experience.

He shadows George, watching carefully as they roll through the corners. Finally, in tight traffic, the veteran makes his move and owns the lead, with George close behind. Three laps later, in frantic traffic, George gets into turn one just a bit too hot, and he spins, losing nearly a full lap before getting back under way.

Mendenhall is clearly the class of the field and cruises home without challenge. George gasses it all the way back to sixth at the finish.

Back in the pits, George talks with a couple of guys about the race. He is serious and unsmiling, perhaps thinking once again about Monday morning, when like all the other guys here, he'll go back to work.

He is asked what happened with the spin, and he talks slowly.

"Well, I, uh, I, uh..." his voice trails off, and he looks around, searching for the right words.

Suddenly, a smile plays upon the corners of his mouth. It grows, and soon a wide grin is there. "I guess I just screwed up," he says, letting go with a laugh.

Now, all of a sudden, it is clear why people write a check to buy a Legends car: for a few minutes, there was nothing else in life more important to this guy than this race car, and winning a little old race. All the troubles and struggles that come with life were truly forgotten, just for a little while. And if you asked the other seventy-nine guys here, they would probably tell you the same thing.

Mendenhall talks of his victory and about being a Legends driver.

"I ran a late model for twenty-five years, and I was just about to quit," he explains. "I was burned out, and frustrated that I was working really hard and not going anywhere in my career. A couple of years ago a guy asked me if I would drive his Legends car at Charlotte. I did, and it was so much fun I wanted to do it all the time.

"You know, some of the late model guys I raced against, they laughed at me, and asked me, 'Man, what are you doing in a *Legend*?' But I was having a great time. I mean, all of a sudden, racing was fun again. And I didn't spend every dime I had doing it.

"And you know what it's got me? It's got me a shot at a Busch ride, that's what. I won a couple of national races, and this series gets lots of publicity, and some time back a guy called me about running a Busch car. Would that have happened if I was still running the late model?"

He shakes his head and smiles, answering his own question.

But what of Walkup, who before the race talked of having a good time and there being no need to be serious? After the checkered had waved, his car tangled with another machine, parking them both in the infield.

Walkup's door flew open, and he stormed toward the other car. Onlookers quickly restrained him, as he struggled for a moment to get to the other driver. Finally, he cooled off, and climbed back into his car and headed for the pits.

Later, as he was leaving the pit building to head for home, he flashed a wide, sheepish grin, and said quietly, "Davy, they get me excited when they drive like that."

Just a few everyday guys, having fun on a Saturday night. No reason to get excited. Or is there?

GET 'ER UP AND GOING

MARCH 1996 - NATIONAL SPEED SPORT NEWS

H er heart is broken but her spirit is intact.

Linda Holdeman is busy today; answering phones and taking care of all the details that go into running a race track. In just a few days Winchester Speedway will open the 1996 season, and, like promoters all across the country, she is trying to make sure everything is in place for a smooth start.

But there is more happening here than just another season opener. It is the first real step toward Linda going on with her life after she survived a winter filled with shock, suffering, and grief. This was the winter, you see, that took Roger away.

Six years ago, she and Roger Holdeman were married. They were meant for each other, really, and they acted like teen-aged love birds every day of the year. Laughing, living, and loving, they forged a romance that could seemingly sustain them through anything. He had owned Winchester Speedway since 1970, and she had a long background in track promotion and management. They were more than lovers; they were partners.

But it all went away so quickly.

In January, Roger was diagnosed with cancer of the liver and pancreas. Doctors quietly told him there was nothing they could do. The couple walked from the medical building to their car, and on the ride home Roger very calmly told Linda that she had to be strong; that they needed to prepare for the day she would be alone. As he drove toward their home at Winchester Speedway, amid a gray, melancholy winter day, Linda wept.

Within eight weeks, it was time to let Roger go. He died quietly and peacefully at home, and on a bitterly cold February morning the snow and the wind punished those who came to say goodbye. A promoter, it seems, can't even get a break from the weather for his funeral.

After just a few days to deal with her grief, Linda was forced to get back to business.

"This weather is making me crazy," she says, managing a smile amid her struggles. "We wanted to get a practice session in for the racers, but with the weather..."

Before his death, she and Roger spent as much time as possible planning the opener, even though they both knew it would be a solo act by that time.

"I feel so sad, it seems almost impossible that this place is going to be up and running without him," she says, her eyes filled with sadness. "Sometimes it just overwhelms me. I've got so many friends who call over here to check on me, they must think I'm going to go bonkers or something. But we've got some wonderful people helping us, people who worked with Roger long before I came along, and they know what needs to be done."

When you examine the situation at Winchester, it becomes evident the past twelve months could not have been any tougher at any track in the country. Early last season she and Roger decided to invest a significant amount of money into repaving the historic oval. A paving crew removed the old asphalt, then watched as three days of torrential downpours turned bare dirt into a quagmire.

When the surface finally dried, weather continued to delay them until a total of three dates were lost. They finally completed paving in July, yet the surface was fraught with problems and controversies as USAC sprint cars and midgets visited. As a large crowd looked on, the midget card was canceled and $8 per person was refunded.

"That one hurt," Linda admitted with a wince.

The paving contractor then worked "superhuman" shifts to resurface the track, and as the season wore on it finally came into its own. In fact, competitors today say the track is flawless, perfect.

Linda has always been one of the most successful in the business at signing sponsors. But in 1995 she faced another example that signing sponsors is one thing, and getting them to pay can be quite another.

"We had one firm that went bankrupt, and we had some other problems with another," she explains.

"Other problems" were that a sponsor had signed an Indianapolis agency, which allegedly took receipt of the sponsor's funds, but never delivered the money to Winchester as agreed.

All told, about $25,000 that had been budgeted never showed up on the ledger. Ah, well, Roger said, we've made it through tough times before, we'll just come back next season and make 1996 a kick-ass year.

"We called last year the 'Summer from Hell,'" said Linda. "Little did I know it would turn into the 'Winter from Hell,' too."

And the weather over the past month has been, well, less than cooperative. Fewer than fourteen days prior to the opener the county was hit with a record snowstorm, piling drifts on Winchester's fabled surface more than three feet deep. Snow, rain, and high winds have all greeted Linda, her son Kevin, and the crew each morning.

But you know what? She is still optimistic. Absolutely, positively optimistic.

"Given that the track is in fabulous condition, and that the racing here is always good, I think this could be one of our greatest seasons ever," she says. "We're just a little bit behind physically from where we'd like to be, but we'll be ready Sunday."

Anyone who knows her knows she is capable of going on. But she is human, and like all of us, still struggles to deal with the overwhelming grief the past sixty days have brought.

"(Roger's) fingerprints are all over this place," she says, her voice quivering. "His heart and soul are here. My heart is broken, but I want to be enthusiastic and get the place up and going for Roger.

"During his last few weeks, how many times Roger said that to me, 'Get 'er up and going.' He was so wonderful, so caring, and more than anything else he cared about the history and the heritage of this place. I want to continue that for him, and for everyone around here who loves this place like he did."

Author's note: Linda Holdeman later sold Winchester Speedway, and now works with the NAMARS sanctioning organization.

DADDY JACK'S BIG NIGHT

MAY 1996 - NATIONAL SPEED SPORT NEWS

It was Daddy Jack's big night.

Jack Nowling looked stressed as he worked, jamming the fuel nozzle into the sprint car's tank in the infield of Anderson Speedway. Through the translucent hose you could see methanol flowing downward from the large tank that lay at a sharp angle, six feet above the ground.

He was giving life to this hungry sprint car; life that he hoped would bring him the Little 500 victory he has been seeking for so, so long. Fourteen times he has prepared a car for this grueling race, and although he has been close, he's never grabbed the brass ring.

After a few moments the tank is full, and with a jerk Nowling removes the mechanism. A round aluminum plate within the fuel opening snaps into place, sealing the contents without a drop of spillage.

Nowling hangs the hose on the tank, and looks around for something else to do. The hours spent working under the blazing sun have left him tanned and tough, and the tension of the moment is on his face. Team members continue chores and prepare for the start of the race, a start that will come in about two hours.

His driver paces around as well, watching Nowling fuel the car. David Steele is just twenty-two, a red-hot Florida talent that so far this year has put the Midwest on notice that he indeed is the real deal, winning a USAC sprint race and setting a speed record at Phoenix International Raceway two months ago.

Steele looks like an inquisitive kid, poking around the car after Nowling had finished. He pressed down on the fuel opening, and the moment it opens a small amount of methanol splashes in the air, pouring down the sides of the tank.

Steele grins sheepishly, and Nowling grimaces and grabs a cloth and wipes up the mess. He doesn't speak, almost like the father who bites his tongue as he watches his kid grow up.

In a way, that defines this relationship. Nowling has had some talented drivers aboard his cars, but he's more enthusiastic about this kid than anyone before him.

"David is as good as they get," he insists. "When we hooked up a couple of years ago, he just didn't have any self-confidence. I've worked with him and worked with him, trying to make him understand that he's way better than he once thought he was."

Certainly Steele has been the willing pupil. He is soft-spoken and polite, pleasant and friendly, looking up in awe at Nowling and Nowling's years of experience. It is almost ironic, the strong relationship between personalities that just couldn't be more different: Steele, a shy, quiet kid who looks like a high school student; and Nowling, a rip-roaring big man with a hearty laugh and a quick profane joke, full of life and living.

But it is clear these two have found a powerful bond, and it may well be time for both to shine. They are confident, happy, and fast. They have come North this year not just for the Little 500, but for the entire USAC sprint schedule, a tough proposition with tough customers ready to challenge their dreams.

Earlier this afternoon, Steele crashed heavily in the Hulman Hundred at the Indiana State Fairgrounds. The old mile has bitten some of the best, and the kid rubs his knee as he tells about a hard, wild ride that he won't forget for a while.

"That's the thing that's changed about David," insists Nowling. "A couple of years ago, a crash like that would have just destroyed his confidence. Now, he understands it's part of the deal, and knows you've got to forget it and go on."

Nowling stands there hands on his hips, looking stressed and strained. Of course, the big guy always looks stressed and strained. He's quite friendly, really, but he looks fierce as he flits around at the speed of light, always working, working, working.

He is asked about tonight's race strategy, about how long they can go before they must stop for fuel.

"Yeah, that's what we've gotta do..." says Steele, walking over. "We need to figure out how many laps we can go, and plan when we're gonna take our stops."

"You don't worry about that," Nowling retorts, gruffly but with a smile, putting his big paw on his young gun's shoulder. "You just think about driving and winnin' this bitch."

Steele grins, shaking his head and walking away chuckling.

Nowling beams, watching him.

"It's our year, ain't it?" he says, going back to work.

About an hour before the race, it's time to grid the cars. The crew pushes the car in place, proudly sitting on the pole, a first for both Steele and Nowling. The car is orange and white, with a silver No. 14 on the tank. It is an ironic sight for anyone who has followed the Little 500 over the past twenty years.

Nowling's cars have always been a dark-colored No. 66, and fellow Florida rival Harold Wirtjes has always campaigned an orange No. 14. But Wirtjes, now in the autumn of his life, quit a year or so ago to help care for his ailing wife.

"Harold asked me about a sponsorship, so we started working together," says Nowling. "Then (his wife) died, and he asked if I would paint the car orange and run No. 14."

It is clear Nowling would look more at home in the middle of a barroom brawl than at a church social, but the softness of his words at this moment reveal that inside this big man is a heart about two sizes too big.

In a few moments, they will fire the cars, and 500 grueling, tense, exciting, heartbreaking laps will follow.

"It's our year," he says, shaking hands. "It's our year."

228

The kid is soon buckled down, and the cars form up in the scintillating eleven-rows-of-three pace laps and prepare for perhaps the most electrifying moment in sprint car racing. Steele looks to be ready to deliver tonight, leading early. He is smooth and patient, running a smart, flawless race.

But they stretch their fuel window too long, and on lap 398 Steele sputters to silence while leading. He coasts to his pit for quick fuel work, and Donnie Adams moves past to take the lead. Soon, Adams has his own problems, but now Brian Tyler is in command.

Tyler and his crew have risen to the occasion on this night. They are strong and fast, and have made their second scheduled stop and ride two laps up on Steele. There is a long, long yellow, under which Steele can only idle around the track in frustration, watching his chance to race with Tyler and get his laps back evaporate with every circuit.

They go green with just thirty-two laps to go, and Steele must perform the impossible task of passing Tyler three times. He gets the first one right away, now needing two more passes to win.

Isn't it just too cruel? Nowling stands in his pit, hands on hips, watching as the Little 500 once again slips from his grasp.

But wait! Tyler suddenly pits on lap 475, out of fuel himself. Steele hammers the throttle, passing him once...then again to take the lead...and a couple more times for a cushion as Tyler rejoins the field in second. "Just ride, just ride," Steele's crew barks into his earpiece. He backs off the throttle, making sure this one stays firmly in their back pocket.

They flash under Kenny Wright's crossed checkered flags as photographers blaze away, their lights giving a Hollywood glitz to a gritty, tough night of racing.

"I just feel so good for Jack, and Harold (Wirtjes)," says Steele. "They've been coming up here so long, and they've been so disappointed...I'm so happy they finally won this thing, nobody deserves it more than they do."

"It's our year, didn't I tell ya? Didn't I tell ya?" shouts Nowling, more hyper than ever. "God, we did it. I knew he could, I knew this kid could get 'er done. He's just for real, he's a hell of a racer, he did it just perfect."

Nowling nods toward Tyler's Contos Racing pits, and admits they were tough to beat.

"(Tyler) did a hell of a job," he says, "but we weren't going to let it get away this time. We were just due, that's all there is to it."

Now the crew starts to think about packing gear and heading to the motel, but Nowling will have no part of it. Shouting and happy, he appears to be ready to party all night.

And why shouldn't he? It only took him fifteen tries to get here. He's only got about a dozen years of partying saved up for Anderson. Buckle up, hang on, and prepare to enjoy. It's Daddy Jack's big night.

OVERNIGHT SENSATION

JULY 1996 - NATIONAL SPEED SPORT NEWS

He was born in Florida, grew up in Alabama, teaches people how to drive a sprint car, and he calls himself a hillbilly. And, he lives to race.

Kevin Thomas peeks over the shoulders of mechanics working on the Guy Applebee sprint car, asking questions and offering advice. They tell him to get lost, in so many words. He laughs, and heads to the trailer to fiddle with his helmet.

We are still a few minutes ahead of the feature, and Thomas pauses a moment to think about 1996 and how he has, over the past couple of seasons, become hotter than a three-dollar pistol in the wing-free open wheel racing of the Indiana heartland.

He is thirty-eight now, not yet old but certainly not a kid. His father, Ray, grew up in Kokomo, and successfully raced "sportsman" cars, an early open wheel car that preceded sprint cars in the area. When Kevin was just eight years old, Ray got a job in Mobile, Alabama and moved his family South.

"I always call Alabama home because I grew up there," he admits, waving his hand in his typical energetic mode of conversation. "But I've got a lot of roots here in Indiana, too."

Like most other racer's kids, when he was twenty-one he decided to race. He put together his own car, and every weekend made the 800-mile round-trip tow from Mobile to Riverside Speedway in West Memphis, Arkansas. It was a lonely, tough way to race, but it was all he had.

"I worked for Miller Beer at the time, going around to bars and stores, setting up displays, stuff like that," he recalls. "Every weekend was the same, I'd leave Friday afternoon, drive through the night, sleep in the car till Saturday afternoon, race, drive through the night back home, wake up Sunday afternoon and wash the car.

"One day they said, 'You're gonna need to decide if you want to work for Miller Beer, or spend time with your hobby.' I asked the guy if I could get back with him on Monday, he was shocked I would even need to think about it. But that was the end of the job thing."

The job thing became the racing thing. It was the spring of 1982, and Thomas tried to figure out what to do. He had always wanted to see the Gambler Chassis shop in Hendersonville, Tennessee so he loaded his car with everything he owned and drove there. The guys at Gambler told him of a "big show" at Tri-State Speedway in Haubstadt, Indiana so he rolled on down the highway.

"I got to the track and pitted next to Jesse Plummer, and you know Jesse, he's such a friendly guy he could strike up a conversation with a dead person. I was standing there, and Jesse said, 'Hey, boy, where's your crew?' I said, 'You're looking at him.'

"Jesse and his guys helped me out, and it turns out I made the show. The only tires I had were these old Firestone drag tires, it was kind of pathetic. But we made 'er."

When the race was over, Thomas loaded his car and changed clothes, then slid behind the wheel of the truck.

It suddenly occurred to him he didn't have a home to drive to. So he slept in the truck that night, still parked in the pits.

"The next morning (Tommy) Helfrich (promoter of Tri-State) came down and asked if I had broke down, I said, 'No, I just figured this was the safest place to sleep tonight.'"

Basically, he's made Indiana his home ever since. He has raced with wings and without, on pavement and dirt, and today is a journeyman sprint car driver who is one of those "overnight sensations" that only took sixteen years to get noticed.

231

He won twelve features last year, and has seven so far this season, despite all the rain that has hampered Midwest racing. He fulfilled a life-long dream early in July when he won the Sumar Classic for USAC Silver Crown cars at Terre Haute Action Track.

His drive in the Sumar race...what a classic! He took the Galas car, which had struggled for the past many races, and parked it along the inside rail, his arms slashing and tugging, keeping the machine where he wanted it to be. As others rode the rim and fought the tough race track, there was Thomas, the picture of patience, running faster and faster until everyone else simply couldn't touch him.

Nothing spectacular, just a journeyman doing his job. Winning a Silver Crown race is a big deal; it's a very tough series with plenty of capable cars and drivers on any night. But at this stage of his career, Thomas is realistic about whether a big victory can really make a difference.

"Maybe if I would have won it earlier...I don't know," he says, his eyes revealing that he can't help but wonder what-if. "But, I've had a helluva time, getting to race and make a living at it, it's been great. I can't let myself worry about what could have been, or stuff like that. You know?"

He slept in cars, and garages, and it certainly was a helluva time. A new girlfriend every week, plenty of friends with whom he could share a cold beer, and if he had $10 in his pocket he felt rich. It is very, very clear that there isn't much he would change about his life since making that lonely trip north, fourteen years ago.

But things are very different today. He now has Lisa, a beautiful wife and friend, who loves sprint cars about as much as he does. He's got (shudder) a house to pay for and bills like every other Joe.

He insists he will race two more seasons, no more.

"I'm getting too old for this stuff," he insists. "I've had my neck broke twice, hurt my back, broke both kneecaps, hurt my hand, that stuff still hurts when I wake up every morning.

"You know there will come a time when you've got to be realistic, and my time is coming. But I sure can't complain about anything, like I said before...it's been a helluva run, no matter where or when it ends."

But don't let this guy mislead you into thinking he's ready to give it up right now. Slide him into a decent car on a slick race track, and you're missing the boat if he isn't on your short list of favorites. He teases about his age, but is still sharp and quick, with the cunning that comes only to a veteran.

He has won the Indiana Sprint Week title four of the last five years. He's a threat to win the championship at any track where he runs regularly. When he is introduced today, there are more cheers for Kevin Thomas than ever before.

Just two more years? We'll see. But until that time comes, he will crank it up with the best of them. An overnight sensation, who has paid his dues in spades.

THE 'BURG LIVES ON

SEPTEMBER 1996 - NATIONAL SPEED SPORT NEWS

The bright orange moon slowly rises above the Hoosier tree line, and darkness comes grudgingly on a late-summer evening. Kids munch cotton candy and snow cones, while moms and dads and uncles and aunts sit in the covered grandstand and fill the brief intermission with talk of race cars.

For just the second time this summer, life is seemingly right at Lawrenceburg Speedway. This famed and beloved bullring has come to life just as other tracks are winding down, trying to get in a couple of shows to save a tiny bit of the season.

Not far from this clay oval the Ohio River flows peacefully. But earlier this year the mighty river flooded this valley, covering the speedway with millions of tons of water and silt. When the water receded, promoter Mel Johnson would spend the better part of the summer picking up the pieces and fighting to return the facility to race-ready form.

On this night, he has succeeded. Just two weeks ago winged sprint cars opened the season and tonight the USAC Stoops Freightliner series rolled into town. After qualifying and heats for sprint cars and a couple of support classes, the track was still plenty fast; just the kind of surface this place is famous for.

The crowd seems eager and hungry for action, and the locals talk about how their Saturday nights had been empty earlier this summer without the 'Burg in the picture. But as the feature lineup is pushed onto the track, life is back in order. The scent of burned methanol fills the air, and tiny bits of clay are slung skyward as cars warm their tires and begin to find their proper starting spot.

There is an aura at a moment like this, something that is sometimes obvious even though it cannot be seen. It happens only when a crowd is truly in synch with a field of race cars, when there seems to be a genuine excitement and appreciation for what a field of race drivers are about to do.

It is not present at every race, of course. But it is here tonight as the crowd jumps to its feet and roars and waves, with twenty-two gloved hands poking skyward and waving in return. The flagman grabs the green one, furls it, and shows the polesitter the universal sign that the moment of truth is at hand.

In a moment, Kevin Thomas steps hard onto the throttle, with the field following his lead and kicking up dirt and dust, their roar bouncing off the roof of the grandstand and filling the ears of the paying customers. It is a moment of chaos and danger and excitement and thrills that is the essence of the sport.

There is something to be said for confidence and how much better it makes a race driver; right about now Kevin Thomas is about as confident as he can be. He's in the midst of a great year; he's out front; and the bottom groove is still sweet and inviting.

But Dave Darland is coming, and soon the noise of his engine fills Thomas' right ear. It's a classic Hoosier confrontation: Thomas on the bottom and Darland riding the outside cushion. It is a scene these two have played out time after time, and it is clear on this night that it is going to be a brawling, brutal sprint car fight right down to the final lap, the final turn, the final flag.

Patient and smooth, Thomas holds on for several laps until Darland can simply no longer be denied. He gets past Thomas and holds the lead, before Thomas fights back, now on the outside as they work through traffic.

Finally, Thomas feels his car grow more and more loose, as his right-rear tire has over-inflated itself in the heat of the moment. Darland is soon back in front; but Thomas is still right behind, and as they take the white flag Thomas makes one last inside try as they go into turn one. But his car is simply too loose and he nearly spins. He carefully straightens the car, now glad to hang on to whatever he can get.

Darland roars off the turn with a nice lead, and all eyes are on his white car as he travels down the backstretch, the race seemingly in the bag.

But wait! There is another ending to the story on this night. Mark Cassella had earlier battled both Thomas and Darland as he rode in third, and as he moves down the backstretch the crowd stands in unison as it is suddenly obvious that he is coming, coming, coming, and he just... might...catch...him...

Darland moves to the bottom, perhaps to block Kevin Thomas, who of course is not there. As he does, Cassella stays in the throttle very hard, staying outside for one final try.

It is, say veteran fans, the classic Lawrenceburg move. Last lap, turn three, ride your right rear against the cushion, stay on the gas, let the cushion carry you around the corner, keep your momentum, and...*Zoom*! You come off the corner like a rocket, praying and hoping nothing gets in your way because you are now going so fast that if you crash here you won't stop flipping till Wednesday and...

Cassella's red car rides the rim onto the main straightaway, and as the cars come to the finish line he clearly has more momentum than Darland. As they pass under the checkered, Cassella's front bumper is a couple of feet out front.

Darland apparently has no idea this has happened, and drives in front of the grandstand, where he pops his belts and jumps into the air, his fists raised in jubilation. But the crowd hoots and yells, somewhat politely, perhaps knowing Darland will never be the kind of person who is booed. Cassella soon arrives, the fire still belching from his engine as he shuts it down.

Now the crowd is in full crescendo, rewarding him for a brilliant drive and thanking him for a fantastic ending to an already great race. He jumps from his car and runs to Darland, shaking the stunned driver's hand and giving him a bear hug.

It is the moment for which moment these fans have hungered, and they stand for several minutes, buzzing with excitement and talking about how this one will hang around in the memory banks for a long, long time.

It is just the kind of moment the 'Burg needed. It takes more than a flood to stop sprint car racing. The Ohio River should know better.

K.O.'S FINEST HOUR

SEPTEMBER 1996 - NATIONAL SPEED SPORT NEWS

He has enriched us with his jokes and stunts; written outrageously funny letters to trade papers; jested about his bogus business interests; and has even talked about running for president.

But here at Indiana's Terre Haute Action Track on Wednesday night, Kevin Olson enjoyed his finest hour.

Everyone loves the comedian, and for the past twenty-plus years Olson has been happy to oblige. He is zany, witty, and off-the-wall, with a constant sense of humor about himself and the world that surrounds him.

But within that happy, goofy exterior, is a lionhearted racer who knows what it means to reach far, far within himself to come up with that extra something that separates champions from hopefuls.

Without sounding harsh or cruel, it is unlikely Olson would have made the short list of favorites to win the 44th Hut Hundred for USAC midgets. There were more advanced cars in the pit area; there were other teams with more money; and yes, there were younger, more aggressive race drivers who seem to be the darlings of the moment.

Hours before the race, Olson surveyed the scene and talked of his career, and revealed he has a clear understanding that time has not stood still for him or anyone else.

He came here the first time twenty-three years ago, when he was a fresh-faced twenty-year-old kid. He's been trying to win this race ever since, and as youth gradually gave way to middle age, he's watched other men carry off the hardware, year after year after year.

"I'm getting old, and I'm not brave anymore," he said, the joking somewhere far away at this moment. "I understand that younger guys, they own the sport now. I've enjoyed my career, and I want to keep racing for a long time, but I understand where I am in the cycle; that I'm not going to be the rising star, no matter what."

But as he looked toward this legendary half-mile oval, his voice grew softer, quieter.

"I've just always wanted to win this thing..." he says, the tiny changes in his facial expression revealing far more about his frustrations than his words. "We've been on the pole three times, we've been awfully close, but never got it done. And now I know that at my age it is probably not going to happen."

With that, he headed into the trailer to suit up, as his crew prepared the car for qualifying.

He timed in twentieth, in the middle of the field. He had to make his way into the feature through a qualifying race, where he finished third. He would start thirteenth, nearly invisible behind stars such as Tony Stewart, Kenny Irwin, Jr., Jason Leffler, Tracy Hines, Robbie Flock, and Billy Boat.

The Action Track, in all its legend and glory, is often two very different race tracks. There is the relatively slow, methodical "huggy-pole" around the inside guardrail; and a wild-and-wooly, fast and exciting ride up on the cushion. That's the groove that put "Action" into the Action Track.

Tonight, everyone apparently wanted a piece of that action. Car after car headed to the top, roaring through the turns, slinging clay, drivers putting their foot in it until their engines would beg for a breather. Everybody, that is, except Olson, who seemed to putt-putt so slowly through the corners right down along the inside guardrail that he should have been using emergency flashers.

But a funny thing was happening; as fast as everyone looked on the top, they just couldn't shake Olson.

He stayed in the top five through the early stages, but by the midway point appeared to be losing ground. A few others had run the bottom early in the race; but by this point virtually every car was running outside. As car after car passed him, Olson began to have doubts.

"I kept saving my tires, hanging in there," he later admitted, "but when they were passing me I really thought we missed. I thought we were going to lose one more chance to win this thing."

"Good things," goes the old saying, "come to those who wait." Olson waited and waited, until the good things began coming. Tony Stewart and Kenny Irwin, who clearly had the field covered, crashed their team cars out of the race in the same incident. Then Randy Koch, who drove a splendid race to take the lead with eleven laps to go, apparently ran out of fuel on a restart with just five laps remaining.

In a jumbled, chaotic moment that would thrill the crowd and test the nerves of the men in the middle of the fray, came the sight of Olson's No. 66 on the inside, forging to the front of the pack to lead lap 96. Four more times he would come off that fourth turn, with Jason Leffler running way outside in never-never land, trying desperately to get past Olson.

He took the white flag, and suddenly it began to dawn on this huge crowd that...Hey! Ol' "Beetle-bomb" is gonna win this thing!

He brought his ride home safe and sound under the checkered; a champion who proved he's still got a few good runs left. He cut the engine and climbed out amid sheer jubilation and a very raucous outpouring of genuine affection from the grandstands.

"You just don't know what this means to me," he said moments later, his eyes again saying more than his words ever could. "I'm old, I've got a lot of patience, that's what I have to rely on. We just did it the best way we knew how, and it worked.

"I know I'm never going to be a big-time racer like some of these guys are going to be. But this race, it's really, really important to me, and winning it is a great thing in my life."

For a moment, Olson the comedian was nowhere to be found. Instead, here was a serious man who was proud, and truly touched by what he had just done. The lion's heart had just grown another size or two.

In a moment though he was back to his old tricks, laughing with his crew and his fans, lipping off about some loony joke or funny line and making everyone around him giggle.

Enjoy the laughter, because when you laugh, something inside of Kevin Olson shines more brightly. Just don't be confused about this racer, who tonight showed us what can happen when a professional gets every ounce from himself and his equipment, and when the last flag waves is standing exhausted and elated over his rivals.

He's wrong about one thing, of course, when he says he will never be a "big-time" racer. We all know he's already there, and he will stay there, at least for the time being. And that's no joke.

HOLD ON, HERE COMES HEWITT

OCTOBER 1996 - NATIONAL SPEED SPORT NEWS

Indy car racing, are you ready for Jack Hewitt?
He might be coming, you know. A few days ago he plopped his forty-five-year-old bottom into the seat of an Indy car for the first time. It was an opportunity for Hewitt and several other drivers to get through their Indy Racing League driver's test, running a 1993-vintage machine at Phoenix International Raceway.

This opportunity, by nearly anyone's estimation, comes about fifteen years later than it should have. Politics and the landscape of Indy car racing made people like Hewitt invisible the past decade or so. As a result he just kept crawling in and out of sprint cars; sometimes four and five nights a week, paying the bills and building an open-wheel career that nearly any driver would envy.

Of course, merely passing his rookie test at Phoenix is just one tiny step. He still must find a team to give him an opportunity to drive competitively. But he believes it can happen; you would have a hard time finding anyone strong-willed enough to convince him otherwise.

So if you're an Indy racing fan who happens to have lived on Mars for the past decade or so and have never heard of Jack Hewitt, you might want to sit down, brace yourself, and get ready for a genuine character to show up at Orlando in January with his helmet bag and a ton of enthusiasm.

A recap of Hewitt facts: He began racing in the early 1970s, the son of Don Hewitt, Ohio sprint car star; almost three hundred USAC Silver Crown and sprint starts since 1976; Silver Crown champ in 1986 and 1987; won twenty Silver Crown events, (nearly one victory for every five starts) since 1981; thirty-nine sprint car first-place trophies, fifth all-time; 1985 All Star Circuit of Champions sprint champ; fifty-six All Star feature triumphs (second all-time).

But what's important is not just *what* Hewitt has done all these years, but *how* he has done it.

If there were ever a group called the Tough Racer's Club, Jack Hewitt would be the poster child. He defies definition; he can be physically tough one moment, scuffling with an on-track rival; then soft as a kitten with a little kid the next. He is outspoken, bull-headed, politically incorrect, and full of laughter. Despite enormous charisma and people skills, and a real gift with words, he sometimes believes that a punch in the eye is the most effective way to get his point across.

Kind of a blend between John Force and John Wayne.

There is probably not an open wheel driver today with more fans than Hewitt. Sprints, midgets, whatever, his introduction nearly always brings the loudest, most boisterous applause. Whatever legions he has attracted he has earned; this man is far too proud and stubborn to do anything just to get people to like him.

He is a bit like a very spirited horse: you might keep him on your farm, and get along with him, but you'll never really break him. He simply has too much heart to be owned by anyone.

That's why the thought of Hewitt in Indy car racing is very, very interesting. It's a fair statement to say that the culture of Indy car racing over the past twenty years has evolved into that of an upper-crust, well-heeled group that places a premium on pizzazz and polish and a full set of teeth. Nice and neat, with nobody rocking the boat.

For example, when was the last time an Indy driver punched out one of his rivals?

Not that punching someone is a good thing; it is not acceptable behavior anywhere today. But there isn't any question that much of the human, rough edge was honed off of Indy racing years ago. Maybe that's why the popularity of Winston Cup racing has soared, while Indy racing has experienced decidedly slower growth over the same period.

So here comes Hewitt, a likely outlaw among the so-called good guys. His arrival just might be a gust of fresh air at just the right time, when Indy racing appears to be headed in a new direction.

Whenever Hewitt faces the media, he says exactly what's on his mind. That blunt honesty is going to ruffle some feathers; some will say he's too callous or rough while others will cheer that somebody is finally telling it like it is.

If you think Indy car racing will smooth and mold Hewitt into its own image, think again. For twenty years, he's been a USAC star; but nobody has fussed and feuded with the organization more than Hewitt. He'll loudly criticize and raise hell over a ruling or a judgment call; and for its part USAC has stiffed him on at least one occasion like he was a stray dog.

Each really needs the other; but they get along only grudgingly, kind of like in-laws who have learned to get along only because they need to.

But no matter what one thinks of his personality, there can be no question about Hewitt's ability to drive a race car. His resume is filled with great rides from the back, in a less-than-perfect race car, never giving up.

Consider last week's test: On that Phoenix afternoon, he literally sat in an Indy car for the first time. When his turn came, he climbed into the car and took three or four slow laps along the bottom, warming the car and getting settled in the cockpit.

The driver's test consists of four phases: Officials like to see a driver begin at the 25-second range, then shave a half-second with each segment, finally turning laps in the 23-second bracket.

With some prior coaching from John Paul, Jr., Hewitt was finally given the green flag to begin the first phase. Within four laps, he was already running in the 23-second bracket. This on a hot, sunny afternoon with the boost turned way down to simulate next year's horsepower.

"Now I know how people like Lyn St. James have been able to do this for years," said Hewitt later, with a wry grin.

So, Jack Hewitt hopes his future includes seat time in an Indy car. You should hope so, too. Because whether he can make a successful run at it or not, his mere presence will make the scene more interesting.

I can hardly wait.

Author's note: Jack Hewitt qualified for the 1998 Indianapolis 500, where he finished twelfth.

BREAKING THROUGH

OCTOBER 1996 - NATIONAL SPEED SPORT NEWS

As rain drizzled on Winchester Speedway from gloomy skies, Brian Tyler stood under a canvas roof in his pit and stared at the banks of the legendary half-mile oval.

Today, he was celebrating his twenty-ninth birthday, and what a present he had chosen for himself. The USAC Stoops Freightliner championship, free and clear with no strings, all his to carry home and stick in the achievement box.

He thought about the past season and smiled. It has been eight months of racing, from Phoenix to Pennsylvania, thrashing and working, all for the honor of putting his name on the list with men such as Parnelli Jones, Roger McCluskey, Gary Bettenhausen, Larry Dickson, Pancho Carter, on and on through forty years of glory.

This is what he's been aiming at, steadily and gradually. He grew up in southern Michigan, a race track brat who watched his older brother, Bill, drive sprint cars throughout the area. At age eight he started riding competitively in motocross racing, until he was thirteen. When he was still a teenager he climbed into a sprint car, and the seat has not yet let him go.

He is a quiet man, too quiet for his own good when you consider the yackety-yak everyone expects from today's race drivers. But as quiet as he appears on the outside, there is always a fire burning deep within.

He came to this series a few years ago with a reputation and an image for which he could personally take the credit (or blame). On a dare from friends, he marched into a barber's chair and demanded a Mohawk. Then, also sporting a very fashionable earring, he showed up to run the daunting hills of Winchester Speedway.

Surely Barney Oldfield rolled over in his grave.

"I guess it took a while for people to forget stuff like that," he laughs.

In 1993 he tangled with Steve Butler at Eldora's 4-Crown Nationals, and punched the four-time champion following the race, earning a very hefty fine and more reputation.

"It was the wrong thing to do," he now says.

But amidst all the shenanigans, there was something that shined through almost unnoticed. Somewhere along the line, we all discovered that this guy could drive a race car. And then some.

Although he had some good runs prior to joining the Contos Racing team in 1995, it is clear the association has been the most significant development to date in his career.

It's funny, isn't it, that one of the quietest guys in the Midwest goes to work for one of the quietest teams?

Contos Racing is a ten-year-old dream of just about the most unassuming CEO you'll ever meet. Larry Contos oversees his family's Anderson, Indiana-based business of eight large grocery stores and several restaurants, along with several significant tracts of commercial property.

It isn't a secret Contos has the money that goes along with being a successful businessman, but if you've heard stories of wealth and power you've never heard them from him. He always changes the subject glad to talk about race cars and such, but always looking quite uncomfortable when he is the subject.

Contos loves racing, and really loves sprint cars. So he bought a race car a few years back, and came into the sport with the perspective of having fun instead of a must-win mindset. And it's worked, because he's smiled a lot as the years have gone by, sometimes winning and sometimes not.

He hired local driver Jason McCord three or four years ago and they have developed a friendship that goes well beyond just driver and car owner. When Contos decided to run two cars in 1995 with USAC, he needed a driver who was absolutely versatile, who could run dirt and pavement. McCord made a recommendation.

There's a guy from Michigan, he said, who can run them both.

Yes, he can.

Tyler responded by winning Contos' first USAC feature right out of the gate in their first season on the paved Louisville oval.

Managing race drivers, it could probably be argued, is something like trying to keep order in a kindergarten class. Pride, jealousy, resentment, rivalry, all can become factors when competitive men roll out to do battle on Sunday, especially among warriors who wear exactly the same paint. This, says Contos, has never been a problem with Tyler and McCord.

"These two have never had one problem like that," he insists. "They've always raced each other hard, yet they've helped each other at every turn. There's no secrecy; they just truly help each other. I've never had to deal with any of that. I mean, these guys room together, they've *got* to get along."

That's because Tyler immediately left his Michigan home to move to Anderson when Contos hired him. The first person Tyler called was his girlfriend.

"I told her, `you'd better call your parents and see if your room is still open, because you're gonna have to move back home,'" he says, laughing. She must have laughed as well, because she is still a part of his life.

This year, like any other, has been one of peaks and valleys. Tyler was the model of consistency, missing only two main events all year. McCord was in the thick of the points battle as well, until he shattered a shoulder blade in a wicked crash at Bloomington in July.

Ironically, as McCord's world darkened, the opposite was true for Tyler. His chief rival at that time was Doug Kalitta, who missed some key events, giving Tyler the momentum he never lost.

McCord recovered and resumed racing in August, and played a key role by giving up his seat at Hales Corners when Tyler crashed during a heat race.

"I'm really, really happy for (Tyler)," insists McCord. "He's a great guy to race with, clean and fast, and I'm as happy for him as I would be for myself."

Now, the problem for Tyler is he can no longer be the quiet unknown at the track. The USAC title brings prestige and honor and makes a statement that among many good racers, this is the team that stood up when all the numbers were counted. These are the winners.

"I guess I haven't really grasped what it means," he says of the title. "It is a hard series, a lot harder than people would really understand. You're racing against the very best on pavement one night, then the next night you go to a dirt race and go against the USAC guys plus the local dudes, who are all fast. Every week, you just keep plugging away."

And they did, of course. This is the day to savor, to enjoy, to grin and tip back a beer and laugh, knowing nothing can take an ounce of it away.

It's odd, really, that the guy once viewed as the off-the-wall renegade has turned into perhaps the most intense player in the lineup. Days before the race, the game face goes on. No laughter, no jokes; the hours filled with concentration and commitment to doing what it takes to win. Closer, closer, closer, he's inched toward his objectives. This title is merely another step.

He stands outdoors in the gloom, and the sun begins peeking through. Of course it does. Every champion deserves some sunshine. And for Brian Tyler, it's liable to be bright for a long time.

THE CHRISTMAS VISIT

DECEMBER 1996 - NATIONAL SPEED SPORT NEWS

The old man stared impatiently at the traffic light, his hands gripping tightly on the car's steering wheel. He didn't want to be here; really, as he looked around at the gray, wintry scene that surrounded him, he didn't want to be anywhere.

Fred was depressed. Christmas was here once again, like all those years before, and the colorful decorations sparkled outside homes he drove by. "Christmas is for kids," he continually barked, not allowing any cheer to pierce his unhappiness.

Long ago, he had been the hero: winning races and enjoying a fast-paced life that took him all over the country. But age took the dashing good looks, and time stole whatever fame he had earned, leaving him a forgotten old man. In turn came bitterness; anger that the world that once embraced him with adulation had turned its back on him. So he tried to forget the old racing days, and didn't stay in contact with many of his old pals any longer.

But his wife kept reminding him about Charlie, and their annual reunion. Each year at Christmas, Fred and Charlie always visited, a custom that went back almost fifty years. The past couple of visits had taken place a few hours north, in the nursing home where Charlie was living out the rest of his days.

Today, he didn't want to see Charlie. Not really. He hated driving that far; he hated nursing homes, and the fear they brought him; and he hated the fact that each visit might be his last.

And he hated Christmas, and the helpless feeling of having nothing left to give his old friend.

He turned his car into the parking lot of the facility, pulling up to a handicapped spot toward the front. Clutching his cane, he struggled up and out of the car, steadying himself as he walked inside. He could hear the annoying sounds of Christmas bells, softly ringing from the church across the street.

Near the entrance, he saw himself in the reflection of the glass doorway. He stopped and stared, marveling at how he had changed. The gray hair; the deep, wrinkled face; the belly; the slight shuffle in his walk. God, he thought, how could it have gone away so quickly?

His heart filled with dread as he walked the hallway, stopping at the nursing station to ask directions to Charlie's room. He told himself he would stay just a few minutes; let's get this over with and get out of here.

"Charlie hasn't had a visitor yet this Christmas," a young nurse mentioned as she gave him directions. As he began to walk away, she quietly told him Charlie was very near the end.

He entered the room and was startled at Charlie's appearance. It was bad enough that a heart attack almost killed him a couple of years ago, but then came the stroke that left him nearly paralyzed, a prisoner in his own body. But his eyes sparkled as he saw Fred, and Fred scooted a chair alongside his bed and sat down.

"It's good to see you, old friend," he began, holding Charlie's hand, knowing the man could hear but not answer. He began making small talk, about the weather, about politics, about a lot of things that really didn't mean very much at all.

After a few minutes, he began to feel like he was talking to himself, looking as Charlie stared out the window at nothing at all. He shifted uncomfortably, finally saying he really needed to get on his way, to get home before dark.

He was surprised at the strong grip from Charlie's hand; and the old man's pale blue eyes darted to his, as if looking directly at his soul. The man's mouth moved slightly, and no words came; but his eyes begged Fred to stay, just a little bit longer.

"All right, let's talk for a while," Fred said, releasing Charlie's hand and settling back into his chair.

He began talking about their early days together, and something began to come over him, something warm and pleasant. He suddenly could recall days long ago forgotten; happy days filled with excitement and enthusiasm.

He talked of when he and Charlie were boys, playing in the lush green fields not far from here, trying to laugh away the hard times of the Depression. And of the day they wore their new army uniforms, so crisp and proud, their dark hair combed neat and sharp.

It had been more than fifty years; but the words began flowing easily from Fred. It was almost as if he had pushed them far back into a corner of his mind, not allowing them to be seen or heard by anyone, even himself, now to be suddenly and inexplicably released in a torrent of memories and experiences. He was amazed at how much he could recall, and how vividly.

He talked of how they both discovered their love for cars and racing, when they were fresh out of the army. Late Saturday nights and bright Sunday afternoons that were filled with sunshine and fun, two young men who were living life to the maximum.

He laughed out loud at some of the stories, while Charlie lay nearby, listening to every word. He couldn't speak; he couldn't respond; but as the stories flowed, his eyes twinkled and a tiny smile played upon his lips, and he would occasionally nod his head and laugh.

Fred's stories of their old racing days were bright and colorful, filled with rich detail and passion. Fred had forgotten all thoughts of today; instead, he had found that rare bridge to yesterday, and his words had allowed both men to take the trip together.

Fred's eyes focused on his left hand, resting on the arm of the chair. No longer was it pale and spotted with age; instead, he saw only a lean, tanned arm resting on the outside brake, brightened by the sunshine of a thousand yesterdays.

He turned to Charlie, lying in bed. Gone was the man he had visited, replaced by the Charlie he had known so long ago. He saw the old Cromwell, perched on the man's head, the paint peeling slightly around the many rock chips that dotted the front of the cap. Charlie's broad smile was as bright as the sun, a picture of happiness and contentment.

It was now quiet, and Fred leaned his head back into the chair, the room's warmth making him drowsy. He closed his eyes, feeling warm and happy in his memories, and in a moment had drifted off to sleep.

He awoke with a slight start, the nurse's hand gently shaking him from his slumber. The window was dark, the winter sun gone until morning. Very quietly, she knelt next to the chair, and moved close to Fred.

She softly told him Charlie was gone; he must have passed on in his sleep. Fred nodded to say he understood, and rose from his chair, his trembling hands clutching his hat as he stood unsteadily at Charlie's bedside.

He looked down on his friend, who lay still and silent, finally a contented, peaceful look of happiness on his face. His struggles in this world were over; instead, he would make his long-awaited trip to a better place.

Fred could hear bells from the nearby church, reminding all that the joy of Christmas is upon us. He thought of his holiday anguish, and his fear he had nothing left to give his old friend.

He now realized he did indeed bring precious gifts. The words he spoke taking them both to a beloved time of long ago, had led his friend home, one last time. A gift only he could deliver; a gift worth more than silver or gold.

He looked out the window at the nearby Christmas lights, and finally saw the beauty of Christmas, beauty that had been there all along. Softly and quietly, he found the words he had ignored for so long; words that now could be spoken with the emotion and feeling they deserved.

"Merry Christmas, old friend..."

LOUIS SAYS NEVER GIVE UP

JANUARY 1997 - NATIONAL SPEED SPORT NEWS

Several miles west of the sprawling, flat floor of the RCA Dome in downtown Indianapolis, there is a carved bust of Louis Chevrolet. Standing near the entrance of the Indianapolis Motor Speedway Museum, it bears three words any racer would be wise to remember: "Never give up."

On Saturday night, a couple of good old racers did not give up.

Racing on the artificially sticky floor of the stadium here is an exercise in patience. A tight, tight little track offers plenty of opportunity for banging, while the surface changes its character more often than a politician. Early in the day it is greasy and slick; as it takes rubber late in the night it becomes so tacky that midgets bicycle as they navigate the corners.

One hundred laps can be torture; if another guy's wheel doesn't get you, the fumes might.

There were stars here this night; guys who sell tickets and are destined for sensational careers. But there were also a couple of quiet men who rose to the top, men who seem invisible in today's blaring world.

Russ Gamester and Ted Hines are second-generation racers who would probably bleed motor oil through an open wound. At thirty-plus years old, they aren't kids any more; but it's hard to think of them as veterans, because (trust me) neither of these men has peaked yet in their careers.

Gamester won a USAC midget championship a few years ago, but seems to have faded from the limelight a bit since then. He still works at trying to progress, but it's been some time since he's won any big races. But he hasn't given up.

Hines has become a journeyman midget racer; put him on any track that takes patience and finesse, and he's a good bet to be in the money. He's been out-horsepowered for several years now; but he hasn't given up, either.

Few remember Louis Chevrolet, and probably even fewer care. But *there* was a guy who knew how to forge on. He was a hard-nosed character who lived an exciting life in an exciting—and brutal—era of racing, a man who was as brilliant as he was difficult to get along with.

He made several fortunes during his lifetime; unfortunately, for every big gain there was a bigger loss right over the horizon. But did old Louis give up? Never.

Even the cars carrying his name aren't really "Chevrolets." General Motors founder W.C. "Willie" Durant discovered Louis when Louis was a thirty-two-year-old driver and mechanic for the Buick team in 1910, and Durant had the idea that a new automobile for the exploding passenger car industry needed to be both innovative and carry a well-known racing name.

Louis offered both. They struck a deal and Louis immediately began designing and building a car. But perhaps he was an early outlaw; his visions of what would be a great car were very, very different than Durant's ideas which were rooted in good old business logic.

Durant wanted a car that could be sold cheaply, like Henry Ford's Model T. But Louis, like a true racer, wanted horsepower. To hell with the cost.

In late 1912, Louis presented Durant with the Chevrolet Six Type C Classic, to be sold for $2,150 (it would be 1955 before the list price of a Chevy passenger car exceeded that amount). At a length of 120 inches, it was the longest Chevrolet ever built. It had a massive 299 cubic-inch six-cylinder engine that was praised by the motoring press as being very well put together. Thinking he was a millionaire, Louis and his wife went to France for an extended vacation of almost one year.

When they returned, Durant had changed everything. He discontinued the Type C, replacing it with a smaller car. None of this sat well with Louis, and in 1914 when Durant told Louis he should stop smoking cigarettes like a common man and use cigars instead, Louis told Durant exactly what he could do with his cigars.

Louis held a sizable portion of Chevrolet stock at that time, and sold it all back to Durant for $1,500.

Louis would design racing cars and components for the next decade, often with great success, but every time he would be positioned to make any money, something would happen, often something completely out of his control, that would make the gain vanish right before his eyes.

As a race driver, he earned a reputation as a fearless daredevil who won his share of races but crashed on a frequent basis. Through his sixteen-year driving career, he spent nearly three years in hospitals recovering from racing injuries. A total of four mechanics who rode with him were killed.

Of course, he never gave up.

He survived the loss of a brother (Gaston), a feud with another brother (Arthur), bankruptcy, the rise and fall of his aftermarket racing parts business (Fronty-Ford), another financial bust in the passenger car business (Frontenac), and the collapse of his new company during the 1929 stock market crash (the Chevrolet Aircraft Corporation).

In the most cruel irony, he eventually got a job as a common mechanic at the Chevrolet plant in Indianapolis, making an hourly wage as he worked on the fine automobiles which carried his name.

Eventually time caught up with Louis. He had a stroke in 1934 that greatly sapped his health, but he recovered somewhat. He lost a leg in 1941 to health complications, and died June 7 that year in Detroit, fighting until the very end.

Of course, Louis' life was over long before kids like Gamester and Hines were brought into this world. Still, it is good to know that the world still sometimes rewards a person who won't quit.

When they rolled out to take their spot on the grid Saturday night, it didn't look good for either Gamester or Hines. Up front were the heavy hitters; Stevie Reeves and Tony Stewart hogged the front row, with guys like Johnny Parsons, Lou Cicconi, Jr., Jay Drake, Mark Dismore, Tony Elliott, Andy Michner, Davey Hamilton, and Doug Kalitta all licking their chops throughout the field.

Hines sat in tenth spot, while Gamester was all the way back in the tenth row of the twenty-four-car field, on a track where passing can be very difficult.

At the start, Hines rocketed to third, while Gamester began picking off cars one at a time. Reeves led, but was clearly struggling with his car before Stewart took over and looked to be the man to beat.

But Stewart got caught up in traffic and spun, and at the thirty-lap mark Hines was the leader. Gamester was fourth.

Hines led for a while, with Ronnie Johncox forging past with about forty laps to go. Gamester got around Hines as well.

Johncox had everybody covered, as his VW was strong and hooked perfectly to the sticky pavement. But Gamester and Hines battled lap after lap fighting for second.

But with just fourteen laps to go, Johncox sputtered to a stop, out of fuel. Suddenly, the two quiet racers were up front, and appropriately enough they immediately began rubbing wheels and fighting till the finish.

They raced it all the way, exactly as it is supposed to be done. Good friends, they didn't give one another an inch, but they kept it clean. In the end it was Gamester standing atop his roll cage saluting the crowd, as Hines pounded his steering wheel in frustration with a lapped car that spoiled the final few laps by getting in the middle of the fray.

A couple of fighters, taking it all the way to the end, never giving up.

Somewhere, Louis would be proud.

THE VIDEO MAN

JANUARY 1997 - NATIONAL SPEED SPORT NEWS

Greg Stephens stands on scaffolding, high above the floor of the Tulsa Expo Center in Oklahoma. His brow furrows as he listens intently to voices coming from the black headset he wears, as his hands fiddle with the expensive tripod-mounted camera before him.

It is still several hours before race time here at the Chili Bowl Midget Nationals, but Stephens and other members of the production crew have been hard at work much of the day. It is a typical day for Stephens; lots of work behind the scenes, with the result being high-profile video images with no real signature of the author.

There have been many people praised recently for getting the World of Outlaws "on TV." But truth be known, Stephens has been the single most important person in bringing sprint car racing into the mainstream television medium, long before anyone proposed the live coverage the series now enjoys.

Yet, as important as he has been, he has been virtually invisible to the masses who enjoy his work. That veil of anonymity was lifted a bit recently, however, when Stephens was recognized by the National Sprint Car Poll as the Media Member of the Year, a long-overdue selection.

He is a boisterous, outgoing person, who thrives on attention and loves to be right in the middle of things. He is a die-hard open-wheel fan; and aside from the competitors themselves, there has been no person closer to the Outlaws scene for the past ten years.

It wasn't all that long ago that Stephens was just another working man, with a full-time job and a life not unlike that of millions of other Americans. He worked in the St. Louis office of the Peabody Coal Company, just across the big muddy from his Illinois home. He was also a race fan, and in 1980 he bought a J.C. Penney portable VCR camera and began filming some area races just for fun.

In 1983 he lost his job, the victim of internal politics at Peabody.

"I was devastated," he says of the loss, "but it was the best thing that could have ever happened to me."

Less than a year later, he went to DuQuoin, Illinois to tape a USAC midget show. He met Greg Oldham and Danny Laycock, who at the time worked for the production company for ESPN's "SpeedWeek" program. Oldham encouraged him to pursue the filming more aggressively, and suggested Stephens consider upgrading his equipment and submit footage on a free-lance basis to the growing segment of racing-related programs on cable television.

"A guy named Randy Gosnell had a Silver Crown car and also owned a (video) production company in Indy," recalls Stephens. "Late in 1985 we got together, and we planned on starting off by producing a show on the 1986 Hoosier Dome midget race in Indianapolis. I had quit my other job by this time; I was committed to finding a spot for myself making a living filming racing stuff."

The production of the Dome race turned out to be far less successful than Stephens expected, so he and Gosnell parted ways almost as quickly as they had gotten together. Stephens bought some gear from Gosnell ("I got a tripod, a portable deck, and an editing recorder, all three-quarter inch stuff, for $2,000, and it was worth about $9,000"), formed a company called Motorsport Video, and headed for Florida for Speedweeks.

He shot the East Bay Nationals, and worked at Daytona as well.

"There I was, working victory lane at Daytona on a full credential, it was amazing," he laughs. "I was up on the roof of the Speedway and I ran into Oldham. He asked me, 'Did you ever think you'd go from shooting with a home VCR camera to the roof of the Daytona Motor Speedway in just a year-and-a-half?' It just happened really quickly."

Stephens traveled throughout the country that first year, covering special events like the Little 500 sprint car race and sending footage to programs such as "SpeedWeek," "MotorWeek Illustrated," and "This Week in Motorsports."

By the middle of the summer in 1986, Stephens made an important decision that influenced the direction of his life. He decided to follow the World of Outlaws circuit as a priority.

"I love open-wheel racing," he explains of his decision. "They were the major series, and to me that was the most exciting thing out there. But I also had to make a living, and there seemed to be a lot of interest in the Outlaws, but they didn't get much exposure on television. So it was an opportunity."

It was a difficult life, but one Stephens relished. He converted a Ford van to a tiny production studio and would roll from venue to venue right along with officials and racers, becoming one of their own.

The kid had joined the circus.

Stephens would roll into the parking lot, unload his camera and walk through the pits, getting interviews and headshots for the night's race. He would set up high above the action before hot laps, filming virtually every racing lap that night. When the race was over, he would hurry to his van, producing a highlight video from all the footage.

Next he would seek the nearest airport, where he would express tapes to studios where his clients produced their respective shows. Later that night, guys like Steve Kinser and Sammy Swindell came right into your living room, thanks to Greg Stephens.

The old gray van now boasts more than 500,000 miles on the odometer, and it, like Stephens, shows no sign of letting up.

"I like goin'," he says simply.

There is never a day he wishes he were back at Peabody, or any other conventional job.

"I've never made a ton of money at it, but I'm happy at what I do," he insists. "The Outlaws guys have accepted me as one of their own, and I think some of them appreciate what I do, some I don't know if they do or not. But you have to do something like this because you love it, not because you'll make a lot of money."

As television offers more and more live coverage, Stephens hopes to move on to do some live directing. In the meantime, he has never been happier following the series, especially since meeting Kim, a special girl who seems to like racing almost as much as he does.

"It's been fun getting Kim involved in all this, I was really happy to find such a good person who loves racing.

"I've got friends all over the country, and that's been the real treasure of the last ten years. It almost hurts their feelings when I don't stay with them when I get to their area of the country; that's how good some of my friends treat me.

"That's been the thing that really makes me feel good about what I do, that I've had the chance to see the country and meet so many great people.

"I think about all the good times I've had with the racers, playing golf with guys like (Steve) Kinser and (Ron) Shuman. Wow, we've really had some good times."

But it has taken ten years to receive some national recognition for his work.

"The Sprint Car Media Award, I've been kind of disappointed I wasn't at least on the final ballot sometime before now, but getting the award makes me feel better.

"Sometimes I've been aggravated that I've worked pretty hard and nobody really seems to realize that it's been my film they've seen on TV. But the racers, and writers, guys who really understand how the deal works, they realize I've been there. And it's made me feel good that people within the sport had some appreciation for my work."

Those of us who have known Stephens since he started know how much he has impacted the sport of sprint car racing over the past ten years. Now, with the Media award, the rest of the country perhaps will realize it as well. It's a shame it took ten years for it to come, but it's never too late to say thanks.

Especially for the guy who got the Outlaws on TV. Night after night after night.

THE DEAN

FEBRUARY 1997 - NATIONAL SPEED SPORT NEWS

The rental car bumps gently across the Phoenix parking lot, my eyes uncertain as they scan the building, looking for a familiar sign.

Clint Brawner once worked here, or at least that's what the memory banks keep insisting. It is a quiet Sunday afternoon in this sprawling western town, the sun shining from the winter skies and warming all it touches.

More than a decade ago, on a February day much like this one, Brawner entertained a visitor from the Midwest. I was just a race fan on that day, looking to meet one of the most colorful and well-respected chief mechanics of a bygone era.

In his time, Brawner was known as "The Dean of Indy 500 mechanics." He first ruled the world with Jimmy Bryan, the larger-than-life, broadsliding boy who also came from this desert valley. He later brought A.J. Foyt to Indianapolis for the first time, and still later introduced a shy, small Italian kid named Mario Andretti to championship racing.

It was one helluva run for The Dean.

The telephone call that day, twelve years ago, is a clear as if it were last week. Pick up a local phone book, look up "Brawner, Clint" and —zing!—dial a legend.

"Sure," he said then, "I've always got time to see a visitor."

I arrived and parked near the back that day, and entered the garage through an open back door. The scene inside was truly remarkable: parts and memorabilia piled literally ten feet high, with something that resembled a pathway winding through the mess. I gave a shout to announce my arrival, and in a moment heard a muffled reply from somewhere near the front of the building.

I wound my way through the maze, rounded a corner, and there he was: straw hat; deep, leathery lines drawn on his face; bandana tied around his neck; white T-shirt; a left arm that jutted crookedly as he walked.

He was friendly, and we talked all day. He was sixty-nine years old at the time, retired from Indy car racing. He spent his days here, relaxing among his junk, thinking back on hundred-hour work weeks and monumental stress. He sat in his swivel chair and talked of Bryan, and Mario, and A.J., his words providing a living lesson in history. The student was awestruck, to say the least.

It was an inspirational conversation, for it revealed that history was not merely old statistics and facts; rather, it is the life experiences of real, live people. And there was the real, live Clint Brawner, living legend, spending time with a stranger, willing to share the stories of his life.

257

His career was filled with excitement, and grief, and anger, and joy, and success. Each emotion seemed to be carried to an extreme level at various times, both good and bad. There was the unabashed joy of seeing Andretti drive the Brawner-built Hawk to a surprising win at Indianapolis in 1969; there was the indescribable sadness of watching his best friend Bryan die at Langhorne in 1961.

We talked that day until the sun grew heavy, slowly sliding to the west. He grinned and waved as we left the lot.

In a couple of years he was dead, tired of fighting the cancer that had chased him for quite some time. Six weeks before he died, he buried his wife, and I sometimes wonder if he had lost his reason for living, and just gave up. But no matter; death is a personal thing, not meant for others to question.

Now, a decade later, there is no Brawner to sit down and talk with. He lies a few miles from here, resting in a quiet plot not far from his pal Bryan, under the tall palm trees that line these streets. It is sad to know he is gone; but it makes that day so long ago all the more satisfying, knowing that the memory of a delightful day with The Dean will be forever.

The breeze is gentle on this day, and pleasant. It feels good, standing here looking at the old shop, staring and trying to clearly remember the layout of that day. Physically, there are many changes, the most noticeable a tall, white stucco wall that rises and blocks the view of visitors. The sprawling parking lot of the bank that sits on the corner spreads right to the very edge of the property, as if today's prosperity is trying to push yesterday aside.

Not far away, cars rumble through the intersection of Seventh Street and Glendale Avenue. The traffic light blinks, a horn is heard, and in moments a gaggle of cars roll past, drivers accelerating to go somewhere for some reason or another.

They don't seem to notice the little garage, nestled between the bank and the photo shop. Their eyes look neither right or left, instead peering straight ahead. It is as if the world is oblivious to the fact that a little, tiny bit of racing history happened here, when Brawner prepared the famous Dean Van Lines cars that mesmerized a generation of race fans.

A laugh makes its way to the surface as one recalls Brawner's grumpy distaste for Indy car racing, circa 1985. "A folly," he fiercely labeled it; not at all as worthy as the wars that he fought. One wonders what he would say about the current state of affairs in the sport. Would he be grumpier still? Or would he believe that the sport is finally headed in the direction he longed for? If only he were here to see it all.

Of course, if he were here, we would be sitting inside that old shop, listening to a vast wealth of racing experiences and stories. Instead, I can only stand here on the outside, looking at the changing landscape of our world and reminding myself that while a man's history might be eternal, his life is not.

Even for the great ones. Like the Dean.

THE OHIO TRAVELER

MAY 1997 - NATIONAL SPEED SPORT NEWS

The car is only four years old; it has seen less than a half-dozen races. But there is something about that orange "zero," painted with black outlines on the cream-colored background, that looks nostalgic.

Rick Ferkel stands over the machine, wrench in hand. He is preparing for hot laps for the Masters Classic here at Iowa's Knoxville Raceway, a special race featuring drivers who have reached age fifty and beyond.

It is an odd scene; here in the late 1990s with a Hall of Fame driver standing under the fading Iowa sun. It is as if our eyes and our mind are tricking us, lulling us into a make-believe world that never changes.

The world waits for no man, of course. Ferkel is fifty-eight years old now, still stout and vigorous but with hints of age playing on his face. He is asked if this scene, this moment, makes him wish for other days.

"I'll tell you what this does," he says, his speech coming in the familiar rapid-fire bursts, "if you do well, you start thinking that maybe you should be doing it all the time.

"And I'm not so sure I shouldn't."

His eyes look directly into your soul, and you know you are getting the straight stuff.

He's always given us that straight stuff, really. Maybe that's why this man, called the Ohio Traveler, built a following of fans that stretched from ocean to ocean, border to border. No matter how hard the tough old world of sprint cars could be, it could never beat the gentleness, or the smile, from Rick Ferkel.

"But you know, for me to keep racing today...when I raced, I was never very good at promoting money. I was really weak in that area. So it would be the same problem today, trying to find a motor deal, or money, or whatever. It would be the same old problem."

Up until just a couple of weeks ago, he was wrenching for a team, but that gig is over, at least as of this moment.

"I'm not independently wealthy, so I've got to start beating the bushes hard. Maybe I'll mechanic...I don't really know what I'll do. But something will come together, I'm sure about that."

He is asked if it feels weird to be fifty-eight. He grins broadly, with a twinkle in his heart that is revealed in his eyes.

"It sure does. You ask yourself, 'hey, how did I get this age? Where did the time go?' It's kind of amazing, really."

Years ago, when he was young, he chose the path that took him racing, and today, like most racers, doesn't have a lot of money to show for it. He is asked if he regrets not spending those years building a business, or working nine-to-five toward a pension.

"No," he says, answering very, very quickly. "And I don't think any real racer would regret that decision...because racers don't think in terms of stability. You think you'll race forever."

Soon, it's time to race once again. He climbs into the car and buckles up. His hands work quickly, as though he could do this exercise in his sleep. Like a businessman tying a tie, he gets his belts tight and his helmet on without even thinking about it.

The sun is dropping just below the Knoxville fence, the first hints of a brilliant sunset on the horizon. High overhead, in the deep blue sky, a commercial jet leaves its contrail as it seems to chase the sun westward. It's hard to imagine that a hundred or so people would want to be somewhere other than here at this moment.

He fires the car and takes his spot, and soon is working the low groove alongside Clay Bontreger. After a few laps, he takes the car to the top, bouncing off the black cushion and powering from the corner.

Ahhh, yes.

He rides home third in his heat, and the blue sky eventually gives way to blackness and sparkling stars. Before we know it, it is feature time, and he lines up on the pole. He has won this race twice before, and it's not hard to see the fire burning inside him as he leads the field to the flag.

Ferkel leads a couple of laps before Billy Englehart, last year's champ, gets by. He then contends with Mike Brooks, and soon is riding third. He is clearly not as fast as Englehart or Brooks, but he's holding his own. Late in the race Jerry Crabb moves up to do battle, and he leaves Ferkel nothing but fourth at the flag.

A few minutes later, he's shed his driving uniform and works in familiar jeans. The engine, provided by Tom Klein, is lifted from Ferkel's car and prepared for the return trip.

"Well, it's not fun running fourth," Ferkel laughs, and then the smile runs from his face and he looks serious.

"I'm either gonna have to quit completely, or I'm gonna have to race more," he says, his eyes looking far away as he speaks. "If I mechanic, I can't race. If I race, it's tough to do it without sponsors.

"Maybe I'm being facetious, I don't know..."

Nearby, generators from his and other trailers hum away. A crowd stands around, and several approach Ferkel for autographs. He smiles and shakes hands and signs his name, and is soon back with tools in hand, putting the bodywork on the car.

Kenny Weld is gone; Opperman is far away in so many ways; Scruffy, Amati, Bubby, Gaines, they've all gone home. But Rick Ferkel's shoes are in the dust, toiling away long past midnight, one more night.

Maybe he will race forever. Really. Maybe he will.

JOHNNY COMES MARCHING HOME

JULY 1997 - NATIONAL SPEED SPORT NEWS

It is a hot day, with the merciless sun beating down on the black pavement of Indiana's Winchester Speedway.

It is hours before race time, and a gaggle of people wander about looking at a collection of restored race cars sitting poised for an exhibition run on this storied half-mile.

Johnny Rutherford walks about, shaking hands, smiling and remembering. Was it very long ago, someone asks, that he raced here?

Yes, he says, it was a long time ago. 1963 or 1964, he thinks, pausing to try and place the year, wondering aloud if he has it correct.

He brings his hand to his chin for a moment, and the sun sparkles on the championship ring on his finger. Between then and now he earned nearly a handful of the rings at a big oval on 16th Street in Indianapolis, a place that somehow just doesn't seem very far from here at all.

Everybody in the world, it seems, knows Lone Star JR. Three-time winner at Indianapolis, star of television commercials, and perhaps the best ambassador for auto racing in the history of the sport.

But on this day, he isn't interested in being the star. He's back among the short-track people who raised him.

He came to serve as grand marshal for the twenty-fifth-annual gathering of the Winchester Old Timer's Association. That was the official reason. But he also wanted to come back and visit one of the places that occupy a distant corner of his life, some thirty-five years ago.

The old cars are firing up, and he steps off pit lane and out of the way. His eyes, still sharp and quick at fifty-nine years old, gaze at a vintage 1963 sprint car as it pulls away and heads for the track.

He was just a boy, back then; a happy kid who figured racing would sure be a fine way to live. These cars, and places like this, made him a man.

The story of his early racing days may as well be a love story; because that's really all there was to it, love. He had raced a few stock cars at Devil's Bowl Speedway near his Fort Worth home and eventually he and his Texas buddy Jim McElreath packed their belongings into a camper truck and headed for the Midwest.

"Boy, that is a great memory," he says, thinking of that trip. "Jimmy and I, we didn't have anything but desire, and that's about all we brought with us. But what a wonderful, wonderful time we had.

"We had this old pickup truck with a camper that stretched over the top of the cab, and sometimes Jimmy would get up there to sleep and I'd drive, we'd have all those miles to go between the races.

"I'd get that thing rolling, and we'd top a hill and there would be some farmer on a tractor, fifteen miles an hour. I'd jump on the brakes and I could hear McElreath up above, *wump-wump-wump, WHAM*! He'd roll all the way to the front of the camper...then I would hear the cussing start."

He laughs, a laugh filled with joy and satisfaction. It is obvious, all these years later, that it was a trip that changed his life.

"I went to a race in Lacrosse, Wisconsin. I had not yet ever driven a sprint car. I signed in at the pit gate, and asked if any cars had signed in without drivers. The guy looked down the list and said, 'yeah, the No. 42 car,' and he gave me a couple of others.

"I went and looked at the cars, picked the one that looked the best, and found the old guy rubbing on it and asked him if he had a driver. He kind of hem-hawed around for a minute, and I asked if I could drive it.

"He asked me if I had ever driven one of these, and I said, 'sure I have.' He asked me where. 'Down in Texas,' I told him. He gave me a try and I guess I did okay, because nobody seemed to know the difference."

Imagine that: a three-time Indy winner who got it all started with a little white lie.

"McElreath and I, man, we just had no money at all. I remember when we went racing at St. Paul, Minnesota we didn't have money for a hotel or anything like that. So we would park down by the lake, get our swimming trunks on, and get into the lake to take a bath.

"I remember once we were wading out into the lake, and McElreath saw this little piece of two-by-four floating by, and he grabbed it. I said, 'McElreath, what in the world are you gonna do with that old piece of wood?' He just said, 'Well, I'll show you.'

"We waded out till it was about chest high, and he takes that two-by-four and he floats it right next to him, and real careful like, he takes his bar of soap and puts it on the wood, so he has a nice little soap rack, floating right beside him! Man, stuff like that was just crazy, all the time."

He and McElreath began with the traveling IMCA circuit, where Rutherford eventually landed with the cranky, cantankerous Dizz Wilson from Mitchell, Indiana.

"Old Hezzie, now he was something," says Rutherford. "He was tough and gruff and hard to get along with, but I can honestly say that my learning curve was never steeper than when I was with 'ol Dizz.

"He had a couple of cars, and the driver was responsible to take care of his own car. I had one of the cars, and I towed it with a Ford Ranchero. After every race I'd go over the whole car, and Dizz would check the compression to see if the engine needed work. If it did, I was responsible for pulling the engine and getting it ready.

"I'd ask Dizz which tires we were gonna use at the next race, and he'd show me, and I'd use this old manual tire machine to break down the tires and mount 'em up. It was tons of work, but looking back, it was a great experience for a young man."

He takes his hand, and pokes a finger on his chest near his heart.

"I think about firing up that old sprint car on the country road by Dizz's house, and it gives me a pang of fear right here. Man, it's a miracle I didn't kill myself. One-hundred-twenty mph, out on that old road, with my seat belt on and nothing but goggles on my head. Now, that gives me fear, thinking about it today."

Rutherford and McElreath, still great friends, eventually moved on to USAC where Rutherford became the 1965 sprint car champion.

He thinks of those days, and speaks with a fondness that reveals the great depth of emotion he holds for that period in his life.

"It was just so simple, so wonderful," he says. "Back then they would check the top four of five cars after the feature, and they'd usually do it right behind the grandstand.

"So we drivers would sit back there while they checked the cars, and people would hang around after the races and share their chicken and their beer with us. I know everybody uses this word a lot, but it really was like a family."

Perhaps that's what defines the early era of Johnny Rutherford: a world of extreme danger and hardship, but a world of extreme joy and happiness.

It isn't difficult to imagine he and a few of his cronies piled into an old station wagon roaring across the endless two-lane highways to Winchester Speedway. Through little towns like Pendleton, Emporia, and Mechanicsburg. Past the Blue Moon cafe in Losantville, and Sparky's Dog House Bar in Mount Summit. Past towns where life has not changed all that much since he last rode through, thirty-some years ago.

Today, under the hot sun and among the people he never really left, Johnny Rutherford takes in the memories. They are sweet, like a bright red Indiana watermelon on a warm summer evening.

An old sprint car flashes by, throttle open and singing a song. He grins, and his eyes follow the car as it roars past. The years have come and gone, but JR remembers the music.

Racers always do. They always do.

THE RIVALS

AUGUST 1997 - NATIONAL SPEED SPORT NEWS

They are friends who really don't like one another very much.

It is 1997; twenty years ago two young men found themselves fighting over the same piece of real estate, and they haven't really settled it yet. Since that time, they have put their names at the top of the World of Outlaws lists year after year, after year, after year.

Pick up this week's standings for the World of Outlaws, and there the two names are, sounding familiar and right, in the One and Two positions: Steve Kinser; Sammy Swindell.

There is something historical about that, seeing those two names. It is not a surprise that they have been enormously successful. Of course anyone remotely knowledgeable who has seen them in action quickly puts them in an exclusive league. Rather, it is the incredible longevity of these two that should be toasted by anyone who loves excellence.

They are as different as two men can be; yet so much alike that you think they studied the same manual.

In terms of victories, they have been downright hoggish. Both were so good in the early 1980s that only Doug Wolfgang saved them from themselves, as they threatened to take the excitement out of sprint car racing with their utter dominance.

"It's just no fun," Ron Shuman once told OPEN WHEEL MAGAZINE, "getting your ass kicked every night by Steve and Sammy."

No fun, indeed.

This year, the World of Outlaws season is shaping up to be a truly monumental fight to the finish. As of this week, Kinser holds a four-point lead over Swindell, with Dave Blaney third, Jac Haudenschild fourth, and Andy Hillenburg fifth.

In all fairness, defending champion Mark Kinser should be at the top. He missed several Outlaws events earlier this year when he ran selected NASCAR truck events, suffering a significant point penalty each time (the series long ago abandoned its "outlaw" principles). Karl Kinser's car has once again been the team everyone chases, and the car has earned 7,550 points, with cousin Kelly Kinser subbing for Mark when needed.

But there is something amazing, almost historic, about Steve and Sammy fighting for the driver's title.

(That's what they are known as, of course. Mention to any sprint car fan the name "Steve," and they won't ask you for a last name. The same with "Sammy.")

Both are just past forty, and they can't hold off the onslaught of drivers like Blaney, Haudenschild, and Hillenburg forever. In fact, it has been quite some time since they were both at the top of the point list. So we should covet this moment, because it could be one of those magical moments in history that is still too common to be appreciated, but perhaps never repeated.

They have, over the past twenty years, had a relationship that can politely be described as "stormy." They have banged wheels, butted heads, and exchanged punches. Their intensity has boiled over into strong dislike at times, but they always seem to settle back to an uneasy tolerance of one another.

If there was ever a venue that encouraged friction between men, it is surely this World of Outlaws series. Racing on tight race tracks, in what often look to be terribly out-of-control machines, the potential for contact is enormous. Throw in the fact that teams are out here on the road for weeks at a time, and you've made certain that people are going to get downright sick of one another before very long at all.

But if Steve Kinser and Sammy Swindell worked together down at the shoe factory, they wouldn't be close friends. They are far different personalities, with vastly different views on life in general.

That said, they are mirror images of one another in their competitiveness, their intensity, and their remarkable ability to drive a race car. Throw in the fact that each wears a game face that scares off even the most veteran interviewer, and you think you're dealing with twins.

Kinser is likely the greatest single driving talent in the history of sprint car racing. For seventeen or so years, he enjoyed the benefit of Karl Kinser's unmatched mechanical genius, leading to the age-old question: was it Steve...or was it Karl?

The answer: It was both. They had what could be called "synergy." Each was individually great; put them together and their combined greatness was more than the total of the two.

But anyone who has witnessed Steve Kinser in traffic knows that the man has a gift beyond words. Darting, flitting, doing whatever it takes, he has an uncanny ability to find the tiniest hole and get through clean. It is even more remarkable when you consider the frantic pace in which he must work: twenty-plus sprint cars, all bouncing seemingly at random, at full speed, and here comes Kinser, smoothly going through the field, making it look easy.

Sammy is the technician: He thinks about the car, tweaking, tweaking, tweaking, using the mechanical understanding with which he was gifted. Yet, despite an enormous knowledge of the sport, he is so quiet many men have found him nearly impossible to work with, because they don't know what to make of such long periods of silence.

"Working with Sammy is a trip," ace mechanic Deuce Turrill once said. "You might get up in the truck with him after a race, and him literally go four hundred miles without saying one word. A lot of guys just can't deal with that."

Once Swindell is strapped in, he is on a mission. Early in his career, he picked up the nickname "Slammin' Sammy" after track announcer Terry Baltes observed him bouncing hard into the Eldora cushion. But Swindell's hard-nosed, aggressive driving made him few friends on the race track.

He has mellowed somewhat in recent years and his changing driving style has earned him even greater success—and respect—behind the wheel. He has developed a much more broad range of talents, with the natural ability to be either subtle or rowdy, and the wisdom to know when to use both.

Today, the two men shrug off most talk of their rivalry. They are very polite when asked about the other, and even in the most unguarded, off-the-record conversations, each refuses to speak harshly of the other.

On the other hand, you'll likely have a hard time getting them to say anything positive about each other. It is almost as if they don't want to melt the icy exterior, the barrier, because they know they must stay "up" for each other every night.

It is not unusual to find them parked side by side in the pit area, yet saying nothing to one another the entire night. Each still, after all these years, "feeds" off of the other. On a crowded race track, when their ears pick up the scream of someone alongside, and their peripheral vision reveals it to be their arch-rival, they race just a tiny bit harder into the next corner.

At that, they have been a splendid help to one another, whether they realize it or not. Racing is far more emotional than physical; they have provided each other with a special motivation that has elevated each of their games.

There have been classic confrontations: In the early 1980s at Kokomo, when Sammy beat Kinser on the last lap; Kinser returning the favor with a mind-boggling last-corner pass at the treacherous Indiana State Fairgrounds in 1991.

Although they are unfailingly polite in post-race interviews, it isn't difficult to imagine some intense swearing within the private confines of their helmets when they cut one another off, or bang wheels, or snooker each other with lapped traffic.

"All race drivers are alike in one way," the savvy Karl Kinser once observed, "age gets them all eventually."

And so it will be with Steve and Sammy. They are just past forty; both are secure financially and could likely quit today and live comfortably. But they aren't even close to that point, because they still seem to have plenty of energy and desire to stay "out here" on the road, chasing each other and all the kids who come along.

Of course, we know how this will end: It is 2045, in the sunroom of a cheerful Florida nursing home.

Two ninety-year-old men face one another, their wheelchairs rolled up to a small table on which a worn, weathered checkerboard rests.

The ticking of a nearby clock is the only sound. The men stare at the board, neither speaking, neither moving. Finally, Steve Kinser reaches forward, his frail hand grasping one of the few pieces left on the board.

Trembling, he takes a long time to carefully move the piece forward. In a moment, more silence. Finally, Sammy Swindell leans forward in his chair, and his left hand reaches the red piece nearest Kinser's final black token. Slowly, carefully, Sammy jumps the last piece and the game is over.

Neither man speaks, both glaring at one another.

Kinser clears his aging throat. "Set 'em up again," he says. "We ain't done yet..."

LEAVE ROOM FOR AGNES

AUGUST 1997 - NATIONAL SPEED SPORT NEWS

Agnes Johnston sits on the front step of her camper trailer, feeling just a little bit lost in her own back yard.

It is a lonely corner of the Marion County Fairgrounds in Knoxville, Iowa, about a quarter-mile from the track that has become a likely example of what the future holds for sprint car racing: bigger, richer, and more refined.

For thirty-seven years, Agnes parked her camper right on the midway behind the main grandstand, right in the middle of the excitement and euphoria that is the Knoxville Nationals. But during these past few months, the onslaught of growth that has transformed this event has dramatically changed the layout of the midway, and perhaps the very nature of the Nationals.

Gone are the campers, around which people crowded both before and after the races, gabbing and sampling a cool drink and a sandwich. Replacing them are bright canvas corporate hospitality tents and commercial booths.

Since 1959, Agnes and others offered fans and racers a place to gather, sharing friendship and memories. Every person who visited her camper was offered a meal; you were a stranger there but once.

Now, a couple of hours before race time, just a few people are seated at her campsite, far off the main path. She feels somewhat lost, being so far removed from the hub of activity. She worries that many of her old friends won't be able to find her now.

At seventy-seven years old, her soft white hair and cheerful face exude warmth. If you ever need to define "sweetness" to someone, just show them a picture of Agnes.

She began coming here in 1959, she and her husband Eugene. They parked their camper here for the entire summer, making the drive down from Des Moines each weekend. When Eugene died in 1977, Agnes kept coming here, on her own.

She talks of progress, and softly insists she supports the changes that have come with the dramatic growth of the Nationals.

"I want it to grow," she says, her voice breaking slightly in the soft Iowa breeze. "But I just hope they don't grow me out of here."

A few hundred yards away, Ralph Capitani sits on a golf cart and tries to keep some semblance of order in the midst of the mid-afternoon chaos that precedes tonight's racing. As the longtime race director at Knoxville, Capitani has been instrumental in the growth that has propelled this sleepy Midwestern town to becoming the epicenter of big-time sprint car racing.

"Twenty-five years ago I could stand near the exit of the grandstands after the race, and I knew most of the people," he says. "Now, I stand there and I don't know one person out of fifty. It has just grown so much, become so big, so many new people."

Capitani has seen a profound change in these Nationals. He is very much aware that this is not so much just a race; it is an event.

For as long as anyone can remember, much of the aura of the Nationals has been the atmosphere of fraternity it has offered. Not diluted by any other influences, it has always been THE sprint car gathering, catering to hard-core lovers of the sport who would wade through hell or high water to get here each August.

271

Those who watch support most races; the Knoxville Nationals is for those who care.

After the races many fans stayed on the premises to party, and the track earned a reputation as a place for hell raising. Wet T-shirt contests and crap games were commonplace, and booze and liquor flowed freely.

Capitani, and others involved with the fairgrounds operation, have worked hard to clean up that image.

"Oh, sure, we've really tried to cut that kind of thing out," says Capitani. "This is a family sport. We want families here, and you can't have that sort of thing.

"We know just about everybody here is going to have a couple of beers before the weekend is over. But I don't think you'll see people walking around who have had way too much to drink.

"We want lots of kids coming here," he says, turning and peering over the top of his glasses, "because without them the future of this sport is bleak."

The commercial presence at this facility has been anything but bleak. Amoco pours many thousands of dollars into the event as the primary sponsor; T-shirt sales (and residual income) are huge. Nearly every imaginable product or service related to racing is offered in a trade show.

Capitani gazes at the area where campers once were, now looking at the corporate hospitality tents that replaced them. Nearby, huge concrete pillars rise from the ground, supporting a vast expansion of the grandstand that boosts the overall seating capacity here to nearly 30,000.

"I know a couple of people who are probably upset that they were moved," he says of the campers. "We tried hard to accommodate everyone, and that's pretty difficult to do. Most everybody has been pretty understanding."

He thinks of Agnes and her friendly old camper.

"I thought about putting up a map, to make sure people could find her," he says. "It looks like everyone figured out pretty quick where she is now."

He turns toward the black oval that has made this county famous, and talks of the future.

"We've just scratched the surface," he says, eyeing the towering grandstand and the busy crowd, oblivious to his golf cart in the midst of it all.

He talks of exciting days, the good times in store for sprint car racing. He is one of many key people in this sport that share that vision that we've only just begun.

He is very much aware of the allure of the Nationals, and of sprint car racing, and speaks quietly of not wanting to toss out the baby with the bath water. If it becomes clean and smooth and polished and sanitary, will it still look like sprint car racing?

Capitani thinks so, and he is clearly optimistic. He is correct that this sport, like any living entity, must grow or die. Like a big purple monster that must be fed each morning, that growth must be fueled by money. And big money, for sure, will require that the image and essence will continue to be refined.

More corporate tents will come, just as surely as the sun blazes on this hot afternoon. Those tents bring money, to feed the growing monster.

But there ought to be room for Agnes and others like her, for they laid the bricks on which these splendid towers of concrete and steel are built.

Sweet little ladies are as big a part of the American story as sprint cars and apple pie. Let's not leave them out of the coming chapters.

THE MOVIE PARTY

NOVEMBER 1997 - NATIONAL SPEED SPORT NEWS

After the sandwiches and tall tales, it was the movie that grabbed their attention. Eight hundred people, schmoozing and munching sandwiches, telling lies and stories, and enjoying themselves immensely.

It was called the "Roar from the Sixties," a one-night affair in the impressive Petersen Automotive Museum, where people gathered to remember their connection with a decade that ended nearly thirty years ago.

It is kind of amazing, really, that this many people would gather to celebrate something that took place so long ago. But their affection and memories are strong, and they came with open hearts and belly laughs, to embrace friends from another time.

They mingled and gabbed throughout the large room in which the evening's ceremony would take place, raising the noise level to a lively hum. At the appointed time a large screen in front of the room flickered to life, revealing filmmaker and author Dick Wallen's latest volume, also called "Roar from the Sixties," released in tandem with a brilliant 600-page book of the same name.

The screen looked to be fifteen feet tall, but it was not nearly large enough. For you see, the characters in this drama were indeed larger than life.

Not far from the screen, some of those characters grew quiet and focused on the screen. Parnelli Jones, Al Unser, Rodger Ward, Johnny Rutherford, Len Sutton; all looked at themselves in more youthful days.

Soon, nearly everyone in the room was seated and quiet, absorbed in the film, the narrators' voice echoing through the room. They visited places like Phoenix, DuQuoin, Springfield, the Indiana State Fairgrounds, New Bremen, and Langhorne.

During the times while cars were shown on the track, it was hard not to grit your teeth as you watched men race wheel-to-wheel with nothing more than a tiny roll hoop over their head. Flimsy uniforms, open-face helmets, and hospital rooms that couldn't help much anyway, they were all a part of the package.

For those of us who were too young to catch the live version, it is difficult to understand this crazy, tumultuous, dangerous era. But as you watch the faces on the screen, you begin to understand why eight hundred people traveled from all over the country to be here tonight.

It was a time of love, and devotion, when men raced purely for the indescribable joy of competing. The money was far from grand; the conditions were appalling; but their intense desire led them to pursue their dream regardless.

Their fans knew this, or so it seems, and they have responded with the finest, most pure affection possible: devotion. They have never forgotten their heroes.

They saw smiling faces on the screen, men who grinned broadly at the camera during candid scenes in the pits. Bobby Marshman, Eddie Sachs, Don Branson, Jud Larson, Jimmy Clark...you winced, because you know how the story ends for them. Of course they didn't know; but they smiled all the way.

You begin to understand the profound heartache that their rivals still carry today.

Later, when the evening is over and the audience is filing out and heading home, Rutherford, Jones, and Ward are still standing on stage, signing autographs and shaking hands. They still stand and sign; it is almost as if they still have dust on their shoes and sweat on their brow.

Jones is asked what it felt like, seeing himself and his former rivals on film.

"It made me realize how dumb we were," he says with a laugh. But in a moment his voice is quiet, his eyes are clear and sad.

"I think going through that time, we were young and kind of wild at first," he says, almost softly. "Then when you realize that you survived, even though so many of your friends did not, it makes you appreciate life all that much more."

Rutherford walks up to join the conversation, and agrees.

"You have to understand just how painful that time was, because it seemed like we lost somebody every week," he says. "You never forget those guys. I mean, you're grateful that you can be here yourself, but at the same time you miss all those who didn't make it."

But those who survived are certainly beloved and still adored. It is so curious, while contemporary championship racing today struggles for identity and a place in the world of sports, these men enjoy powerful devotion from a fan base that has never forgotten them.

Soon the building is empty, and it is time to go home. A soft, light rain has fallen, shining the streets of Los Angeles and letting the tires sing as they carry you away. It is hard to forget the men of the Sixties.

THE CHRISTMAS ANGEL

DECEMBER 1997 - NATIONAL SPEED SPORT NEWS

Maybe it was the glow of the Christmas lights that lifted his mood. Tony was smiling as he walked toward the old building, with cold air hanging his breath in white vapors as he walked.

The door creaked loudly as he entered, and he saw the taw, lean figure of his father facing the workbench. As the door closed, the older man turned to see who had entered his quiet workplace.

"Hey, Pop," Tony called out, as the older man smiled. He walked toward the stained workbench, pulling up a tall stool as he shivered off the cold. A nearby radio offered a hint of an old pop music Christmas carol, barely audible over the hum of an ancient heater hanging overhead.

"What'cha workin' on?" Tony asked needlessly, his eyes falling on bicycle parts strewn across the worn surface.

"Wendy's bike," the gray-haired man said, peering at his son over a pair of reading glasses perched squarely on the end of his nose. His eyes, gleaming amid a region of softly wrinkled skin, were warm but piercing. "Seems like her husband didn't have the time."

Tony squirmed on the stool, shifting his feet from the floor to the foot rail, then back again.

"Okay, I hear 'ya, I should fix my wife's bike," he said, smiling sheepishly. "Don't bust my chops too much, I've been busy at work."

The guilt played on his mind, and he stared at the shiny parts for a moment before continuing.

"Have you heard from the motor guy?" he asked, walking over to the stripped shell of a race car that sat in the middle of the aging concrete floor. "We don't want to get too far behind in getting this thing back together, you know. Spring will be here before we know it."

His father's expression never changed as he spoke softly and slowly, as if equally dividing his attention between his work and the conversation. "Oh, I reckon I know when spring comes. I've got the car done in time every year before, and I'll get it done this year too," his voice trailing off.

"He said he'd have the motor ready a couple days after Christmas," his father continued after a moment. "I figured I'd run up there and pick it up a couple of days after Christmas. Thought maybe you'd run up there with me."

"Nahh, too busy," Tony said, leaning down to pick at some paint flaking from a frame rail. "Just don't wait too long...I don't want to get behind."

Tony walked around the car and remembered the past season, already thinking about next year.

He thought of the winter almost two decades ago, when as a seventeen-year-old boy he had talked his dad into helping him put together a race car. It began a special relationship between them, one that saw his father spend countless hours trying to keep the best car possible under his boy.

They had seen wrecked parts, trophies, helpers, and a few small sponsors come and go, and they had seen all of it together. Tony's mind began to reel with the memories, and it dawned on him that none of it would have been possible without his father.

He recalled the night when he had crashed heavily, knocking himself senseless and nearly destroying the car. He remembered sitting in the seat, trying to clear his head, and hearing the din of approaching voices. Amid the chaos, came the strong, calm voice of his father, asking Tony if he was hurt.

And the night, so long ago, when there was an on-track incident that spilled into the pit area. Tony was a young, raw kid at the time, and as he climbed from his car a confrontation with another driver and the driver's crew ensued. Outnumbered and frightened, Tony marveled at the strength of his father, calmly refusing to be bullied or show his fear. He commanded the irate crew back to their car, refusing to be cowed, hardly raising his voice in the process.

He realized his father was a man's man, strong and tough and fair and kind and decent. All things Tony wanted to be. He now realized who had taught him the right way.

It suddenly occurred to Tony that everything he had become, both as a racer and as a man, was a direct result of the love and example set by the graying, familiar figure at the workbench.

He stared at his father and at his strong hands working on the bicycle, lost in his own world. He thought of the Christmas of long ago, when he sat on his father's lap and sang songs and talked of Santa Claus. He thought of the strength his father had always given, in good times and bad, and he thought of the love that apparently knew no bounds.

His eyes misted, and he wondered what had happened to make the time pass so quickly, to this day when he himself struggled to find the strength to be a father, a leader, a man. For the first time in his life, he understood there was a debt owed, one that was long past overdue.

"Pop," he said softly, his voice so quiet it was hardly more than a whisper. "Pop...thank you."

His father continued working, oblivious to the emotion his son had suddenly discovered.

"Thanks for what?" he said casually, not looking up from the workbench.

"Just thank you for...for all the things you've done for me," said Tony, struggling to keep his voice from breaking.

His father put down his work and turned with a curious look. For a moment their eyes met, and each saw something of themselves in the other man's face.

The father stared at the son, and he saw a man he could be proud of. The little boy who had once held his hand, now standing before him with a maturity that had never before been fully revealed.

"Well...okay, I guess," said the older man, searching awkwardly for the right words. "Sure...you're welcome."

There was a pause, and each knew there was more to say. But neither knew where to begin, so they said nothing, allowing the look in each other's eyes to say the rest.

After a moment his father turned back to his work, nervously whistling the tune, "Jingle Bell Rock."

"Pop, I need to run," Tony said quickly, grabbing his jacket and heading toward the door.

The old door creaked loudly as it was opened, but before he could step outside, his father called out.

"Hey, Tony," he said, turning away from the bench. "Merry Christmas."

"Merry Christmas, Pop," said Tony, smiling and stepping out into the cold. He pulled the door closed behind him, and started down the sidewalk he had walked a thousand times as a child.

He stopped at the old frame window of the shop and stared at the man inside quietly at his work. His ears tingled in the cold, and he blinked and brushed his eyes to clear his vision.

He remembered a story the old man told him years ago, about a Christmas angel who stays with you forever, protecting you and bringing you good fortune. He had always wondered if he would see such an angel; but as he stared at the strong figure through the window, he finally understood: he had been there all the time.

FEATURE
STORIES

DICK GAINES REMEMBERS

AUGUST 1988 - NATIONAL SPEED SPORT NEWS

Like the many years before and since, the 1974 Knoxville Nationals represented the very best sprint car racing had to offer. But that year will always be remembered as one of the most exciting in the history of the prestigious event, as those on hand witnessed one of the toughest showdowns ever held. For Dick Gaines, the 1974 Knoxville Nationals represented his finest hour.

Gaines and car owner Karl Kinser brought with them plenty of momentum into the little Iowa town that memorable August. The pair had been winning features throughout the Midwest, in what Gaines remembers was a very innovative chassis handcrafted by Kinser. While Gaines called Mitchell, Indiana home, Karl kept his shop in nearby Oolitic.

The two men were at the opposite end of their respective careers at that moment, although neither could possibly have known it at the time. Gaines, who began driving stock cars at age eighteen in 1949, had switched to sprint cars "sometime in the mid-1950s," and by the early 1970s had become something of a legend among his Midwestern contemporaries.

He teamed up with Dizz Wilson in the early 1960s, and the pair became so successful, everyone simply lost count of the number of victories they amassed. Like all great teams, they had their ups and downs, and when they went their separate ways in 1971 Gaines found himself bouncing from ride to ride.

Karl Kinser bought his first sprint car from Wilson shortly before that, and he put fellow Hoosier Larry Miller in the car. The ancient sprinter left much to be desired, and soon Karl was planning to build a new car for Miller. With the 1971 season finale coming up at Tri-State Speedway in Haubstadt, Miller had already made plans to run somewhere else. Gaines got a phone call.

"Karl knew I was looking for a ride, and he asked me if I would run the car for one show at Haubstadt," Gaines remembers. "I jumped at the chance, because, even though he didn't have much experience, Karl was a sharp cookie. I wanted to see how I could go in his big old car."

The "big old car" was known as Bertha. It was a lumbering machine, powered by a 454-cubic-inch mill, and it was sometimes fast. Plywood wings would be allowed at Haubstadt, and Gaines set fast time and won his heat race. But on the first lap of the main, he tangled with another car and got upside down, ripping the wing from the car.

"I knew we were sunk, because I didn't think the car would have a chance without a wing," he admits. "But Karl got it going again real quick, and when we started racing she started workin' real good. A valve got sick in the motor, and I lost some power, but it actually made the car bite better. I wound up winning the race, and I knew right then that I wanted to keep running with Karl."

Kinser was sufficiently impressed to offer Gaines the "Bertha" ride for the following season. He cautioned that Miller would have first chance at the new machine Kinser was building. That was good enough for Gaines, and the two struck a deal.

"Miller just didn't feel right in the new car, if I remember right," recalls Gaines. "I finally got in the car, and after a week or two we had it going real good. Miller got mad and quit, I guess he was sorta hurt. But I knew me and Karl were gonna win some races."

Win some races, indeed. The pair became virtually unbeatable at Indiana haunts like Paragon and Lawrenceburg, and they were no less effective on pavement. Gaines sat on the front row of the Little 500 at Anderson in 1972 before breaking, and in 1973 won the first of his two victories there. That victory was good for $2,500 cash, big money at the time, and it was paid in silver dollars, which was so unwieldy it had to be carried home in a wheelbarrow.

By the summer of 1974, the two were not just winning, but dominating. And there was no end in sight.

"Karl and I worked together almost perfectly," Gaines remembers. "He was a hustler, and he was the smartest guy around. He would *live* sprint cars, and he learned a lot about them in a short time. He listened to me, and took my experience, and we were both tougher because of it. We didn't feud or fight, we just always got along."

Gaines had made several Knoxville Nationals appearances, but had never had the equipment needed to run up front at the fabled track. In 1973, while he and Karl were nearing the top of their game, they ran the Nationals and flipped, ending their trip. But in 1974, they came west ready to win.

"Not very many people out there knew of us," insists Gaines. "We were well known around the Midwest, but we hadn't run out there much at all. Oh, some of the guys who had raced against us respected us, because they knew we were fast, but many of those other guys we'd never seen before."

But some of the favorites, such as Jan Opperman and his famed Speedway Motors machine, had been seen by all. There was no doubt they were the guys to beat. The Welds, Kenny and Greg, and many of the IMCA stars were the pick to take the big money.

"We felt like we could win," Gaines says today. "We always felt like we could win, honestly, every time we raced. Karl had built a really strong 406-inch motor for the Nationals, and I had an awful lot of confidence in our car. It was built by Karl and Denny Mitchell, and that thing would really work.

"Right before Knoxville, we went to Eldora for a big show. Actually, Karl didn't go with us, he had a second car that Calvin Gilstrap was gonna run at IRP (Indianapolis Raceway Park). We tried a humper tire on the right rear at Eldora, with about five pounds of air in it, and we really dusted their plow. I set fast time and won everything. We headed to Knoxville ready to do real well."

While he had earned a secure spot in Saturday's main event at Knoxville, Gaines found himself starting in the third or fourth row. At the green, he quickly made his way to the front and was soon side by side with one of the greatest of the sport, Opperman.

"He was running real good on top," he recalls. "I felt like I was faster, but I knew I could never pass him on the outside. I felt like I could get under him, but we were lapping cars right and left, and I didn't want to get caught real late in the race behind somebody and have him pass me back."

So Gaines bided his time. He slid close to Opperman on several occasions, as the two ran nearly flawlessly throughout much of the race. Opperman began pushing harder, and Gaines would hear his tires "humming" as he bounced off the cushion.

"He was really standin' on it hard, and I thought maybe he would heat up his tires and lose a little bit of speed. I wanted to stay right with him, right till the last corner, and make my move."

Getting in front of Jan Opperman was one thing. Staying in front of him was quite another.

"I had lost races by a guy getting past me on the last lap," says Gaines. "I didn't want him to have a second chance, once I got around."

As the pair took the white flag, Gaines began preparing for his charge. He had noticed that while the top of the track was getting dry, the bottom was still sticky and Knoxville black. As they went into turn three, Gaines pushed his machine to the cushion, inches behind Opperman. As he felt his tires bouncing on the very edge, he turned left and began a slide to the inside, with his momentum carrying him alongside his foe as he fought for traction. His tires found the tacky surface of the bottom, and he reached into the very heart of Karl's powerful engine.

"I punched the throttle and felt the car get a hold real tight on the track. Man, that old hog just pinned her ears back and I said, 'Bye-bye, Jan,' and we headed for the checkered. I could see him as I went past, and as soon as we got to the flag stand, I knew I had won."

It was instant euphoria for Gaines, and he waved his arms in jubilation. As he pulled to a stop at the finish line, the entire team was beside themselves with excitement.

"We liked to killed each other with all of our huggin' and jumpin'," he laughs. "I honestly felt bad for Jan, because I knew what it was like to lose a close one like that. They interviewed him on the PA, and he said something about the good Lord wasn't with him tonight. When they interviewed me, I kind of laughed and said, 'No, he was riding with me.'"

While some thought this was a bit brash, Gaines insists he was sincere.

"I had always felt that the Lord had given me a gift to drive a sprint car, and that night was the greatest of all. That one made me feel like I was really blessed."

Gaines and Kinser went on to other triumphs, although they would not win Knoxville again as a team. They did capture the Little 500 again in 1976, the same year in which they had their first real quarrel that led to a split.

"We were running at Paragon one night, and the car was not workin' worth a dang. I had to manhandle it through the corners, and I was hurtin' my old broke-up ribs when I bounced around. After the heat I came in and Karl and some of his buddies were tellin' me, `Wow, that thing's really handlin'".

"I told them that it was workin' just awful, and that they were crazy. Karl got ticked off, and said somethin' like, `well, you know you don't have to drive it,' and I got mad and told him what he could do with that old car.

"Well, I walked off and got in Keith Ford's car, which was Karl's old No. 22, and Karl put a guy named Buckwheat (Larry Gates) in his. I ran fourth and beat them, and Buckwheat came in after the race really huffin' and puffin'. I guess he told Karl, `you better go hire that guy back, he must be some kinda horse.'"

Gaines' feelings were still smarting, however, and the pair remained separated. Karl phoned shortly thereafter, and offered him a ride in a newly developed car he was building.

"I told him I thought he owed me an apology," Gaines remembers. "And he told me, `Well, I don't apologize to nobody, but I built this car just for you. Now are you gonna drive it?' We kind of hem-hawed around, and I told him I would. He never did say he was sorry, and I reckon he never will now."

Late in 1976, the new car proved to be the best machine Gaines had ever driven.

"I've never had a car work like that one did, never. It would work so perfect that you almost couldn't make a mistake. It grabbed onto the track like nothing I had ever seen. It was really fantastic."

But in October 1976, Gaines' driving career was changed forever on the first lap of a feature at Champaign, Illinois. Gaines found himself flipping violently on a steel guardrail at the end of a long, fast straightaway. He flipped completely out of the track, and had to be pried out of the car. His vision and internal organs badly damaged, he began a slow recovery that winter.

"Karl came to see me before the 1977 season, and told me he built another car. He told me it was mine if I was ready. But my vision wasn't good enough yet, and I told him I just couldn't. He told me he was gonna put a young kid, Steve Kinser, in the car, and I told him I thought that was a good choice. Seems like it turned out to be just that."

Gaines did drive again, but the magic was gone. He retired to relative obscurity in Mitchell, tending to his mobile home business, his used car business, and other interests. Life is good now, he insists, and he is so busy he doesn't even get time to go watch the sprinters anymore. Nobody today seems to remember, anyway, he says, what happened so long ago.

But for Dick Gaines, and those who witnessed that scintillating night in 1974, the memories are rich and sweet indeed. With the black soil of Knoxville long behind him, he knows: he was the champion.

"YOU NEVER FORGET THE BIG ONE"

MAY 1989 - OFFICIAL LITTLE 500 PROGRAM

W hen he thinks of his racing career, he lets his memory drift back to 1958. For on a rainy, unforgettable night in May all those years ago, Wayne Alspaugh accomplished something a local guy has never done before or since: win the Little 500.

"I guess you never forget the big one," he says with a chuckle. "And that (the Little 500) was the big one."

A native of Anderson (Indiana), Alspaugh was one of the most popular drivers in the area. He began driving Roaring Roadsters with the old Mutual Racing Association in 1948 at the season opener at nearby Winchester. He made his first Little 500 start in the inaugural event in 1949, aboard Leo Stohler's machine out of Markleville, finishing twenty-third. He continued to run the Mutual circuit, then later the All-American Racing Club (AARC), founded by racing rival and friend Tom Cherry.

Immediately following the 1957 race, Alspaugh began driving for Anderson's Howard Hall, a car builder recognized as one of the era's most innovative craftsmen. Hall's machines had already carried Tom Cherry to victory at the Little 500 in 1952 and 1954. Today, Hall is looked upon as being far ahead of his time, trying new ideas such as large Cadillac overhead engines and front-wheel drive. At the time, Hall was campaigning the famous No. 2 machine.

"For running outlaw (non-USAC), Howard's car was always one of the best," Alspaugh admits. "We won twelve straight races with it in 1957."

They qualified second quick in 1958, behind Bill Kimmell in Dizz Wilson's Offy. Alspaugh jumped into the lead at the green, and led the first few circuits before Kimmell took over. The two swapped the lead before Alspaugh took over on lap 153, and soon after it began raining. Kimmell developed mechanical trouble, and the race was red-flagged and resumed the following night.

Alspaugh then had a different set of challengers with whom to contend: Ronnie Duman, in Harold Beck's Ford; and Johnny White, in Hoy Steven's famed GMC. Duman took the lead on lap 343, and White slipped by as well.

But Alspaugh made his stirring charge, taking the lead from Duman on lap 389. He soon found himself behind the pair, ready to lap them in traffic.

"I just paced the rest of the race behind them," Alspaugh remembers. "I knew that as long as I could see them, they weren't gaining on me."

After he took the checkered flag, the first person he saw was Hall.

"He was jumpin' up and down, he was so happy. I remember I was so tired, so dirty, and I almost couldn't believe what I had done. It's nice to remember things like that."

Alspaugh and Hall remained together following the victory, enjoying success on the AARC circuit which included Winchester, Dayton, Salem, and other paved tracks. They finished twenty-first in the 1959 Little 500, then came back to earn a fourth there in 1960. Shortly after that, on June 26, tragedy struck at Winchester.

Alspaugh was racing with Bob Pratt on lap fifteen in the feature when he and Pratt tangled. Alspaugh's car spun wildly into the infield pits, slamming into the small concrete walls that separated the pit stalls. The car struck and killed Hall, and then burst into flames. Alspaugh, uninjured, managed to escape with his life; but Hall's death had broken his spirit.

Alspaugh had lost not just his car owner, but a friend. He quit driving, and didn't attend a race for several years.

"I pretty well stayed away for a while," he admits. "I really didn't want to get interested. When my son Gary got involved in racing in the late 1960's, I finally could go watch again. It took a long time."

Today, Alspaugh resides in the little town of Middletown, a few miles from Anderson Speedway. Every year he can be found at the Little 500, greeting other old-timers and enjoying the memories.

He is still something of a celebrity around Anderson Speedway, because those who were there still remember. On a thrilling 1958 night, the hometown boy made good.

AN AMERICAN ORIGINAL: BARNEY WIMMER

MAY 1989 - NATIONAL SPEED SPORT NEWS

Here's a quick quiz: who has put a wrench on the most Indy-winning cars? George Bignotti? Clint Brawner? A.J. Watson? Nope, it's Barney Wimmer.

How about this one: what post-war "outlaw" mechanic saw his driver win an incredible forty-three of forty-four starts? Karl Kinser? "Speedy" Bill Smith? Davey Brown? Nope, it's Barney Wimmer.

Unless you're old enough to remember President Eisenhower, you probably have no idea who Barney Wimmer is. But quietly working in the Indianapolis Motor Speedway museum maintenance shop on the southeast corner of the complex is one of the most talented and colorful men who has ever been involved in racing. He is one of the few men who actually do justice to the old cliché: an American original.

The Indy victories? Well, Barney didn't actually win Indy. But since 1963, he and sidekick Bill Spoerle have been responsible for one hundred percent of the work done on the vintage IMS museum racing machines. Today, at seventy six, Barney goes to work every morning and puts in a full day in the relative solitude of the museum, using the knowledge acquired through fifty-five years of wrenching race cars. His hair is short and silver now, his steps slower, and life on the road has been replaced with a home in a trailer park across from the Speedway on Georgetown Road.

His story? Let him tell you.

"I grew up around my dad's garage in Altoona, Pensylvania. Worked there every day after school. In the early 1930s Joe Ventre (he was a school buddy of mine) and I got together on a sprint car. He furnished the parts and the money, and I did the work. We ran Lebanon, Landesville, Kutztown in Pennsylvania. Joe got killed in the car at Jennerstown when he got together with another guy and flipped 'er. Wasn't his fault. I was sure as hell sad, but it didn't sour me on racin'.

"I kept foolin' around with racin' till the war. I got shipped to Middletown (Pennsylvania) with the Army Air Force at the air depot. I was the chief inspector for the government on the aircraft engines that were rebuilt there. I met Deb Snyder and Emory Collins when I was workin' there; they were technicians with Packard, which rebuilt some of the engines. They knew Jimmy Wilburn pretty well, and when the war was over in 1945 Wilburn came out East to start racin' again. Snyder and Collins knew me pretty well by then, and they told Wilburn I'd be a good man to work on his car when I finished up my commitment with the government. We hooked up and went racin'.

"Jimmy won the first AAA race after the war at Lakewood Speedway in Atlanta in 1945. Sam Nunis promoted the race, and Jimmy lapped everybody but Ted Horn. We went to Indy in 1946 and there were only two new cars in the whole damn field. Jimmy drove an old Alfa Romeo, busted the block and didn't finish. Early that winter he bought a new sprint car Ernie Blum built, at least the frame and body. Only paid $400 or $500 for it.

"We went outlaw in 1946 because AAA cut its engine size to 220-inch. We only had stuff for either a 240-inch or 270-inch, so we figured we'd have to run someplace else. We ran the Midwest fair circuit for (IMCA founder J. Alex) Sloane, ran places like Lincoln, Des Moines, Kansas City, St. Paul. We also ran CSRA in Ohio and Indiana.

"Just because we were outlaws, people didn't look down on us at all. Jimmy got a second car going, and we put Ben Musick in it. In 1947, we ran forty-four races; Jimmy won forty-three of them and finished second in the other. Ben had lots of seconds and thirds too. You might say we were goin' pretty good. Wilburn only weighed 135 pounds, just a little guy, but I'd put him in the same class drivin' as (Tommy) Hinnershitz, Jud Larson, Jimmy Bryan, Gus Schrader, Deb Snyder, Ted Horn, and Emory Collins. At the time they called Jimmy 'King of the Outlaws.' We painted the cars gold with black trim and people called them 'The Golden Bullets.'

"We was always known for havin' the biggest Offy engine, but that wasn't so. We had the stuff to make anything from 240-inch to 297-inch. There were some 318-inch engines out there, but we didn't have one. Jimmy drove a car in 1940 for Ralph Morgan and they had a 318, but Jimmy broke a piston in their fourth race and ruined the block. All that talk started when we went to Hamburg, N.Y. in 1947 and Jimmy won big. Everybody started screamin' 'big motor! big motor!' I put my money down on a protest, but nobody covered it, and they didn't tear us down.

"We put a five-inch crank in a 270-inch block, and by God, that makes a 297 no matter how you figure it. I was damned confident every time they screamed about it, but nobody ever covered my money. Not once. They swore and be-damned that we had the big motor, but nobody would put up the money.

"Jimmy quit in 1950, went to work at Chrysler in Kokomo (Indiana). I went to work for Joe Baker, who made some parts for racing people. Another guy and I took some parts to Darlington, S.C. to deliver and some were for a guy named Pat Clancy, who had Indy cars. Pat took one look at me and said, 'Sonny boy, I just hired you.' I told him I was workin' for Joe. He said, 'You *was*.' I didn't resist too much.

"We ran the AAA circuit with drivers like Duane Carter, Bill Cantrell, Jimmy Davies, Al Herman, Jack Turner, and Al Keller. Sponsor was Bardahl. Carter did real well, and when Davies was drivin' we finished third at the Speedway in 1955.

"I stayed with Clancy till after the Speedway in 1957. I was always looking for greener pastures, I guess. Went to work for Mari Hulman and Elmer George on the HOW cars. We used to tell everybody that HOW was for Hell on Wheels, but it really meant Hulman and (Roger) Wolcott. Wolcott gave Mari a car and she had her first sprinter. We did real well, won the (USAC) Midwest sprint title that first year. Elmer was a hell of a race driver on the banks. Never scared him a bit. He was a good guy.

"They sold the cars in 1963, and I went to work for the Speedway at the museum. I like workin' on the old cars. On the modern cars, they're way out of my line. We've restored some newer ones, like Donahue's 1972 winner, and that was a challenge, too, but when we got done (former car owner) Roger Penske made it a point to come by and tell us we did a good job on the car. That was damned nice. We do about one car a year. Now we're workin' on a 1931 Cord Model L29 convertible. That one is tough. We get some real basket cases out there.

"About the last racin' I did was in 1963, just after I went to work for the Speedway. Foyt bought one of Elmer's sprint cars and I went along with him to help out. We got along real well. We went to Williams Grove and he got into an argument with Johnny White after their heat. There was some fighting, but Foyt didn't do any of it, he just argued with White. The story went around that Foyt decked White and USAC called him on the carpet. They asked me what happened and I told them they had the wrong guy. Foyt was exonerated.

"When I set up a car for my drivers all those years, I did exactly what they wanted. I never argued with them, even if I figured their idea wouldn't work. Hell, I figured they knew what they wanted. I was that way with every driver.

"I still go to the races a lot, sprint cars and things. Today's racing is more modern, but you have to change with the times. There are a lot of things today I don't approve of, but it makes things safer and better. I think that the old racing, in my day, was for rugged people. I know we sure had some fast livin' back then. Guys like Jimmy Bryan and I, and a bunch of the other fellows, we were always out havin' a good time. We liked to drink a little bit and dance with the ladies, you know.

"I'll be seventy-seven in September, and I still go to work every morning. I figure you can't just lay around and dry up. People ask my secret to livin' so long, and I tell them, 'Good booze and good girls...no bad ones!' Lots of people don't know, but Harry is my real name. I started wearin' glasses back in my dad's garage and everybody called me 'Barney Google' after the old cartoon character.

"I've seen lots of tough times and lots of good racin'. I never wanted to do anything else. If you look at the old pictures of Jimmy (Wilburn) on the dirt with those old knobbies kickin' up a rooster tail clear over the fence, you know why it gets in your blood. I never could get it out of mine."

WALKING AWAY

DECEMBER 1990 - OPEN WHEEL MAGAZINE

In the beginning, there was enthusiasm. In the end, there was none. When it was gone, Lee Osborne disappeared from the racing society.

This past season marked the first since 1965 that the "Wizard of Oz" was not driving or building sprint cars. OZ-CAR, the successful chassis-building firm Osborne founded in 1984, has been sold to Ron McMahon, his former partner. Osborne can today be found about twenty yards east of the OZ-CAR operation in homey Jamestown, Indiana putting together hot rods. You know, street machines, coupes, roadsters, T-buckets. That's a long way from sprint cars.

Call it burnout, call it fatigue, call it what you want. The fact is Osborne was tired of racing, and lost nearly all of his desire for with the sport. When you've devoted nearly every waking minute for more than twenty years to a career, he explains, sometimes you've just got to change.

"I just wanted to do something different, something other than what I've done for so long," he admits from his small, quiet office. "I thought about a lot of different things when I decided to quit, trying to decide where I wanted to go and what I wanted to do. I thought about high-performance boats, lots of different things. But I've always been a car guy. I liked the idea of buildin' these old street rods, and it's been fun."

Osborne has paid his racing dues nearly all of his life, beginning with his start in a modified in upstate New York in 1965 at age twenty. He had owned cars of some type on the street since he was eleven years old, incredibly enough, so it was only natural that the competitive fires would someday ignite. He bought his first sprint car four years later, moving to Lebanon, Pennsylvania to work for the late Dick Tobias. Tobias, who Osborne admits was "like a father to me," tutored the young man and kept food on the table when times weren't so good.

"The guy saved me in 1970 and 1971," he remembers. "Back then, your first years in Pennsylvania, you just didn't make any money. I worked for Dick and ran my car in the summer, running all over Pennsylvania."

Far away from Pennsylvania is Indianapolis, and the big track on West Sixteenth Street. Osborne knew that's where he wanted to be, and with stars in his eyes he moved to the Midwest and USAC in 1974, with his heart set on the Speedway. Like lots of guys before him, and lots of guys since, it just didn't happen.

"It was about that time that guys started buying Speedway rides," he says, "but yet a lot of guys didn't. I really planned on being one of those guys, a guy who could make it to Indy because he was a good race driver. But it just never came about."

So Osborne ran with USAC, and slowly became an outlaw. He eventually ran with the fledging All Stars in its early years, and was a season champ in the organization's formative years. He also hooked up with the World of Outlaws. He made a living the hard way, doing his own work on virtually every component of the car. He loved it, until a June afternoon in Oklahoma City that changed his life.

"We were running with the World of Outlaws then, and a group of us met with their officials about rules after a Saturday show. There were several of us, myself, Bobby Allen, Karl Kinser, who were trying to get the (WoO) officials to adopt a 410-inch cast iron engine rule. But it was the guys with the big trailers, the people with the deep pockets, who wanted aluminum engines. They were a lot more influential than us simple racers, and that's who the WoO listened to. They just couldn't bring themselves to adopt a sensible engine rule, so they didn't make a decision at all.

"I got up the next morning, got in the truck, and drove home. I just couldn't see anything but a $40,000 debt at the end of the season with that situation. So I went boating in New York for two weeks, went back to Jamestown and started building race cars, but I didn't work as hard as I'd been working.

"You know, when I look back, those guys who pushed for the aluminum engines, they're not around anymore. The (WoO) listened to a bunch of high-dollar, short-term car owners who lost interest and moved on to another game. And the rest of us have been paying for it ever since."

From that point, Osborne never drove again. Two years later, McMahon became an equal partner in OZ-CAR.

"Our philosophy (in the early years) was that 'if we can't make you a winner you're a born loser.' Steve Panarites did a great deal of the work then, and I remember that every car we built in 1984 won at least one feature. Some won a lot. I didn't make a lot of money back then, I guess I never did make a fortune building race cars. But I made a living, and that's what I wanted in the first place."

The decision to leave the business came in 1989, in the midst of some changes in Osborne's personal life, including a divorce. Suddenly, he was a single, middle-aged guy with a new career.

"Actually, my divorce was just a small part in all of this," he reflects. "My wife pursued a career, and just kind of went her own way, and that's fine. I just really got the bug to do something different; I didn't want to keep on building race cars. So I sold the remainder of the business to Ron, and put up this building next door, and here I am."

His decision required him to change the way he lived, not just his job.

"From the time I got into sprint cars, I had worked seven days a week all year round, with just a half-day off for Christmas. You have to have a certain energy level to do that, and you don't even realize it's there. Then, when you go do something that doesn't require that same amount of energy, you've got to talk yourself into having a smaller energy level. That's been the most difficult thing in all of this.

"I had twenty years of my life that were just fantastic, and I wouldn't trade it for anything. But I also wouldn't do it again."

Osborne maintains a very limited involvement in the sport, primarily by wrenching the A.J. Foyt/George Snider champ dirt car, a team he describes as "lots of fun to be around, they make it fun to go racing." His son Todd, now nineteen, has moved South to work on Kenny Schrader's Winston Cup team, after several years of wrenching various sprint cars and building a respectable name for himself.

"I just don't go to the races anymore, unless it's a dirt race or some kind of event that Todd's involved in," he admits. "Unless there's a particular reason for me to go, I just don't get fired up."

While he points to burnout as the sole factor in his career change, his friends have given him some good-natured ribbing about his changes. With the divorce, the new venture, and yes, the young girlfriend, he was the target of some mid-life crisis jokes. But he just smiles and explains it away.

"My whole life's been a crisis," he says. "How will I know when I have my mid-life?"

BIG MAC

SEPTEMBER 1993 - NATIONAL SPEED SPORT NEWS

The big man leans over the microphone, his large frame swaying slightly as he stares intently through a glass window, gazing on the fascinating scene of the U.S. Nationals. The vast crowd stares along with him, watching as two Top Fuel cars prepare to be launched into a numbing explosion of energy fewer than six seconds long. This is the soul, the very essence of drag racing. At the center stands Dave McClelland.

The man with the golden voice is known officially as the Voice of the NHRA, but he is really much more than that. Stare into his eyes, and you realize that inside this fifty-six year old is the heart and spirit of a teenage kid, with an absolute zeal and passion for drag racing that will be with him forever.

He was a kid of twenty-one on that memorable night in 1958, looking on as Don Garlits and Eddie Hill readied for a match race in Carlisle, Arkansas. Nearby, on a flatbed trailer, stood the track announcer, describing the impending event. Suddenly, the man just locked up. His voice stilled, staring into the night as anxiety and stress apparently overwhelmed him. The track promoter stood alongside in panic, and McClelland ran to the trailer and asked if he could try.

He hasn't let go of the mike since.

"My crowning achievement? Survival, I think," he begins, smiling broadly, as the deep baritone voice seems to bore right into your consciousness. "Also, I've tried to develop the ability to adapt as this sport has changed. And it really has changed since I started, no doubt about that."

He points to the vast crowds, the sophisticated equipment, the corporate sponsors, and the strong media presence as evidence the sport continues to grow. Yet his presence behind the mike the past thirty-plus years has kept the aura, the atmosphere, on which drag racing was built.

"He's had an incredible impact and influence in the sport for a long time," insists NHRA President Dallas Gardner. "No one is irreplaceable, but Mac's got to come close."

While many men his age often long for the simpler days of the past, McClellan is adamant that the best days for drag racing are yet to come.

"*These* are the good old days," he insists. "I loved those early days, and I wouldn't change a thing, but trust me, these are the good old days."

In the early days, racing was a sideline to his job in television and radio, for which he discovered an interest while attending Central Missouri State College and Iowa State College in the mid-1950s. He wanted to be a football coach, and played defensive tackle on a scholarship. After about six weeks, he decided that wasn't the plan after all.

McClellan was a car guy, and in his Midwestern world a major transformation was taking place, one that would change us all. The Ford flathead had ruled the streets, but was being upstaged by the new Chevy overhead. America was changing, putting on a younger and more dynamic face as youth arose to take charge. McClellan desperately wanted a '34 Ford three-window coupe, but his dad said no. Because he had been denied, he vowed to become even more interested in cars.

He arrived in Little Rock, Arkansas in the winter of 1956, taking a job as a studio cameraman at KARK-TV. For the next thirteen years he worked at various radio and TV jobs, including a stint at KSLA-TV in Shreveport, Louisiana where *everything* was live. News anchor, news director, program manager, he did it all. But in his heart he wanted to be racing full time.

He was growing closer to drag racing as he announced events, including the inaugural U.S. Nationals at Indianapolis in 1961. He got his pilot's license in 1967, primarily so he could maintain a three-race weekend schedule that allowed him to get home on Sunday night.

"I knew since 1958 that I loved drag racing to the point where I wanted to make it my life," he remembers. "But, you know, you've got the reality of making a living, paying the bills."

His move to full-time racer came in 1969, when he was offered the job as general manager of Southland Dragways in Houma, Louisiana. Two years later, he moved to Dallas International Motor Speedway ("the super track of the era," he says) as vice-president and general manager. But in six months, he found himself out of work after some corporate shuffling.

He had served on the microphone at every NHRA national event since 1961, and on Labor Day in 1971 joined the organization full-time, overseeing the press area and continuing his announcing. Later that year he moved himself and his family to southern California near NHRA headquarters.

It was on a Los Angeles freeway in 1973 that it all nearly came to a grinding, violent end. He was happily tooling along when he slammed into the back of a large truck that was moving onto the freeway from an entrance ramp ("I was going sixty-five, and he was going about twenty-two," he recalls), ramming the car hood into his face and allowing the steering column to plunge into his chest.

Doctors in a nearby hospital were stunned as attendants wheeled McClelland into the emergency room, as his internal organs were clearly visible through a gaping hole in the middle of his chest. They told his family to expect the worst as they didn't hold much hope. A few days later, after fixing his broken ribs, McClelland walked out of the hospital.

That was the year he helped bring NHRA drag racing to television. The one-hour show continues its run on ESPN, making it the longest-running motorsports show in the business, now featuring nine episodes each season. He continues to serve as the voice of the show, extending his reach to millions of viewers.

That voice, he readily admits, is a gift from God. Since adolescence it has been his to use, and he has tried to take care of the gift.

"I use headsets to help preserve my voice," he explains. "You have to learn how to put the energy level into your voice without screaming. But I'm like anyone else; as I get older I notice it takes me a little longer to recover from heavy use of my voice. Used to, I could announce five straight days and recover in one, but now it takes longer."

While the voice is a gift, his informed and friendly style is the result of many, many hours of practice and work. He knows the inside and outside of how to announce an event, and he wants to help other people learn it too.

"NHRA has an announcing seminar for younger guys who are active and trying to learn more about the business, and I supervise that," explains McClelland, who has also called Formula One, sprint cars, tractor pulls, you name it. "We want to try and bring along new talent. Someday—for whatever reason—I won't be here. You need to have competent people who can take over."

His lifestyle has changed over the past fifteen years, beginning in 1981 when he was diagnosed with adult onset diabetes, and he stopped drinking alcohol. Then in 1991 he suffered a heart attack that resulted in a triple bypass. He now watches his diet and exercises regularly, and admits he feels better today than when he was younger.

"It's kind of like the old story, if I had known I was going to live this long I'd have taken better care of myself," he jokes.

He likes to develop creative ideas, and when he joined Argus Publishing in 1978 he came up with the idea of the Super Chevy Sunday which has become a very successful event throughout the U.S. He also created the Performance Plus program for TNN. That creative drive prompted him to go off on his own in 1985, enabling him to work on "Many, many different projects," including racing commercials, television productions, on and on. Yet, the heart of his passion continues to be the microphone.

He has become something of an old friend for drag racing fans, who instantly recognize his voice. He has a reputation among competitors as a man of integrity, one who can be trusted.

"He's one of the people I go to when I want to discuss issues and get good input," says Gardner. "He's a great advisor. He epitomizes the people who truly have the sport's best interest at heart in everything he does and everything he says."

"As far as announcers go, he's extremely knowledgeable because of his years of experience," says Lee Beard, crew chief for Ed "The Ace" McCullough. "That's important, because drag racing fans are very educated. They learn about the technical end through the announcer. Dave is a great vehicle between the race car and the fan."

McClelland can bring the perspective of a race driver to the discussion, as he has competed in plenty of bracket races, and currently holds a Pro Stock license.

His eyes fill with excitement when he thinks of the future of drag racing.

"We have an exceptionally bright future," he explains. "Our program continues to be straight competition, very simple. The advent of 300-mph runs has captured fan interest, and we're getting better at staging an event. Corporate America is waking up to the fact that drag racing is a viable marketing tool. We've seen a dramatic improvement in facilities. Add it all up and you see we will keep growing, continue to get bigger and better."

He continues to work from his Glendale, California base, logging thousands of frequent flier miles each year as he chases drag races and television production dates. His wife Louise, an attractive, friendly woman with a soft Louisiana drawl, travels with him nearly all the time.

"Looking back, I was very self-centered," he says. "When my son was born in 1960, I was off running a race the very next day. Louise has been very tolerant, very giving, and that has allowed me to do all the things I've enjoyed in racing."

The couple often visits their three children and five grandchildren, enjoying a fast-paced schedule they have maintained for nearly all their adult life. It still hasn't slowed.

"When will I quit? Hell, I don't know," he says, with a friendly smile. "I never dreamed I'd get to this point, really. I think back and remember that in the beginning, the idea of a full-time national drag racing announcer was so far-fetched. Sometimes I can't believe what has happened to me. But I feel great, I enjoy it, and I really love this sport. As long as I feel that way, I don't know why anyone would want to stop."

SUPERMAN HAS SILVER HAIR

MAY 1994 - OFFICIAL LITTLE 500 PROGRAM

Racing is a game for young men, so the saying goes. Yet there in the center of the crowd, standing tall and flushed with success, is Frank Riddle, the sixty-five year old Florida superman who has forever changed the perception of the older American for Little 500 fans.

Since 1978 he has become a cornerstone of the Little 500, and likely one of the most popular drivers over the past fifteen years. While most racers seem to quietly fade away from the hot seat of competition as the years roll past, Riddle seems to get stronger. Now, he's ready to suit up again for his thirteenth start.

Make no mistake about it: Frank Riddle is not a sixty-five year old man who happens to drive a sprint car. No, he is a sprint car driver who happens to be sixty-five years old.

The difference is simple. Many guys still racing past sixty, with a few exceptions, are stroking it. They are having fun and trying to stay out of the way. But Riddle is a legitimate, on-the-gas racer who still wins, and he will smoke past you in a heartbeat.

In his twelve previous starts at the Little 500, he has posted some impressive numbers. Five pole positions, more than any driver in history. Two victories, four top-five finishes. He has completed 3,653 laps, good for thirteenth on the all-time list. Only two drivers (Tom Cherry and Bob Frey) have led more laps than Riddle, who has paced 1,018 circuits. And three times he has broke or crashed while leading the race.

All of this has been accomplished by a man who was already forty-nine when he discovered the Little 500 in 1978.

He started his career in 1948 at the old Phillips Field in Tampa, running a car he bought from the junk yard for $35. He focused his activity in Florida throughout much of his career, racing jalopies, supermodifieds, and finally sprint cars.

He teamed with mechanic Harry Campbell in 1976, and credits Campbell with finally taking him out of Florida toward national exposure in the North. They won the Ohio 500 sprint car series that year, a series of 100-lap races at five Buckeye tracks.

Two years later, they raced at the Little 500 for the first time, and even though they only finished fourth, Riddle knew right then it was a special deal.

He and Campbell returned in 1980 with a new coil-over car that would make Riddle a fifty-one year old USAC sprint car Rookie of the Year, along the way setting track records at several venues.

They won the pole and were running up front at Anderson that year when both were collected by a flipping Danny Smith. After that season, Riddle was fired, replaced by Dave Scarborough. Two years later the car was up for sale; Riddle bought it, and has been running it on his own ever since.

He captured pole position at the Little 500 four straight years from 1983 to 1986, winning the event in 1984 and 1985.

"Winning that first one, that was sweeter than anyone can imagine," he describes with genuine emotion. "Then I kind of surprised myself in 1985, not because I didn't feel capable, but winning that race, you've just got so much working against you, so many things can go wrong. It's very tough to win one, and when you get two in a row that's almost unbelievable."

In twelve starts in the 500-lap grind, he has proven to be just as tough as the next guy, rivaling anyone in stamina and strength.

"I've never needed relief, so far. My legs give way on me, my knees, from mashin' the pedals, I guess. Sometimes when I get out of the car these guys think I'm gonna pass out, but it's just that my legs are hurting."

He has struggled over the past few years, however. He crashed in 1986 and 1987, and in 1989 he finished fifteenth.

In 1991 he returned in Jack Nowling's Quikload Trailers machine, leading almost half the race before pitting and changing a right-rear tire on lap 295. They could never get the handling back on the car ("I couldn't hit my butt with a bass fiddle," he says), and eventually finished fifth.

In 1992, Riddle tangled with another car and was parked after just sixteen laps, and in 1993 he was uninjured in a scary crash that also involved every racer's nemesis, fire.

Still, Riddle believes there is plenty of racing left in his career.

"I still feel competitive, and that's important to me. When I'm in people's way, when I'm a hazard, I'll have no trouble giving it up. But as long as I'm still going good, I'd like to keep racing. Plus, I'm still having a lot of fun with this. That's the main thing, this is a tough business and you've got to be having fun."

He would like one more Little 500 victory, but admits it's getting tougher every year.

"The advantage our car used to have, that's gone now. Our car still handles real good at Anderson, but lots of other guys; they're pretty fast, too. I don't know, though, I'd sure like to win one more."

He retired in 1988 from the railroad, after more than forty years as a locomotive engineer where he was sometimes known as "Hot Rod."

"I ran them trains just like my race car," he says. "Wide open."

He bought a small farm near Thonotosassa, Florida where he and his wife of forty-six years, Martha, raise cows and cut hay. Once a month his old railroad buddies get together for lunch, and when he doesn't show up they look at each other and wonder where "Bones" is.

Usually, he says, he's off racing somewhere. After all, that's what sixty-five year old guys are supposed to do. Aren't they?

THE LEGEND OF BOBBY GRIM, PART 1

DECEMBER 1994 - NATIONAL SPEED SPORT NEWS

B obby Grim leans back in his chair and lets go with a deep, heartfelt laugh, one that echoes through the room. He is talking of past and present, telling a story from his heyday years behind the wheel of a race car.

He is seventy now, long removed from the glory days when he was slinging clay from the great IMCA haunts of the Midwest. Long past his successful career at Indianapolis, and long past the victories he scored behind the wheel of a midget.

Today he stands as a bright, fascinating window to an earlier era, when he was king of the dirt tracks. Some remember him as one of the greatest dirt track artists in the long history of sprint car racing. But when he sits down to talk, the personality trait that is most endearing becomes immediately evident: despite his legend, despite his success, he's still just good 'ol Bobby Grim.

Sprint cars tried to kill him, as did a couple of midgets. His heart almost quit a couple of years ago, and cancer came calling last year. He's managed to hold them all at bay, and now seems to be on the road to recovery with his handsome wife, Betty, at his side, living the golden years on their way to forever together. Just like years ago, he isn't a big man, but he's tough and he never gives up.

That was one of the hallmarks of his storied career. As others lost their lives or simply faded away, the kid from Coal City, Indiana kept going. Drafted just after high school in 1943, he fought with General George Patton's Third Army across Europe in 1944 and 1945, sending his G.I. pay home to his family.

When he was discharged in 1946, he returned to Indiana and couldn't find a job. On a cool August morning that same year, he climbed into a primitive Studebaker-powered sprint car at Jungle Park Speedway in western Indiana, and his need for a job was filled in the form of a hard steering wheel gripped tightly in his hands.

He gained immediate acceptance among his competitors, with his quick wit and bright smile. His talent was obvious, and he soon was running near the front. He was a regular on the Midwest Dirt Track Racing Association (MDTRA), known as the "Kerosene Circuit," racing at Hoosier tracks such as Jungle Park, Franklin, Mitchell, and Scottsburg.

Cliff Griffith was the circuit champion in Hector Honore's car in 1947, and near the conclusion of the season he decided to put his own car together. Honore asked Griffith's advice on whom his replacement should be, and he suggested Grim.

At Mitchell a few days later, Honore informed Grim, "You're drafted again." It wasn't "Would you like..." or "Will you..."

It was a match made in heaven. Honore had acquired an Offenhauser engine, and a continuing hunger to win. Grim was the young, eager man he needed. Over the next eleven years, the two would stay together through thick and thin, wearing on one another and enjoying remarkable success. They raced with the CSRA and IMCA until 1951, when they decided to concentrate on Al Sweeney's IMCA fair circuit.

What a time they had! Grim and his competitors, driving like maniacs across the plains and prairies, from one county fair to the next. They lived in their cars during summer months, and although there were great rivalries on the track, they were fast friends everywhere else. They partied, had lunch in faceless, nameless diners in all corners of the country, and generally lived every minute of every day in the midst of laughter and good times.

Grim grew especially close to Frank Luptow, a three-time IMCA champ. Grim was steadily improving his skills, and in late 1951 watched Luptow begin the transition to AAA. Later that next season Luptow was killed in an AAA stock car race at Atlanta's Lakeside Speedway, and Grim was devastated. Nearly two years later he and Betty, Luptow's widow, fell in love and were married.

"Same old broad in all those pictures," she laughs today as they look over photographs from their past, victory lane pictures from who-knows-where.

"Don't hardly seem fair," Grim answers, wearing a wry, ornery smile. "Everybody else got two or three different wives over the years, and I got stuck with the same one."

His memory of those days is clear, when he and Honore would roll into the pits and unload, often with everyone else staring at them and wondering what it paid for second place.

With Luptow gone, the IMCA soon became a heated, tough fight between Grim and Bob "Slats" Slater. They managed to get along, although they sought the same prize and their styles and personalities were very different. Slater poked his nose under Grim at Belleville in 1954, and Grim moved to the outside until there was no more room. Slater kept coming, and when his wheels banged Grim's mount into the fence, it began a violent cartwheel down the frontstretch, taking out fence timbers and flipping Grim like a rag doll.

It had all the appearance of a fatal crash, but Grim survived with some nasty burns and a severe physical beating. A year later Slater died in a crash at Des Moines, and Grim stepped up to dominate the IMCA.

Before his run was over, Grim scored 186 IMCA feature triumphs. He won the championship four straight years (1955-1958), which is especially impressive when one considers he raced against some of the greatest of the era: Jud Larson, Jerry Blundy, Buzz Barton, Marv Pifer, Johnny Pouelsen, Herschel Wagner, Jim Hurtubise, Arnie Knepper, Don Carr and more.

His stories and memories of those years are filled with emotion, the happiness of true friendship in spite of fierce competition, and the profound sadness of seeing men die, some needlessly, in their pursuit of a dream.

Near the end of a feature at Kansas City as Grim was winning, Curly Wadsworth was badly hurt in a crash. When the race was over, Grim and Betty drove to the hospital to check on Wadsworth, and found him on a gurney in the hall, his young wife by his side. The hospital wasn't certain of his insurance coverage, so they refused to treat him. As the three looked on in anguish, Curly died.

"Things like that stay with you," Grim admits, the humor gone from his voice.

He remembers Jud Larson with particular fondness, because the hapless Larson leaned on Grim for financial and moral support as he bounced his way happily through life, without a care in the world.

"Jud was just about unbeatable when he was broke," says Grim, "and Jud was broke a lot."

Still, Grim had him figured out. Many IMCA events were just one day apart, and if an event with a small purse was first, Grim might quietly run second, watching Jud pick up a few bucks.

"The next day at the big-money race, Jud probably still had a few bucks in his pocket," Grim explains, "and that took away his motivation. He was hardly the same guy."

He remembers Larson's brazen, bold passes, where he would slide up the groove to the outside, forcing Grim off the throttle to save them both from disaster.

"He'd come up after the heat race and say, 'Geeeez, Rob, I scared *myself* with that one. I ain't never gonna do that again!'

"And he wouldn't, either...until the feature."

Remarkably, all those victories with Honore came in just two different cars. When Honore drafted Grim in 1947, they ran the light yellow "City of Roses" No. 2, named for the cash crop of Honore's home town, Pana, Illinois. Later, in 1953, Hiram Hillegass crafted a new car, the fabled "Black Deuce" that proudly carried "Bardahl Special" on the hood.

With the combination of the fast, new car and Grim's natural talent, they scored a clean sweep (track record, fast qualifier, heat victory, feature triumph) at the first fifteen events of 1953. By the end of 1954, the car had broken more than two hundred track records, often eclipsing Grim's previous mark. In 1955, they won twenty-seven of thirty-five IMCA events.

Through it all, the dour, difficult Honore was hardly impressed. He was once asked how Grim had been doing and responded, "Well, pretty good, I guess," even though they had won thirteen straight races at the time.

"There were times when we weren't even speaking to each other," Grim remembers. "He knew how I wanted the car set up, I'd race it, and we just didn't say a word. It got difficult as hell sometimes."

Their setup startled many other racers who refused to copy their tactic of running stagger and right-rear weight. Grim, perhaps more than any other driver, helped pioneer that riveting, exciting image of a sprint car right up on the cushion, in a beautiful, controlled slide, the knobbies sending a rooster tail of clay upward toward the heavens.

That scene was common at many IMCA venues, as they often raced on superb surfaces that were normally groomed for horse racing.

"Some of those old tracks were as smooth as could be," insists Grim. "Sure, we also had some run-down places that were full of holes, but some of the IMCA tracks were among the best anywhere in the country.

"We might be turning twenty-four seconds on a half-mile, and guys from out West figured we were lots slower than them, because they might be turnin' their half-mile at twenty-two. They'd come out to our place figuring they'd wax us easy, but then they'd look down those long straights and swallow real, real hard. They didn't know ours was a *true* half mile."

Part of Grim's legend was the fact that his stardom wasn't just important to IMCA, but important to the county fair circuit as well. At venue after venue, in front of many people who saw only one race a year, he was the hero of the county, waving to the crowd after a victory and rolling out of town to another show the following day. He was treated like a star, with people often pressing close to get a look at the champion. Sometimes too close.

"At Nashville (Tennessee), they had a path going across the track that led to an outside concession stand down toward the third turn," Grim recalls with a laugh. "During the race, you might see somebody run right across the track. And people would sit on the inside rail, and stretch their legs out to touch the car with their feet as it went past. God, they were crazy.

"One time a hot dog vendor at Algona, Iowa set up his stand right up against the fence outside turn one. We looked at that and thought, 'Man, does he know what happens when those cars slide through that dirt up there?' I hooked those old knobbies up, and put him out of business on my first hot lap."

By the end of 1958, sprint cars could offer nothing more to Grim. He made the much-debated move to AAA championship racing, and was the 1959 Indy 500 Rookie of the Year. In 1960, he won the hundred-mile championship event at Syracuse, and also began enjoying success in midget racing.

He made a good transition to pavement, earning starts in every Indy 500 until 1969. He was the key driver who helped Herb Porter develop the turbocharged Offy engine in 1966, and Grim made the last Indy start in a front-engine roadster. But eventually the politics of the emerging class of big-money racing convinced Grim that championship racing was no longer fun.

"In 1971 or so, I was in Dan Gurney's car, sitting in line, ready to go out and qualify," he remembers. "Jerry Grant was out on the track and lost an engine. The Goodyear rep and Gurney leaned into the cockpit, and explained that, well, Grant was a contracted Goodyear driver, now without a car. They had a problem. They needed a car.

"I said, 'Sounds to me like *I've* got a problem,' and I unbuckled and climbed out. It was like getting fired in front of thousands of people. God, I was embarrassed. I didn't go back, even as a spectator, for several years after that."

Still, there's no bitterness in his voice. He raced midgets until 1971, when he quit competitive driving and settled into the exciting routine of driving a gasoline tanker throughout Indiana.

He looks back to that morning at Jungle Park with no regrets. There were many smiles, more than enough tears, a lot of sweat, and a little of his blood lost along the way. But he still smiles when he thinks of those old knobbies, and sitting up proudly in Hector's car.

King of the IMCA. King of the Dirt Tracks. One of the greatest ever. That's good old Bobby Grim.

NEXT WEEK: THE TRIP TO JUNGLE PARK

THE LEGEND OF BOBBY GRIM (JUNGLE PARK), PART 2

DECEMBER 1994 - NATIONAL SPEED SPORT NEWS

It was just after dawn that August morning forty-eight years ago when Bobby Grim and his entourage arrived at Jungle Park Speedway. It was a morning that changed his life, when the restless, ambitious young man from Coal City finally found something that went fast enough to suit him.

A sprint car.

It was hours before race time, and Grim wanted some practice laps, so he and his crew unloaded the Studebaker-powered car as the sun began to inch above the horizon. Amid the dew, and the birds in the nearby trees, Grim made the surrounding woods come alive with sound and excitement, the Studebaker pop-pop-popping as he made his first awkward, uncertain laps.

Today he returns to Jungle Park, virtually a lifetime away from that morning. Twenty-two has turned to seventy, and gone is the youthful grin, replaced by a more mature, wry version. His youth has slipped away, and in its place is the wisdom and patience of age.

It is a beautiful autumn day. Leaves twirl toward the ground, finding a winter resting place. Like an eternal cycle, a season is closing. Amid the brilliant change of color, Bobby Grim reaches far back into his mind for those memories of this place, long stored away.

Very little remains of Jungle Park today, and there was certainly no Studebaker engines to be found, nor a crew to cheer him on. But for a few brief, delightful hours, these woods were alive once more. Not with noise, or dust, or the scent of castor oil, but with one of the most powerful, wonderful elements known to man: memory.

Grim's eyes, now behind bifocals, scanned the infield, searching for clues that might unlock doors in his imagination. He walks slowly, looking at what is, and telling us what was.

"I had no idea it was banked this steeply," he begins, gently scooting a piece of the surface with his toe. "I thought the straightaway was flat, but, hey, this thing is steep."

As he talks, passenger cars inch by on a gravel path on the bottom groove of the old track, headed for a canoe rental agency located on the banks of Sugar Creek, just a few feet outside of the back straightaway. They stare at the stranger and his companions, and one imagines that they have no idea of the meaning of this reunion of a man and his memories.

The chunks on the old track look like asphalt, but the surface was never paved. Rather, because the soil was so sandy, track operators gave up on keeping the dust down with water, and began oiling the surface. Soon, after countless applications, the oil made it's way below the surface, forming a hard, rocky race track.

Grim laughs now, thinking about how primitive this place, and the overall racing scene, was in those days.

"If you went off down in one and two, you hit the trees," he explained, his finger pointing the way. "If you're off on the backstretch, you might get all the way to the creek. If you crash in three and four, you wind up out on the highway. If you're in trouble on the frontstretch, you're in the grandstand."

No walls to speak of, just nature's friendly little reminders to keep you on the track where you belonged.

"I didn't care for this place, right off the bat," he recalls. "I left here not sure if I wanted to race any more. We went to Scottsburg a couple of weeks later, though, and I raced on a real dirt track. I finished third, and thought, 'Yeah, this is a lot better deal.'"

As Grim continued his look back in time, a van slowly pulled up, with an older man with tousled, graying hair leaning over the wheel. He stuck out a hand, and we had found Charlie Sentman, former racer, now a seventy-plus stand-up comic (no kidding). He's been the proud owner of this piece of ground for the past twenty-five years.

He made a few laps around this place himself, he explained, back in his younger days, and he nods at Grim.

"I'm not famous like that guy," he says, nodding toward Grim. "I ran with him, but I couldn't get near him. That's your famous one, right there."

Within moments the two strangers had a conversation going, each contributing pieces of the puzzle for one another. Like miners exalting with each found nugget, they laugh as they complete one more story, one more question, one more answer.

"I was following Bill Pavlok here one time," begins Grim, a skilled storyteller with a wry, sharp wit. "I didn't want to mess with him for twenty laps, so I wanted to wait until the last couple of laps to try him. I got right up behind him, and I could see his brown shirt billowing out of the cockpit, flapping in the wind.

"I started to get under him in three and four, and something broke on his car, and he just went—zoooom—straight out off the track. There's a big 'ol tree out there, and poor old Bill, he hit that damned thing.

"By then I was by him, and I glanced over my shoulder, and I saw a guy in a white shirt laying on the race track, and I thought, 'Holy Christ, 'ol Bill got throwed out on the race track!' I was rolling down the frontstretch, gettin' the car stopped, and it occurred to me: Bill was wearing a *brown* shirt.

"Turns out some kids had climbed up the tree from the highway there, and when Bill hit it, it knocked one of 'em plumb out of the tree."

"I was here that day," Sentman chimed in. "That kid jumped up, and ran like the dickens out through a hole in the fence. Never did see who it was.

"You know, some years back, I was talkin' to a local fella, and he was telling me, 'I was up in a tree out there years ago, and a car hit it and I fell out, right on the race track, and ran like hell out of there.' Turns out it took me twenty-five years to figure out who that kid was."

While there isn't much left of the old speed plant, the track surface is easily identified, all the way around. One lonely section of grandstand remains, standing strong and proud, oblivious to the forces of time as they slowly erase the track from physical existence.

It was last used in the early 1960s, when an errant midget killed a spectator and Jungle Park was closed. It was left to die when Sentman purchased the land in 1969.

"This section of grandstand was still in pretty good shape when I got it," he recalls. "The others had just about all fell down, but this one, it was real strong, but it needed a roof.

"I put a new roof on, and I have no idea why I did that. I guess I just wanted it to last longer, to show people what this place once was."

His eyes work their way up the grandstand, studying the structure. His hand rests on the splintering rail, and he is a bit unsteady. But his resolve is still strong.

"I'll probably put one more roof on it," he says.

Soon, it is quiet again, and Grim is reflecting on the day that changed his life. This place opened the door, he admits, to a lifetime of great, great treasures. He won four straight IMCA titles. He won nearly two hundred features. He captured the imagination of a dirt-kicking, broadsliding, knobby-loving nation, sitting bolt upright and looking straight ahead.

But he did something more than win: he survived. Hector Honore's fabulous, famous Black Deuce tried to wallow him into the hereafter at Belleville, and he survived the rocks and clods from Langhorne to Minot to Shreveport.

He left many colleagues behind, and with each of them left a piece of his heart, hanging his head in sorrow. Frank Luptow, Jud Larson, Don Branson, Bob Slater, all died behind the wheel. Grim always pushed on.

Standing nearby is Verne Trestor, who has ties to Grim that reach far, far back. Trestor was four years old when Grim took his first ride here. While Trestor's father announced races at Jungle Park, young Verne sold programs in the crowded grandstands.

Like all kids, he had a hero, and Bobby Grim wore the title well. At each race meet, Trestor saved one nickel from his program sales, and when the feature was over, he greeted Grim with a cold soda. It was a moving sight, back then, the child with the broad, soft eyes reaching carefully upward with the cup, passing it to the calloused, worn hand of the race driver.

Forty-eight years later, Trestor wanted to be here, because the memories are his as well. What passion is as great, what friendship as strong, as those of the child who has turned into a man who can still see the magic in his hero?

The three stand together, talking quietly as they relax, never seeming to run out of steam. The sun makes its trip across the sky, and evening is soon around the corner. As the sky begins losing its fire, and the sunshine fades, Jungle Park begins to look more melancholy.

The shadows in the trees look darker, more sinister, as if they still await an errant race car, ready to send its driver to the Promised Land. It brings to mind the wretched, dangerous reputation this place had, rumored to be a man-killer of epic proportions.

In reality, that reputation was exaggerated. To be sure, it took a few, but no more than its share. Still, one must, in the context of today, be amazed that men were willing to risk their lives in such primitive machines, on such primitive race courses.

Grim was willing. Perhaps he, like others in his generation, simply didn't know any better. Regardless of the reason, he and his kind are disappearing all too quickly. They represented a powerful, exciting period, when money meant far less and honor meant far more.

As he walks on this race track, he looks comfortable. No regrets, no complaints, just good memories and a cheerful laugh. This man's trip back to the past was coming to a close, and he was climbing into the modern-day automobile that would take him back to the present. It had been a memorable journey.

THE MAN WHO SAVED THE SPEEDWAY

MAY 1995 - NATIONAL SPEED SPORT NEWS

He was the man who turned wood into steel.

It was a half-century ago when the shy man from Terre Haute emerged as the unlikely savior of the Indianapolis Motor Speedway. Anton Hulman, Jr., known as "Tony" to nearly everyone, was called upon to rescue the deserted and neglected speedway from the brink of extinction.

In doing so, he left an indelible mark on racing that remains evident today, despite the fact this month marks the passing of fifty Memorial Day celebrations since he answered destiny's call.

The mood in the United States during the summer of 1945 was one of hope, tempered by harsh realities. The nation had endured ten years of depression, followed by forty-three months of brutal, bitter war. But the end of hostilities appeared near. The thousand-year Reich of Germany had been reduced to ashes after just one decade; the Japanese had been pushed back to their homeland, seemingly prepared to fight to the last man in the name of their emperor. Everyone knew it would be over. But when?

Racing, like many other forms of recreation, had been dormant for so many months that there was genuine doubt if it would resume with any vigor or strength. Through those dark clouds of doubt came Wilbur Shaw, a three-time 500 winner from nearby Shelbyville, Indiana. Shaw had served as Firestone's director of aviation products during the war, and was tabbed to perform a 500-mile test of a new passenger car tire made of synthetic rubber during the winter of 1944-1945.

Shaw arrived at the Speedway, and was devastated at what lay before him. Huge potholes dotted the turns; the wooden bleachers were falling down; grass was growing in between the bricks that comprised the speedway surface. Several years of total neglect had taken their toll; the once proud facility looked like very much like a dilapidated Hoosier farmstead.

Shaw approached Eddie Rickenbacker, who indicated an interest in selling the 433-acre facility at war's end. With the conclusion of the war in August 1945, Shaw was in the midst of finding a way to save the Speedway. But while Shaw had the tenacity and vision to lead the charge, he needed one major ingredient: money.

Offers from corporate investors were made to Shaw, with troubling strings attached. Each company wanted, in exchange for its investment, a guarantee that only its product would be used at the Speedway when racing resumed. Shaw, knowing such exclusives would damage the credibility of the sport, searched on.

He found Tony Hulman.

Tony was a third-generation leader of the Hulman empire, a privately held conglomerate based in Terre Haute. He was introduced to Shaw by Homer Cochrane, an Indianapolis investment broker who was helping Shaw arrange financing. After a detailed presentation in September to Tony and several key associates, Shaw was stunned by Tony's philosophy toward buying the speedway.

"I don't care whether or not I make any money out of it," said Tony. "The Speedway has always been a part of Indiana, as the Derby is part of Kentucky. The 500-mile race should be continued."

Soon, the deal was struck, with the transaction to be completed at an afternoon meeting on November 14, 1945 at the Indianapolis Athletic Club. Although the exact figure paid for the facility has never been made public, it has been widely accepted to be approximately $750,000. One popular bit of folklore that lingers to this day has a low-profile Tony signing the check in the men's washroom, because his wife was opposed to the idea.

The challenging task of getting the facility in shape for the 1946 race began immediately in earnest, with Shaw named president and general manager of the Speedway while Tony served as chairman of the board. Wartime shortages of steel and supplies were addressed, and renovation and replacement of existing seating areas was a top priority. A shortage of qualified carpenters was creating serious problems when a strike at the nearby Allison plant idled hundreds of men. Shaw employed any striker who knew the difference between a hammer and a saw. However, once practice began, productivity sagged; any time a car moved on the track for practice, workmen put down their tools to watch.

Tony Hulman watched as his money was spent freely for improvements, and worried. While he had made it clear to Shaw that profit was not an objective, he been equally clear that expenses must be offset by revenue.

Soon, it was the morning of the first major post-war racing event in America, May 30, 1946. Tony left his hotel room at 9:00 a.m. and headed for the track, where he encountered a traffic jam of monumental proportions. Vast numbers of people, ready to shake off the blues of depression and war, had turned out for the race, and Tony's doubts had vanished.

"I guess," he later related, "it was the first time there were really as many people there as was claimed."

It was a defining moment in his life, because it renewed his belief that the Indianapolis Motor Speedway was not a property to be owned, but an institution to be nurtured. He made a commitment that each year would see physical improvements; and any increase in spectator turnout each year meant an increase in purse money as well. It was a philosophy he never abandoned.

Although Hulman was content to remain behind the Speedway scenes during those early years, his life changed forever on an unseasonably cold day in October 1954. Shaw, along with two other men, died when their small plane crashed into a cornfield near Decatur, Indiana while returning from a trip to the Chrysler Proving Grounds in Detroit.

Shaw had been the man who had uttered, "Gentlemen, Start Your Engines!" each May. Shaw was the man in the public eye, the symbol of the Speedway.

But in that defining period, Tony Hulman became the face and voice that would be associated with the Speedway for years to come. In May of 1955 he stepped to the microphone to give the command to start the engines, forever linking his image to that powerful, emotional phrase.

After the first few turns at the mike, he eventually agreed the phrase could use more zip. With help from IMS network announcer Luke Walton, he practiced and drilled, until four simple words became the most electric moment in sports: "GENNNTELMEENNNN, STAAAAAAART YOURRR RRRREN GINNNS!"

He was shy, but his position as leader of the world's greatest race brought new attention and adulation to Tony Hulman.

He had seen his first race here in 1914, riding with his father on the National Highway (U.S. 40) to witness Rene Thomas win. He never forgot that day when he was just another fan, and the experience gave him something in common with hundreds of thousands of people every May.

Early in life, he had great success at many things. He was named to the All-American Scholastic team of AAU in 1919; he was a gifted track star in the pole vault, shot put, high jump, and hurdles; he earned seven athletic letters at Yale; he was a world-class deep-sea fisherman.

But a curious thing became obvious: despite his success, he seemed reluctant to brag or boast about it. Through his life, when meeting new people, he would ask questions about them, genuinely interested in their life, rather than being obsessed about talking of his own.

He became the genteel caretaker of the Speedway, a friend to all who entered here. Drivers, officials, fans, all felt very important after talking with him. He insisted everyone call him Tony, and they did.

He was always smiling; he was always kind; he was always friendly. He seemed to especially care for the drivers, probably because he knew how much the speedway meant to them, and he also knew how much they meant to the speedway.

To help publicize the race, he would drive to cities throughout Indiana to ask for help, and nearly all responded by hanging huge banners each spring listing the dates for qualifying and the race. He would often have a championship driver in tow.

Rodger Ward rode along on some of those trips, when Tony's 1957 DeSoto convertible flew down the Hoosier highways from town to town. Inevitably, Tony would roll into a gas station, only to discover he had forgotten to bring cash, leaving Ward to pick up the tab. He always reimbursed Ward for more than the amount paid, but Ward chided him that one of these days he was going to get stranded somewhere when he traveled alone.

One day they piled into the car for another trip. Tony immediately informed Ward that he brought money this time. On the first fuel stop, Tony pulled out an envelope that looked to contain more than $5,000 in cash! But no bills were less than a $100, which the station wouldn't take, with Ward once more coming to the rescue.

Will Rogers never met a man he didn't like, and Tony Hulman never met a stranger. With his slightly rumpled suit and ready smile, he would stop to visit with anyone who wanted to talk. In one well-known episode, he and several others were preparing to go to Trenton, New Jersey for the championship race there in April. As they piled into the car to head for the Indianapolis train station, Tony noticed two clergymen taking pictures of the main gate at the Speedway.

They were from Australia, they explained, and wouldn't be able to stay for the race the following month. Tony insisted they join the travel party going to Trenton, and they were soon on the train, as his guests.

About an hour from the station, Tony asked the conductor what time they should rise in the morning to prepare for the Trenton stop. The conductor replied, "This train doesn't stop at Trenton," chuckling as he walked away.

In a soft, quiet whisper, Tony said, "I think it will."

Late that night, the conductor and other crewmembers could be heard in a heated argument about the party that thought they were stopping in Trenton.

Yes, it stopped in Trenton, the first stop on that line in twenty-two years. So Tony and his entourage, along with two smiling clergymen who had met a friend for life, rolled on down the road toward happiness. Later, Tony would only laugh about having an interest in a railroad.

In later years, Tom Sneva was playing golf on the Speedway course when he sliced a ball that looked like it would clear a fence near the VIP suites in turn two. A black Cadillac was rolling slowly along the road, when someone groaned, "Oh, no, that's Tony Hulman's car!"

The ball smashed through the windshield with a mighty crash, and the car stopped. Sneva just stood and stared as one of his friends ran to the car. Tony just smiled and handed the ball out through the hole in the windshield.

In the fall of 1977, Tony went to a Terre Haute hospital because he wasn't feeling well. He was transferred to St. Vincent's Hospital in Indianapolis, where they discovered a stomach aneurysm. He did not survive the emergency surgery.

It was Friday, October 27, 1977. The racing world mourned the loss of a leader and a friend.

Huge steel grandstands now lined the track. The rough brick surface had been replaced by smooth asphalt. A systematic traffic pattern inside the speedway had been developed. Every pre-war building except one, a barn on the outside of the backstretch, had been replaced.

Championship racing had thrived during Tony's years of leadership at Indianapolis. But there were problems coming to the surface, and today many feel Tony's death was probably one of several catalysts of the political upheaval experienced by championship racing two years later.

There is no question that Indianapolis Motor Speedway became far bigger than Tony Hulman (or anyone else in 1946) could have imagined. But he believed in the Indianapolis 500, and put an infrastructure in place that remains today.

He could not live forever, but his contribution to racing is truly beyond measure. Yet, despite his lofty, famous position, he remained a friend of the common man right down to the end.

His success was not just the building of great wealth and power, because many other men have also done so; rather, what made Tony Hulman so remarkable was that he remained a warm, gentle, loving person to the masses, completely unspoiled by wealth and power.

He left us with a world-class facility, the finest automobile race course on earth. He also left us with another image, though, one that will never be forgotten by those who witnessed it.

Just five months before Tony's death, A.J. Foyt became the first four-time winner of the Indianapolis 500. He was preparing to take his victory lap in the pace car following the race, and insisted Tony join him on the back of the convertible. For the first time in his life, Tony climbed into the pace car and sat on the rear deck with the winner.

As they pulled onto the race course, a roar went up from the crowd. They cheered Foyt, the perennial favorite, but they also cheered Tony, the beloved caretaker. He smiled and waved, his rumpled suit blowing in the breeze.

It would be his last appearance in front of the crowds. People rose and cheered as the car passed, cheering the man who built these grandstands and one of the men who had filled them.

His friends say Tony never looked as happy and fulfilled as he did at that moment. Perhaps it was fitting that the track he loved so dearly brought him one more moment of immeasurable joy.

He is gone now, eighteen years later. But he is still here, in spirit, in every corner of the Indianapolis Motor Speedway. Fifty years later, Tony Hulman is still remembered as the man who saved the Speedway.

STORM CLOUDS GATHERING

AUGUST 1995 - NATIONAL SPEED SPORT NEWS

It is midmorning, and bright summer sunlight spills through the windows of the busy shop. It is another hot, humid Indiana day here in the little town of Oolitic, and the locusts and birds add music to the calm, still air.

Karl Kinser is busy today, another day just like so many before. He smiles and whistles as he works, brushing his hands on the orange shop apron he wears.

Seventeen years ago, he was among a group of racers who changed the very direction of sprint car racing. A ragtag, loose assortment of characters became one at that time, giving birth to the World of Outlaws and forever altering the landscape of open wheel racing in America.

Of that group, he is virtually the only car owner remaining on the circuit. He has logged more than a million highway miles, hauling his race car to venues from sea to shining sea. Fourteen titles and 400-plus feature victories were earned along the way.

It is likely that a significant factor in the departure of many of those teams from the Outlaws circuit was Karl himself. His success has been so utterly dominating that people simply got tired of getting beat. He does not win every race; but he has proven beyond any doubt that you cannot consistently outwork, outthink, or outrun him. The championship score reads like this: Karl Kinser, fourteen; everyone else, three.

He is fifty-seven years old, a bit long in the tooth for a racer but an infant compared to the beautiful hardwood trees that rise from these nearby hills. Men have sweated a living from the earth here for more than 150 years, digging Indiana limestone from under the surface and harvesting trees.

He is in a good mood today, and willing to talk. Crew members Todd Seitz and Jamie Adrian work under his watchful eye, and as they help, he teaches. They are now in the tough part of the season, when the people and the machines are both growing tired. Already, they have raced nearly sixty times this season, and are just about halfway finished.

This is a year of transition for Kinser. For the first time since 1978, he has a new driver aboard. Steve Kinser, who lived, breathed, and dominated sprint car racing right alongside Karl for those seventeen years, is gone. In his place is Karl's son, Mark, a talented young racer whose greatest years lie ahead.

And for the first time since 1989, Karl has elected not to follow the entire World of Outlaws circuit. He picks and chooses, in the same "outlaw" spirit on which the World of Outlaws was founded. Yet, despite missing several races, he and Mark have won as many features (eleven) and more money (more than $150,000) than anyone this season.

In just a few days, Kinser will load his car, his crew, and his tools into his tow rig and roll west, toward some property he owns in Iowa, called the Knoxville Raceway. He doesn't actually hold the deed, of course, but it's his place nonetheless.

He owns eleven Knoxville Nationals titles, and he and Mark currently hold the track record there. Winning Knoxville eleven times would satisfy most men, but not Karl. He wants number twelve as badly as he wanted his first.

"It would be nice to win it with Mark," he says softly. His gentle tone disguises the beast that rages within, the beast that will come roiling to the surface when they roll the Wirtgen No. 5M from the trailer at Knoxville on their qualifying night.

It is then that Kinser is in his element. Stalking, brooding, working, swearing, pushing, he is lost to the rest of the world. Only when Saturday night is over, and his car is the winner, is it good enough.

He has earned unmatched success over the past twenty years, and earned a place in the National Sprint Car Hall of Fame. He won the Little 500 twice, and nearly every other sprint car event worth winning. But he has also worked harder than most of us can comprehend.

"Everything I've done, I truly wanted to make the sport better," he insists. "After all these years, what have I got to show for all this? Hell, I got just a little money put back, but I had about that much money when I started this deal. I shore ain't done it for me.

"We've won some money, sure, but think about how much we've spent to do it, and you figure how much work I've done. Why, I ain't made but about ten cents an hour. Now, I ain't complaining, because nobody made me do nothing I didn't want to do."

Not that they could, anyway. He is strong-minded and firm, doing exactly as he pleases, with nobody to boss him around. To his very soul, he is a product of Midwestern values and beliefs, where things like honor and respect carry infinite value.

"All these years, my word is my life," he says softly. "If I tell you I'm gonna do something, then you can take that to the bank. I've had a hard time learning over the years that a lot of other people don't work that way, but by God, you won't find anybody to tell you Karl Kinser is anything less than honest.

"All these years, I've never ran a big motor, I've never ran illegal fuel, I've never cheated in any way. What I've done I've done flat-ass fair and square."

He is very outspoken about his success, and he has never been afraid of competition or challenge. He graduated from high school at sixteen, then spent the following year on a factory assembly line. He also worked in area sawmills, but since the early days cars have been the centerpiece of his life.

He and his brothers went drag racing in 1955, until the end of the 1964 season when he decided to get a car to race on the many dirt tracks in the area. It was a weekend hobby, and during the week he owned and operated various car lots and body shops. In 1965 he bought his first sprint car.

"We always did go pretty good after we got the sprint car," he says, a vast understatement.

For the next thirteen years he raced all over Indiana, at Paragon, Haubstadt, Lawrenceburg, Kokomo, and Bloomington. His drivers included Larry Miller, Dick Gaines, Butch Wilkerson, Calvin Gilstrap, Ron Fisher, Bobby Kinser, Sheldon Kinser, and finally in 1978, Steve Kinser.

He bought his second car in 1967, an old Dizz Wilson car, before he decided to begin building his own. He had an itch to innovate, and felt he knew how to get it done.

Then came 1972, when Karl put together a car in his little Oolitic shop that would change virtually everything about sprint car construction. Weighing just 1,300 pounds, race ready, the car truly revolutionized sprint car racing, catching nearly everyone by surprise.

"You can't believe the advantage we had," he recalls. "You talk about kickin' ass, that old car just had ever-body covered. In fact, that car is as light as our cars today. And when I told Maxim how I wanted my race car built, my current car, I went down and measured that old car, and that's what we went with."

It was rough-and-tumble, rowdy racing in those days, full of color and excitement.

"Back then, nobody had power steering, and the boys that was good was big, husky sumbitches, because those old cars would just wear you out. You look at Gaines, he's a big 'ol boy, and that's what it took to be good."

Although he won with nearly every driver he tried, it is clear he and Gaines had a special bond. It was Gaines who first put Kinser on the national scene when, in just a few seconds on the black Knoxville gumbo, he pushed his car past Jan Opperman to win the thrilling 1974 Nationals.

They were together from 1972 until 1977, when Gaines' skills were deeply affected after a violent accident at Champaign, Illinois.

"Dick was real good, and that new car just suited him perfect. We could start on the tail, and win races, all the time. In fact, it was easier to win races from the tail back then than it is to win now from the front row. We just were way out front of ever-body."

He laughs as he remembers the wild-and-woolly atmosphere of the challenging Indiana circuit in the early 1970s.

"One time Butch Wilkerson and Dick got together, and it tore the hell out of my car. There was a big ruckus in the pits, and we knew there was gonna be trouble. I got down, you know, kindly to cover myself, and hell, people ran right over me. I ain't kiddin', I got stomped by it felt like a hundred people. You know, laying on the dirt like that, I couldn't tell you if the fight was any good, but she was sure dusty down below. I bet I spit mud balls for two hours after that, and I was black and blue for a week. You never saw such a commotion."

As they ventured farther from home, Kinser saw tougher competition, against people who knew a particular track well. But he was never intimidated.

"When we first went to Pennsylvania, we ran against guys like Lynn Paxton, Smokey Snellbaker, Kramer Williamson, Steve Smith, and hell, they'd lap us. But I never cared, because I knowed we was gonna eventually come back and kick their ass. And we did."

It is lunchtime, or "dinnertime," in Oolitic. Off goes Karl's apron, and we ride to a nearby restaurant. You will always find Kinser here when he is not traveling, at an aging cafe called Marion's. Inside sits F.G. Summitt, one of Kinser's good friends and a devout sprint car follower.

They taunt and tease, and Kinser laughs freely, clearly enjoying the friendship. It's a different world than the tough, competitive arena of sprint car racing.

"All those racers, and other mechanics, I don't really know if they consider me a friend," he says. "I like some of them, but it's always been a pretty serious business, and I'm out there to make a living', and not play around.

"But, yeah, I guess I've got some friends in racing. At least I thought so until this spring."

There it is, out in the open. A deep, profound dispute between two of the most accomplished people in the history of racing. When Steve Kinser returned to sprint car racing in May following a brief Winston Cup effort, he asked Karl if he would consider putting together a second car. Karl wasn't prepared to run two cars, so Steve set about fielding his own team.

But at the center of the conflict was Scott Gerkin, an eight-year employee with Karl, and Steve's close friend. Gerkin soon left Karl to join Steve's new team.

There are many, many facts unknown to anyone but those three, circumstances that are rightly confidential in a private dispute. Suffice to say that while Steve and Gerkin both indicate their desire to patch things up with Karl, his feelings are very clear in the matter.

"I haven't talked to Steve but once since he's been back," he admits, his voice very quiet. "And I don't really care if I talk to him any more."

He is not angry, he says. He is hurt.

"I didn't know you could get your heart broke at fifty-seven years old," he says. "But evidently you can."

He is not smiling or whistling right now.

Soon, lunch is finished and Karl is ready to talk about his old cars. We drive a mile or two through the hills and valleys (called "hollers"), turning onto a gravel driveway at Mark's home.

There, inside a clean, modern shop, sits some of Karl's most treasured possessions. The cars he has restored include a 1955 Cadillac, a 1955 Chevy, a 1954 Chevy, and his special baby, a 1937 LaSalle convertible.

Each looks flawless, another example of Kinser workmanship. Kinser is asked when he found time to work on these cars, and his answer reveals the work ethic that has driven this man.

"Well, they're extra, and their work comes between midnight and 3 a.m.," he laughs.

But it would be wrong to focus only on his work ethic. That would imply Kinser has merely worked harder than everyone else has. Which would only be part of the picture.

He hasn't just outworked everyone, he has outthought them as well. He is that rare breed who can both conceive an idea and create it with his hands. Ideas are a dime a dozen; the man who puts them into practice is worth a million.

Kinser's influence is found everywhere in sprint car racing. Chassis down tubes, wing sliders, aluminum and titanium parts, plastic fuel tanks, slider clutches; all were his innovations. But racing is monkey-see, monkey-do, and as soon as he has developed a new part, it has appeared on other cars as well.

With one exception.

Since 1986, he has built his own engines. Somewhere, in that mass of polished aluminum, Karl Kinser has found something that nearly everyone else still seeks today. And he knows it.

"I know what it is, but I'm not gonna tell you," he says with a coy smile.

Others notice how Kinser's engines have that zing, and while other engines stumble ever-so-slightly for a split-second, his never seem to weaken. How much of an advantage, he is asked, does he have?

"Not much any more," he replies. "It's just about gone."

There are three important factors in winged sprint car racing today: horsepower, horsepower, and horsepower. Thus far this season, Mark Kinser has posted fast time at seventeen World of Outlaws' events. His two nearest competitors have seven each.

Although he has devoted thirty years to the evolution of sprint cars, he believes they have just about reached their zenith.

"How much faster can we go? Not very much, at least I don't think so. Because we're already almost to the point where a human being can't drive 'em, they are just so quick and fast. And I'm not sure we need to go much faster, we're already faster than most of the tracks can handle."

His innovations came from a deep, creative drive, and also from the reality that, as an Indiana poor boy, he had to win in order to survive.

"I knew we had to get faster, because these other boys were fixin' to run 'ol Karl's ass right back to the house. There ain't no mercy in racing. You got to figure it out yourself. I never had no big fortune where I could buy ever-thing. I had to do it myself."

He says there isn't a team on the series today that could race without some sort of outside sponsorship, and his is no exception. Wirtgen, a manufacturer of high-tech highway surfacing equipment, has been on board for a couple of years.

"We've got just about the easiest sponsor to work with, seems like," says Karl. "They love to race, and they help us because of that. They've never asked for much back from us, but we've tried to always represent them right.

"But I told them right up front, a couple of years ago, that they might come out some night and see our car with the hood knocked off, or the wing bent up, and it was because I hadn't had the time to get it nice and shiny again. I told them, 'we're dirt track racers, and the cars ain't always real pretty.'"

He once said that no matter how great a race driver is, age will eventually take him out of the game. He now admits that the same is true of craftsmen, even the invincible Karl Kinser.

"I've gotten tired, and I wonder about going on," he says. "I know I won't do this forever. I've worked like a dog all these years, and for what, I'm not really sure. There's been times when I've got two hours sleep over a three-day period. I've raced when my wife was in the hospital, I missed my kids' graduation, all of that."

He admits he has considered a stock car effort, perhaps the Busch series, with Mark as the driver. Does he think he could make the transition to stock cars on pavement?

"Noooo problem," he says. "That's just a big, long, hard-slick dirt track, as far as I'm concerned. A race car is a race car, there ain't no doubt I would get it figured out.

"But the key is sponsorship. A man would be a fool to go down there without the right money behind him, because he's just gonna fall right on his ass, no matter how good he is. I wouldn't do it unless I could do it right."

In walks Diane, his wife of thirty-five years. She has adjusted to her lifelong partnership with this nomadic man and doesn't complain about the times they missed when he was off racing.

"She has kept it all together, all those years I was gone," Karl insists. "I haven't sat on a lawn mower in eighteen years. She's done all that, every week."

In addition to Mark, the couple has a daughter, Karla, who recently presented them with their first grandchild. All the more reason to stay closer to home.

But Kinser will never be the typical grandfather. His life, and habits, are wildly different than most normal people can comprehend.

"You know, I can never tell you what the date is, not ever. All I know is that we race at Eldora in two days. Because it don't matter what the date is, May, June, or July. It's just two days to Eldora, that's all that matters."

The apron is back on now, and Karl is back to work. Outside, a sprint car is fired on the road in front of the shop, and the afternoon heat is stifling. The heat and humidity have spawned a thunderstorm approaching from the northwest, and lightning begins to flash amid distant sounds of thunder.

Perfect for the mood of Karl Kinser. Knoxville is just a few days away. It will be a hell of a storm.

KENNY WELD

OCTOBER 1996 - OPEN WHEEL MAGAZINE

He emerges from his Brownsburg, Indiana shop and enters the office area, smiling and walking with a quick gait. His hair is virtually gone; his weight has dropped 25 percent from his normal two-hundred pounds. Medicine and natural defenses, along with sheer willpower, struggle to keep at bay the cancer that has invaded his body.

Struggling is nothing new to Kenny Weld. He has lived a life of extreme highs and lows, ranging from the triumph of being regarded as the finest owner/ mechanic package to ever grace the sport of sprint car racing; to profoundly dark days where his freedom, and now his life, are in jeopardy.

But as you look in his eyes, there is still that glimmer, that gleam that tells you Weld has plenty of fight left. Even today, challenged by cancer, he carries himself like a champion, his head high and his eyes boring directly into the soul of anyone he meets.

He sits for a few minutes to talk about his life, and the mistakes he hopes won't overshadow the good things he has done. It is a mountain of a story; it takes a mountain of a man to tell it so honestly.

He has been on this earth for fifty-one years; and since the moment he was capable of cognitive thought, there probably hasn't been a day he hasn't thought about racing. Born the son of a tough, outspoken man named Taylor Weld, he spent his youth watching his dad's midgets race at tracks near their Kansas City home. He saw his two older brothers, Jerry and Greg, begin racing before they needed to shave, and knew there would come a day he would follow them in the cockpit.

In a way, Weld was lucky, because he didn't have to waste much time as a kid wondering what he wanted to be when he grew up. Doctor, lawyer, Indian chief; none of them fit. He was a track rat from the beginning, crawling in and under cars to keep from being tossed out because he was too young for a pit pass.

His father was his first car owner, fitting the fifteen-year-old kid in the seat of a flathead-powered jalopy in 1961. He was a winner from the beginning, almost immediately moving into the high-horsepower supermodifieds that predated modern sprint cars. By 1964, when he was just eighteen, Weld won his first Knoxville Nationals, and he won it again the following year.

"I was just a kid," says Weld of that era. "Hell, I didn't know anything."

If that was true at the time, he must have caught on quickly. He and "Pappy" headed East in 1965, introducing young Kenny to a region that would be his destiny as a great racer. They raced at the Oswego Classic, then learned of an open-competition supermodified event at Williams Grove Speedway in Pennsylvania.

"That year, we realized that (Pennsylvania) was a racing community. I mean, we got a lot of attention. The Williams Grove hundred-lap race, that was that time. We thought, 'Man, what is this?' So that got our attention right away."

By the mid-way point of the 1966 season, Weld continued to race around Kansas City with his father, but his heart remained in the East. He was already a mechanically gifted young man; he decided to try the daunting task of building his own race car from scratch, ignoring the reality that he was not yet twenty-one years old, with certainly a lot remaining to be learned.

Sometimes, it is good to ignore reality. Weld, despite conventional wisdom predicting otherwise, built a car that was so technically progressive it would take his Pennsylvania opponents nearly a decade to catch up. The car, a bob-tailed No. 91, influenced builders from coast to coast.

In a way, that car carried Weld's trademark: innovative, bold, and a winner. Boasting such features as a quick-release steering wheel, an inclined radiator, and an open-tube driveline, the car won more than thirty feature events over the next couple of years, at tough venues like the Grove and Lincoln Speedway.

By the early 1970s, Weld had befriended Ikey Weikert, the son of the high-profile beef farmer, Bob Weikert. They hired Weld to drive the powerful Beefmobile, and the pairing of the dominant driver with the dominant car owner made for quite the formidable team.

Then the hippie arrived.

331

Shortly after Weld joined Weikert, Jan Opperman made a deal to race the central Pennsylvania circuit for the Bogar team, in a No. 99 which came to be affectionately known as "Shitbox One." Between Weld and Opperman, they won more than seventy features in 1972 alone. But while each could have been satisfied with their respective success, all they could really think about was beating each other.

It was, in retrospect, a promotional opportunity made in heaven. Here was the clean-cut Weld, strictly business; and the long-haired, self-admitted pot smoker Opperman. All of this, coming during an era of extreme dissension and change in American society, was played to the hilt by promoters wherever the two raced. Weld looks out the window for a moment when he is asked why the rivalry became so intense, and finally chuckles when he answers.

"He pissed me off," he says, a smile beginning on his lips. "He kept pissin' me off. And he wouldn't leave me alone. I mean, he'd get up beside me and rub on me, bump into me...and it's just, he *knew* it pissed me off. But he'd do it anyway."

Inevitably the rivalry became personal, and as they raced against each other three and four nights a week, capturing national attention, it escalated. Physical confrontation appeared to be right around the corner.

"Yeah, it got very close to that one night...we squared off...and luckily better sense prevailed for both of us."

Today, Weld says the personal rivalry between him and Opperman is "old news." He feels compassion for the hippie, who is today living as an invalid after his disabling crashes in 1976 and 1981.

But one sad aspect of the rivalry with Opperman is that it focused attention on Weld the driver, overshadowing his true mechanical brilliance. Tireless and driven beyond reason, he spent nearly every waking minute on his race car, whether it was his own No. 91, or Weikert's Beefmobile.

He won nearly 175 feature events in Pennsylvania and Maryland, and eight track championships. He also won the Knoxville Nationals again in 1972 and 1973 with Weikert. But by 1975, Weld was beginning to run out of gas. Burned out and unhappy, he moved to modifieds for the next couple of years, building a few cars, but steadily going broke. In the fall of 1977 he and his wife, Maryetta, packed up and moved back to Kansas City. Big trouble awaited.

D rugs, Kenny Weld says today, are just about the nastiest and evil things a person can get involved with. But the environment for disaster was very present for Weld as 1980 approached, and a radical modified race car may have been the catalyst that ultimately brought misery on him and his family.

Weld built a modified for Gary Balough that was very different from any modified in history. Sleek and aerodynamic, it was within the letter of the existing rules, but far outside the spirit of those rules. Balough spanked a talented field at the Syracuse Supernationals in late 1980, dominating the race in such a fashion that rival car owners and fans were shocked. The animosity that poured from the grandstands as Balough celebrated was both loud and emotional. It was obvious that those people did not like what Weld was capable of doing to modified racing. Shortly after that race, officials rewrote the rules with the hopes of banning that car.

Weld had planned on building lots of modifieds. Now, his product was tainted, because it was feared officials would quickly outlaw whatever car he built. So instead of opening a new career opportunity, the Syracuse victory in effect put Weld out of business as a modified builder. With that dream shattered, and feeling broke and despondent, somewhere along the way Kenny Weld got very, very lost.

"I got 'confused' along the way," he remembers, his voice quiet and tinged with sadness. "I got into the 'Why me, Lord?' syndrome. I figured, 'what the hell is going on here? I've worked my *ass* off all my life, and I don't have nothin'.' Let's just say I looked at reward versus risk, reward versus risk...and I had been risking my life ALL my life, for very little potential gain."

Weld was exposed to the dark world of cocaine, and the people within that world.

"I saw people who were only risking time being incarcerated, and the possible rewards were much greater. And I looked at that and I said, 'It doesn't make sense, that this would be so far out of whack.' I was at a pivotal time in my life. And I tried drugs. I said, 'Why is this so illegal? Why does anything that makes you feel good, how can that be so bad?'

"I've since learned, that's the choice that everyone in life must make. If it makes you feel good, and it's illegal, there's probably a reason why it's illegal. Well, I didn't see the flip side of the situation right away, until after you become a slave to it, you become addicted to it, it's all you want to do all day long. It's a nonsense way to live your life."

Weld became a serious user, and dealer, of cocaine. Living out of control, the highs of the drug kept him up days at a time. Racing was no longer a part of his life; instead of thinking about how to beat Opperman or anyone else, Weld devoted his life to eluding authorities.

"It's kind of a macho thing, yes. After a while you're always carrying a gun. I made deals in rooms where me and an eight-year-old kid were the only ones speaking English; everyone else spoke Spanish. I had some pretty frightening experiences, both with people I had to deal with and with law enforcement.

"But it ain't nothing compared to doing a perfect lap at Knoxville. It's nothing like that. I guess after you've done a performance in a sprint car, which is obviously the meanest and most evil type of race car anybody ever knew...after you've reached the limit in one of those things, you're kind of searching for that limit in something else and you'll never find it. That might have been some of the thrill I was seeking, the adrenaline rush that a sprint car will give you."

Despite his habit, despite his desperation, Weld was in that oh-so-dangerous range: smart enough to stay just one step ahead of the law; but not wise enough to realize that nobody beats the system forever.

On St. Patrick's Day 1983, Weld visited a friend who had agreed to store Weld's "inventory." Shortly after Weld arrived, a sharp knock was heard from the front door, and the loud demand, "FBI! OPEN UP!"

Weld fled out the back door where agents immediately collared him. The KANSAS CITY STAR later reported that he had a .45 caliber handgun in his waistband, and that authorities had found twenty-seven pounds of cocaine, and $79,600 in cash, on the premises.

The world, at least in Weld's corner, had come crashing back to reality.

Like nearly every drug user, Weld did not admit he had a problem, not until that St. Patrick's evening. He was charged with possession with intent to distribute; three counts of distributing; and one count of carrying a weapon during the commission of a felony. He was facing seventy years in prison.

As part of a plea bargain, Weld received a sentence that totaled twenty-five years and a $50,000 fine. Shortly thereafter, he began his new life as a federal prisoner. Kenny Weld was no longer a name; he became a number.

"The first day was in the 'big house' in Leavenworth, Kansas. At the 'big house' they've got a gate, that's got a lock just like a boat lock, where they've gotta close one door while you're in the middle, to make sure everything is secure, before they open the second door and you enter that area.

"(Leavenworth) is massive; it is big; and it is intimidating. Well, we went through this first door of this lock, and they started opening up the second door, and I was standing right there at that door, and I was the first one that was gonna have to walk through there, it was right at my nose. Well, that door opens about a foot, stops, and whistles and bells go off, lights are flashing, they had just had a stabbing. So naturally, the guard is pulling me back from the door, and as he does, a guy runs from my left, holding his side, leaking blood all over the place, and trailing blood across the floor, and he falls on a litter that's over on my right. So he had just got stabbed, and they took him to the hospital.

"I don't know if he lived or died...but it was pretty bad impression of my first day in prison; I watched a guy probably get killed."

Weld tried to turn the miserable experience of prison life into a positive.

"I tried to use my time constructively all the time I was there. The first couple years I was a sewing machine mechanic. For the next year-and-a-half I was a welder and a machinist. For the remainder of time in Leavenworth I was a machinist. So I tried to stay constructively busy and I used to try to read the trade publications, and keep up. 'Cause I never worried about 'making a living.' Because that's one thing, the drugs hadn't screwed up my mind and the government didn't take my hands, so I could still make a living."

Part of what made these years tolerable was that Weld's wife and two daughters were waiting patiently for his release. Also, he knew that good behavior would shorten the total time served.

The Federal government has a set of guidelines that determine how long an inmate should serve. Weld benefited from the fact that the judge had ruled that the sentences for the various charges could be served concurrently, instead of consecutively. Plus, looking at the guidelines, based on the fact that Weld had never before been in trouble, it was recommended he serve between forty and fifty-two months; he did fifty-two.

"I have a saying I use a lot...that I like my mistakes to cost me a lot, that way I learn 'em real good. Well, I didn't have to learn this one quite that good. Now, that sounds like I'm complaining because they kept me for four-and-a-half years; I'm not. I think the sentence was just, and I think the time served was adequate. Had I been able to accumulate $10 million and did four-and-a-half years, I'd be laughing. But the fact is, they found everything I had, and when I came out I was broke.

"And they've since found that that's really where the punishment begins...is if you can somehow take the ill-gotten gains, so that the guy who took all the risk, who did all this illegal activity for nothing, and then put him in jail besides, now you're talking about real punishment."

Kenny Weld came back to the real world in September 1987. Maryetta was waiting, and she helped him through the enormous culture shock of going from institutional life to a normal existence. The fact that such love awaited Weld was a great benefit; but the fact was, he and his family were dead, flat broke. So, at forty-two years old, despite a ten-year layoff, Weld went back to the only thing he knew: driving sprint cars.

"I didn't have nothin' else," he admits.

As Weld struggled to regain lost form, he began to realize this would not be the answer to his need to find a livelihood. Instead, an idea that had been with him for several years began to take shape in his fertile mind.

During his prison term, he was sitting on his bunk one day reading a machinery magazine. He hatched the idea of using computers to machine cylinder heads used on racing engines. When he was preparing his race car, that idea came back to him.

"When we were trying to get ready, I was done with the race car, but didn't have a motor to put in it. Bob Westphal was building the motor, and Mike Yelvington was doing the cylinder heads in Texas. And this idea came back to me, the idea I had when I was sitting on my bunk. But I had other things I wanted to do, I wanted to go race."

But Weld broke his arm in 1988 in an Ohio sprint car race, and he realized his driving days were over.

"I could have (kept racing), but the handwriting was on the wall. I mean, I'm not getting any younger...and the eyes are gone, you know. So I said, 'what am I gonna do for the rest of my life?' and the (cylinder head) idea came back to me again."

But Weld had big, big financial problems. Not only was he fined $50,000 at the time of his sentencing, but the IRS also placed a lien on any of his property until income taxes on the proceeds from the illegal sale of drugs from 1980 to 1983 were paid. In a word, Weld was in a box he realized he could never crawl out of.

"I talked it over with my brother Greg, and he signed for the machinery, he gave me a place to work, a telephone to use. I talked to my daughter (Debbie), she said she would own the company...so that's the way we set off."

So Weld Tech was in business, and soon racers and engine builders were raving about the finely crafted cylinder heads that now grace sprint cars and stock cars throughout the country.

"Basically, the port shape, everybody's heard of porting and polishing. That's what we do, porting and polishing. Except I don't think polishing is necessary, and we've proven that. As long as the shape is there, how smooth it is is irrelevant. Basically, what we've created is a way for a machine to go and machine the *inside* of the head. Everybody knows you can machine the outside of the head, because you can see it, it's easy to get to, and it looks pretty easy. But on the inside of the head, it's a completely different story. Very difficult. It used to be done by hand; by guys who had spent a lifetime learning how to do it well.

"And then we further captured a way to exactly reproduce what that guy who did it by hand had created the first time. We learned a way to reproduce it, at will, with a machine. We copied it, we figured out how to map that. And we map it 100 percent, then we convert it into machine tool code, then we tell the machine how to duplicate that. So what used to take two weeks now takes two hours."

So the way cylinder heads are machined was revolutionized, nearly overnight. Another Kenny Weld touch.

"It's just like racing...how do you take a piece of tubing off the wall, and take it all the way to winning a race. There ain't many people who can do it. You've gotta know what it takes to do, from point A to point Z. Well, it was the same thing here. A good machinist, a good CAD/CAM guy, a good head porter, and somebody to finance that stuff, somebody who knows machinery real well...it would have taken five or six people, locked in a room for six months, to duplicate what I did.

"I mean, I've had the best up against me, ever since I started on this thing, and we pretty much...you know, you can't beat a racer on a mission, you can't. You can't beat a racer on a mission. So when I take a concept, and make it total reality, it's the same thing to me as taking a piece of tubing off the wall and taking it all the way to standing on the front straightaway (after winning a race)."

Weld Tech was just what the doctor ordered to help Weld shape the direction of his life.

"Was it a positive force? Absolutely. It was something that consumed me, and kept me from thinking of other things...bad things. Plus, there were some other people on the hook for debt that I...I don't know how most people are, but if I owe somebody money, or if I have someone that is obligated and I have to bear up to that obligation, such as my brother signing the note for the machinery so I could do this, I take that incredibly seriously, to the point that if it takes my last dime...I'm gonna make that payment."

But finances, and cylinder heads, and even racing itself, would soon be the least of his worries.

It began with a pain that wouldn't go away. It was the summer of 1995, and Weld and his wife were in Pennsylvania looking for property to relocate Weld Tech (they eventually selected Brownsburg, Indiana).

"I told my wife, 'You know, my belly really hurts.' And I didn't think much about it...it's just like racing hurt, you know, you just kind of got winged a little bit, so you don't think much about it.

"Then we came home, and I started thinking, 'Dammit, this pain's getting to be a nuisance, now. Starting to bother me.' So I went to a doctor, and she told me to just take some Advil. So I said, 'Well, this ain't an Advil kind of pain.' So I got tired of messing with it, and I walked into an emergency room close to where I lived (in Kansas City), and I said, 'I've got pain, it's abnormal pain, and I want it to go away.'"

The hospital staff took X-rays, which revealed a spot on Weld's lung. The immediate thought was lung cancer, but more tests revealed a cancerous lymph node. It was soon determined the cancer was present in several lymph nodes. The official diagnosis was non-Hodgkins lymphoma, large-cell, multiple-site. He began treatment immediately.

"When I first started treatment, they gave me 75-percent chance of 100-percent remission. I said, 'Hell, that's better odds than (Steve) Kinser at Knoxville.' I went into remission right away; I really responded quickly. That was the fall of 1995. By December, I no longer was in remission, the lymphoma had reappeared. So they tried an intermediate step, with no results, with no success. So they finally went to the highest, strongest, hardest kind of chemotherapy they could do, with all the bells and whistles and experimental things that Kansas University knew about."

It was a traumatic, difficult year, but as 1996 closes Weld remains cautiously optimistic.

"Right now, I'm in remission. Now, doctors won't give you 'odds' like Jimmy the Greek. But everything I've read says that I've got about a fifty-fifty chance of living the next five years."

Perhaps like nothing he has ever faced, cancer has been a massive jolt to Weld.

"Boy, talk about a reality check...when they tell you you've got the 'Big C'...I mean, it is a real reality check. Confronting your own mortality is a good way to put it. It seems to make everything else you've done all your life look very, very insignificant."

K enny Weld is a very brave man. He talks of his illness in an unblinking, straightforward manner. Death is now seriously stalking him, and he is using every bit of his senses and strong will to keep it at bay. But his sickness has brought changes, softening and mellowing the man as he tries to make sense of all this.

He knows he must now stop and examine his life, and he is outspoken in his desires to change his priorities.

"I have been over-motivated all my life...and 'over' denotes excessive, denotes 'something's wrong with that.' There *is* something wrong with being over-motivated. It means you become exclusive, and you tend to ignore, literally, smelling the roses. You don't give a damn about roses, or orchids, or any other flower. They're just scenery, or obstacles in your way.

"It's funny, I can name, almost without fail, over the several hundred races I ran, what tire I ran, what gear I ran, what the weather was like, I can tell you that with almost total recall. But I can't tell you who was with me at the time. So that tells you how you can exclude everything except what you consider to be important.

"I want to try to do a little bit of it over again, only this time with the emphasis on *people*, rather than inanimate objects, like cars. I'd like to realize the personal side of racing again."

He talks with amazement, and gratitude, at the love his family has shown him over the years.

"Let me tell you something about luck. First off, my wife and I got married when we were eighteen years old. Nobody is smart enough at eighteen to know who to marry for the rest of their life, nobody. So it's gonna be a matter of luck, if you marry at eighteen years old, that you're gonna find the one to live happily ever after with. And I did. I've got a queen...she's stuck with me through all that prison stuff, all of that. I'm the first one to tell you...just how much she and my daughters mean to me."

His legacy is of great concern to Weld. It is beyond debate that this man was a major force in sprint car racing. Some say he's one of the best drivers of all time; others say he's one of the top mechanics in history. He's probably the only one who would make both lists. But he is deeply, deeply afraid he will be remembered for neither.

"I know what I don't want," he says, his voice low and tense, revealing the emotion with which he speaks. "I don't want them to think of me as a burned-out old drug dealer. And had I not come back to racing, and just served my time and forgot about it and was working as a welder in Kansas City somewhere, that's what they would remember. But I came back to make a positive contribution...I've got quite a few ideas on what I'd like to do, but I can't start them because I don't know if I've got enough time to complete them. That sounds like gallows humor, but that's a fact. You can't attack a five-year program if you've only got a couple of years to live. And I'm not saying that I do or don't; I don't know what my future is."

Weld talks of different ideas and projects, benevolent concepts that would better the sport. It is encouraging, watching his eyes twinkle as the old Weld enthusiasm and drive creep toward the surface.

Outside, gray November skies begin to drizzle, and clouds gather on the horizon as old man winter prepares to deliver his Midwestern punishment. Weld has weathered the tough storms before, and if anybody can beat this one, he can. His chin is high, and there is still a spring in his step. Cancer is a tough opponent. But it's not yet tough enough to beat Kenny Weld.

Author's note: Kenny Weld died from his ailment on March 20, 1997. Three months later, he was inducted posthumously into the National Sprint Car Hall of Fame.

LIFE GOES ON FOR BECKY BRAYTON

APRIL 1997 - NATIONAL SPEED SPORT NEWS

A jangling phone rattled the late evening scene, and Becky Brayton grabbed it on the first ring. It is a typically hectic night for Brayton as she tries to wrap up details from a dozen different topics while caring for her busy three-year-old daughter.

In a day or so, she will make the three-hour drive south to Indianapolis, where for the next three weeks she will be immersed in the incredible rush of enthusiasm and emotion that is the Indianapolis 500.

One year ago, she experienced a devastating roller coaster ride to which few others can adequately relate. On Saturday, May 11, she shared the thrill with her husband Scott as he captured the pole position just minutes before the Indianapolis Motor Speedway closed for the day, withdrawing a previously qualified entry to do so.

Just six days later, with the pride of the pole-winning performance still crisp in his step, Scott Brayton died when his backup car crashed into the turn-two wall with immense force.

Scott Brayton had evolved over the past ten to fifteen years from a cocky kid to a seasoned veteran, a man admired and revered among nearly all Indy competitors and fans. His death sent a stunning wake-up call that life is fleeting and temporary.

Shocked and filled with grief, Becky Brayton struggled through the next few days before heading back to Michigan to try to deal with the life-changing circumstances. Conventional wisdom might have predicted she would be finished with auto racing.

But Becky has quietly returned to the sport, playing a key role this month with Scott's former employer, Team Menard. As director of public relations, she will help Team Menard negotiate the give-and-take demands of the media, sponsors, and fans.

Her involvement is not limited to that role, however. For the past several years, Becky has operated her own marketing company, helping teams find

342

and keep sponsors. But during Scott's racing career, she moved to the background and supported his efforts, and nurtured their young daughter, Carly.

Today, as she continues to forge on with her life, she finds her involvement in auto racing to be a therapeutic salve that aids her healing.

"It's been really good for me to be occupied," she admits. "I'm pretty busy with several things, I'm still a partner with Brayton Engineering (the family's engine building business) as well. Lee (Brayton, Scott's father) and Jim (Wright) do most of that work, and we're really busy with that. But the marketing business occupies most of my time."

It would have been very easy for Becky Brayton to get lost along the "why me, Lord" trail, but this remarkable woman insists that anger or bitterness toward racing was never in her thoughts.

"No...no, I don't think so. That probably sounds strange to people...I don't know, this whole sport has been in Scott's family forever, for generations, and we all knew it could happen, especially Scott.

"The way it happened, it was such a freak deal, and I just...no, I don't know why, but I never felt angry."

Although it has been almost a year since the accident, it is obvious from her tone that Becky still carries enormous sadness from the loss of Scott. Yet she handles questions and discussion of the subject with an admirable mix of quiet grace and dignity.

As she deals with questions of Scott's death, she tries to remain upbeat, because that's exactly what her husband would insist on.

He was bright, funny, pleasant, and devoted to auto racing throughout every fiber of his being. He was a proud man who worked extremely hard to pick himself up after every setback, and always had the will to smile as he continued the fight.

Perhaps it was the years spent with Scott that helped her absorb that indomitable spirit; more likely, it is that positive thinking is the essence of Becky Brayton.

"Well, you have to be positive," she says, as Carly interrupts with a brief question. "You only have two choices. When something like (the accident) happens to you, you're going to go one way or the other. So, really, I think it is just a function of the way I was brought up, and it's definitely a function of the way Scott was, and his family. I mean, he wouldn't have it any other way.

"At my house, I grew up doing a lot of horseback riding, and if you fell off...you got back on. No matter how you felt about it. And that's kind of how Scott was, too...you just gotta do what you can."

She admits her strong desire to carry on in a positive way is not just for her own benefit.

"I have a daughter, and I have a big responsibility to maintain a positive life, for her. Anyone who is a parent would understand that, because you have a commitment not just to yourself, but to what is best for your family."

Although she is upbeat about her marketing and PR responsibilities, in the weeks following the accident she really didn't see herself continue to be involved in the sport.

"No, I had no intention whatsoever of doing anything (within racing). I wasn't angry or bitter...but I just didn't have the desire.

"The two things that really brought me back to it...was that Scott had commitments to his sponsors...I mean, we had sold programs to those companies and they had built their plans around us. They probably would have understood if I had dropped it, given the circumstances, but...

"But everything still went *on*...you know, with the race cars and things. John (Menard) kept racing, which of course he should have. And we had several sponsorships, Scott and I, and that's the first thing I started working on from home, helping (the sponsors) plan their races. Just a few things, nothing full-time."

Then came the second catalyst that brought Becky back among the racers.

"Right before (the) New Hampshire (IRL event), John Menard called me, and said he had parted ways with his PR person. He said, 'If you could run up there for a couple of days and help me out, I know I wouldn't have to worry about it.'"

She paused, and she laughed.

"And that's how it started. He was on a plane to Europe, he only had two minutes to talk, and I just said okay without even thinking about it. This was the week of New Hampshire, I just bought a ticket and went up there."

Immediately after hanging up the phone, she suddenly realized what she had just committed to.

"I thought, 'WHAT was I thinking of?' But yes...yes, I was excited. At that time, the best thing in the whole world was to be doing stuff, no matter what it was. And it was strange, in a way, to be back around all the racing people."

Slowly, steadily, Becky Brayton began to pick up the pieces of her life and sort out her future. Being back among racing people helped her, she says, because it reinforced her belief in her countless friends in the sport.

"Good friends," she says.

June and early July were dark months, and she began to understand just how important those friends were.

"The whole thing was kind of overwhelming, in a lot of ways...in good ways. The people within racing were just incredibly supportive. And outside of racing...everything the town (Coldwater) did, it was incredible. I was shocked by it, but extremely happy.

"It buoyed my spirits when I really needed it."

She got through that period, then settled into a life where, even though she maintains a strong positive attitude, she still found herself dealing with grief on a daily basis.

"Of course, the shock of it...in an situation like Scott's, there's just so much shock involved. You always know it is possible, but you're still shocked beyond belief when something like that happens. And there's so much...and it was so hard with Carly. As little as she was, I mean, we had to go through all that.

"But it's certainly not the easiest thing in the world (to deal with). But one thing, I think people wonder about me going to the races and stuff, and wonder how I can do that. They must think I'm suddenly reminded (of Scott) when I go to the race track.

"But I deal with it on an everyday basis. There's really very little difference in being at the race track than being at my home, or all the places Scott and I would go together. I mean, we had a whole life away from the race track that reminds me of him every day.

"So that part, it might seem a little cold, but for me, it's an everyday thing, thinking of Scott...not just when I show up in May."

Now, she finds herself working with Tony Stewart and Robbie Buhl, and she is asked if it seems odd to work with drivers other than Scott.

"No, I don't think it's difficult," she says. "How careers are handled is so much a function of the time, the era, the circumstances. Every career is different. The biggest thing in working with others is that you realize how important (PR) is to them. I mean, I've lived it, and I realize the focus you have to give it.

"You have to live it, and you have to give up almost everything (to be a race driver). Scott worked hard, and he loved every minute of it. Seeing others, though, it makes me understand just how hard Scott went at it. He would never give up, he would just keeping working."

Now, as May dawns at Indianapolis, she is optimistic about her role in the sport.

"You always have aspirations, you have hopes that your business or your role will be successful. I'm just going to try to be as successful as possible, trying to grow. Whether that growth will come within racing, I don't know. It's likely, but I'm not set on maintaining the rest of my life in racing.

"Right now...you might as well say it, there is a lot of business opportunity out there. It's what I've always known; (marketing) is how I met Scott. Right now, contrary to popular belief, there's a lot of business happening in the IRL.

"So I'd be foolish not to work within racing from a business standpoint. It would be foolish to turn my back on what I've worked on for many years, now that it is really starting to happen. I don't really know what my plans are. I do have some different goals...but who knows.

"I'm beginning to get excited about my future, and I'm something of an unwilling passenger, because I liked my life the way it was. But I can't control that situation, so I have to just keep trying to move forward and try to go on in spite of how things worked out."

Now, as she heads to Indianapolis and what will certainly be a month under the media's microscope, she isn't entirely comfortable being the subject of their attention.

"This will probably be the last interview I'll do on this subject," she admits. "Not because I want to be difficult, but because I want to focus on my work and get through the month.

"But I don't mind if people focus on Scott. Because he was such a great person, and when we go to Indianapolis I look around and that whole place...it was just *him*. So it's a good thing to remember him.

"But I think if he were here...he would be telling me, 'Hey, all that stuff is fine, but it's done...you need to get busy and get on with it.'"

And that's what she will do. With grace, style, and dignity, she will go on.

THROUGH THE EYES OF BOB TROSTLE

AUGUST 1997 - NATIONAL SPEED SPORT NEWS

It is almost eerie, staring at the scene: a busy sprint car workshop, in a realistic state of minor chaos, with no movement or people. No noise from grinders; no pounding of hammers. Only silence, as if one were viewing a photo of a scene some twenty years ago.

It is a recreation of Bob Trostle's Des Moines, Iowa workshop, located here in the National Sprint Car Hall of Fame Museum in Knoxville, Iowa. It is a fascinating glimpse of history, but after a moment the realization is evident: You can recreate the setting, and recite the facts and figures, but you will never really duplicate the life Bob Trostle has lived.

For thirty-some years Trostle was at the center of the sprint car universe, as both a car builder and mechanic, during a period of explosive growth and excitement. He shaped and influenced the entire sport and introduced America to unknowns such as Jan Opperman and Doug Wolfgang, men who would become superstars.

Life is slower today, as he relishes the wonderfully relaxed pace of retirement. He is still plugged in to sprint cars, though, and will once again have a car at this year's Knoxville Nationals.

Even in retirement, there is one lingering habit: Every Saturday evening he and his wife Dorotha take a leisurely ride south from their Des Moines home to the black dirt and bright lights of Knoxville Raceway. There are some things a man just can't get out of his system.

The eight-year-old boy was fascinated, gazing with wide eyes and a smile through the fence. It was 1941, and Trostle and his father had walked two blocks from their home to the legendary dirt track located at the Iowa State Fairgrounds. The fury of the cars; the aroma of spent racing fuel; the shaking of the ground as the cars thundered past caught the young boy's imagination. It was something that never left him.

But America went to war soon after that day, and for five long years the boy could only dream. When racing resumed in 1946, young Trostle "didn't miss very many" shows at the old fairgrounds.

He was a mechanically gifted kid with a burning interest in cars. Naturally, he dreamed of owning a sprint car, but the modest boy had convinced himself he couldn't afford one. In 1958, he built an altered drag racer, which he raced until Labor Day, 1960.

His drag racing aspirations ended that weekend, when his growing frustration with cheating among competitors prompted him to quit the straight-line scene. His desire to compete needed to be re-channeled, and he finally talked himself into taking a look at his beloved sprint car racing.

"I'd go to Knoxville a couple of times a year," he recalls, "so I still knew a little bit about sprint cars."

The construction and success of his first race car is an amazing accomplishment when you consider how he went about it.

"I went out and looked at an old sprint car, just kind of looked it over. I didn't measure anything; I just kind of eyeballed the thing and figured out how I wanted to do one.

"A couple days later, just before supper, I drew up on paper what I wanted. Then I built it."

Sprint car racing was in the midst of a transformation in 1961. While certain clubs like USAC and IMCA raced sprint cars, most weekly tracks featured what were known as supermodifieds: roll cage, V8 engine, bobbed tail.

Despite the fact he was a complete rookie, Trostle had admirable foresight in his plans. He built one of the first cars that could run as either a super or a sprint car. The car had disk brakes, mag wheels, a tube frame, fuel injection, and a bolt-on roll cage. He also built a sprint car tank as well as a square supermodified tail.

"It didn't take long before word got out on what I was doing, because I built three more frames that winter, before anybody even knew if my car would work," says Trostle.

His cars were successful, and dependable. His business as a car builder continued to blossom, and by 1969 he was ready to quit his regular job to focus on racing.

"I had always had a job that paid my bills and took care of my family, and the racing stuff had to come from money I made extra. So I did a lot of auto repair work, stuff like that, to support my racing."

The workaholic atmosphere surrounded Trostle for nearly three decades, and it became a way of life. Work, work, work, night and day, all year long. It made him edgy and gruff at times, but he never stopped having fun.

"Really, I started building my first car because I just couldn't afford to buy one on my own," he insists. "I didn't have the money to go to Indianapolis and buy a new race car. I didn't know of any Midwestern builders, so buying stuff was just out of my reach. I didn't have any choice but to build cars if I wanted to race."

By the end of the 1960s, Trostle found himself in the middle of what had become a fraternity of outlaw open wheel racers. Kenny Weld, Dick Sutcliffe, Billy Shuman, Roger Larson, Lloyd Beckman, Ray Lee Goodwin, and Chuck Amati began living on the road, instead of running an exclusive weekly show. Each fall they would arrive in Phoenix at Manzanita Speedway for the prestigious Western World championship.

In 1968 a friend of Trostle's had gone to California, and when he returned he brought a buddy of his who had ran some midgets out West. Trostle agreed to give the kid a try in his backup car at the nearby Iowa State Fairgrounds.

Jan Opperman was the kid's name, and of course Trostle had never heard of him. His debut was less than spectacular.

"He went out in his heat race and ran over, and into, everybody out there. All the established stars at the time, he bounced off all of them. The IMCA officials came down and chewed me out, telling me to get this kid the hell out of there.

"It turns out that the steering in the car was broken, and Jan was hesitant to tell me about it because he was new and he thought I'd fire him. We fixed the car up and got through that night, and he went pretty well after that."

Pretty well, indeed.

In 1970 Trostle teamed with Dave Van Patten, with Van Patten providing the workshop and the parts, and Trostle providing the sweat and know-how. They stayed together five years, in what Trostle says was "a great deal for both of us. I needed to be out racing to sell my cars, and Dave got a new car every year."

Trostle and Van Patten split near the end of the 1975 season, and Trostle built himself a car and looked for a driver. He had noticed a kid named Doug Wolfgang, who had a great rookie performance that season at Knoxville, despite appearing in fourteen different cars during the season.

"I needed somebody to help me weld, and I put him in my car as well. I had watched him...I knew he had what it took to be a great race driver. I caught a lot of grief for that, because he was such an unknown. But there was just no doubt in my mind. The guy just had greatness written all over him."

They won twenty-one features that season, including seven at Knoxville.

"Wolfie had never before won a race, and he won the opener that year at Knoxville. It makes me feel good that we won right off the bat.

"Late in 1976, Wolfie thought he had a deal for a new engine, a big horsepower deal. But that fell through, and Wolfie was pretty low. So we talked, and I suggested we try to lighten the car. If we can take weight off, that's the same as adding horsepower."

So Trostle set off in an epic quest to downsize his race car. He and several friends formed a pool to guess how much weight could be shaved, with most guesses in 100- to 200-pound range. He saved seventy pounds on the frame alone, simply by using .095" rails and .065" tubing on the smaller pieces, and eliminating unneeded mounting points.

He shaved nuts and bolts, and made every piece he could out of aluminum. For the first time, he used aluminum engine heads. He cut the size of side panels. He reduced the number of Dzus buttons on the hood. He even went to smaller gauges in the cockpit to save a few ounces.

His 1976 car had weighed 1,954 pounds. He gasped when he scaled the new one, which weighed 1,485 pounds with twenty gallons of fuel. His work had cut 469 pounds off his car, a savings of 25 percent.

He knew he had created something special. To snooker his competition, he ran the old car at East Bay for the Florida Nationals, and waited until spring to reveal his new car.

"I wanted everybody to be already committed to their cars, so they'd have a hard time reacting to us," Trostle admits.

The car won the first four weekly Knoxville shows, and talk began of banning the car as unsafe.

"Lloyd Beckman saved the day for us, because one night he got on the microphone and said, 'Why should we penalize Bob and Doug for doing their homework all winter, while the rest of us were sitting around in taverns drinking beer?' That pretty much ended talk of banning the car. We won eleven straight races at Knoxville, and it turned out that Lloyd was the first guy to beat us there."

That was a dream season for Trostle and Wolfgang, as they won a total of forty-five feature events, including the Knoxville Nationals. By the end of the season, though, Wolfgang left to pursue a deal he hoped would get him an Indy shot, and Trostle was disheartened after a great season.

He was ready to quit, but spent some time in Australia during the winter that helped him rekindle his passion. He returned to the U.S. and hired Shane Carson and had another strong season.

An unlikely series of events in 1980 brought him together with Steve and Karl Kinser, who were just establishing themselves as superstars in the sprint car business.

"I had Garry Rush in my car, and I had two entries filed for the Nationals," he explains. "We broke our primary car the night before the Nationals began, and hurried and put the engine in the backup and went to Knoxville. Garry went out for hot laps and the crank broke, that was our only motor, so we were done, completely.

"Karl and Steve crashed in the heat race, and they were finished with that car. I offered Karl my backup, which was entered for Thursday night. The next morning they were at my shop and we started working. We used their engine, and switched some stuff around.

"It got to be five that afternoon, we were running out of time. I asked Karl what torsion bars he wanted to use, he said, 'I've seen this car run, I'm sure the bars will be fine.'

"Honest to Christ, we didn't touch the bars or anything, just headed for the race track. Steve was fourth-quick, won his heat, and finished second to Sammy in the feature. We worked on the car some more Friday, and ran pretty well that night, then Karl decided the car wasn't quite right, so we thrashed and changed the driveline some, and I had to make a new motor plate for it all to fit.

"It turns out the race was postponed that night because of fog, and Steve wound up winning it the next day. That was a really neat experience, getting to work with Karl and Steve, they were just the best. How could you not like working with two guys like that, who are so good?

"I'm especially proud that I played a part in both Steve's and Doug (Wolfgang's) first Nationals wins."

By 1982, a philosophical war was raging in sprint car racing. Wings were becoming the popular setup, and Trostle was an outspoken proponent of running them at big tracks such as Knoxville.

"I had seen ten guys killed at Knoxville, and there isn't any doubt that wings would make a difference, not any doubt in my mind. I had begged (Knoxville) to adopt wings full time, but it was just not something they were ready to do."

Then, on opening night in 1982, tragedy came at Knoxville. Gary Scott was killed instantly when he was thrown from his flipping sprint car and ran over by other cars on the track, in full view of the front grandstand.

"I was standing on the backstretch, I could see it was a bad accident. I walked over to our car; Tim Green was driving for me. He flipped up his visor and said, 'Damn, Bob, they just killed another one.'

"I could see Scott lying there on the track, and I just looked at my crew and said, 'put this thing on the trailer.' We loaded up and I told (the track) I wasn't coming back until they put wings on, all the time."

The following day, in an emergency meeting, the decision was made to adopt wings at Knoxville.

During the remainder of the 1980s, Trostle continued to race hard, but began to concentrate on helping young drivers move their career along.

"I'll admit it, I like trying to start somebody out," he says. "You get a good feeling helping a young guy and making him better, that is pretty rewarding."

Gradually, he began to phase out his racing until it was only a small part of his life. Finally, he retired officially, although he still builds a couple of cars each year and "tinkers."

He can look back on 313 victories as a car owner or mechanic, including six Knoxville track championships. He built a total of 490 sprint cars, many of which are still competitive.

"I built a 1932 Ford hot rodder, and I'm having a lot of fun with that," he laughs. "This last weekend we traveled to a hot rod show, everyone was sitting around polishing their cars and relaxing. I told Dorotha, 'this is sure different than sprint car racing!'"

He is sixty-four now, with an uncanny memory for detail, and friends literally from coast to coast. He likes to laugh, and talk about sprint cars and the people who made them great.

Two years ago, on the afternoon of the Legends classic at Knoxville, a stroll through the pits revealed a deserted scene hours before race time. Alone in the quiet was Trostle, who was busily putting the final touches on an entry he agreed to field for a friend.

His name was called, and he looked up from his work. The smiling onlooker asked him if, in fifty years, you could still find Bob Trostle on the end of a wrench in the Knoxville pits.

"Well, I don't know why not," he answered, without a moment's hesitation. "I'll only be 112, so why wouldn't I be here?"

ABOUT THE AUTHOR

Dave Argabright is a writer living in Fishers, Indiana. He has covered auto racing since 1981 for publications including NATIONAL SPEED SPORT NEWS and OPEN WHEEL MAGAZINE. His professional honors include the National Sprint Car Hall of Fame "Media Member of the Year," the "Dymag Award of Journalism Excellence," the "Gene Powlen Fan Appreciation Award," and the Hoosier Auto Racing Fans "Media Member of the Year" awards. He and his wife Sherry have four children: Joe, Jake, Amanda, and Chad. He also co-authored the book *Still Wide Open* with Brad Doty.